Universal Principles of Islamic Bioethics

Foundational Maqāṣid-Oriented Study and Critique of Western Biomedical Theory

Universal Principles of Islamic Bioethics

Foundational Maqāṣid-Oriented Study and Critique of Western Biomedical Theory

By

Prof. Dr. ʿAlī Muḥyī al-Dīn al-Qaradāghī

The Secretary-General of the International Union for Muslim Scholars
The Vice-President of the European Council for Fatwā and Research

Translated by

Dr. Hossam Sabry

دار جامعة حمد بن خليفة للنشر
HAMAD BIN KHALIFA UNIVERSITY PRESS

Hamad Bin Khalifa University Press
P O Box 5825
Doha, Qatar

www.hbkupress.com

Almabadi Al'akhlaqiat Aljamiea li'akhlaqiat
altib alhayawii fi al'islam

First published in Arabic by Hamad Bin Khalifa University Press, 2019

First English edition in 2021

Hamad Bin Khalifa University Press

ISBN: 9789927155130

Printed in Doha-Qatar

Qatar National Library Cataloging-in-Publication (CIP)

Al-Qaradāghī, ʿAlī Muḥyī al-Dīn, author.

[مبادئ الأخلاقية الجامعة لأخلاق الطب الحيوي]. English

Universal principles of Islamic bioethics : foundational maqāṣid-oriented study and critique of Western biomedical theory / by Prof. Dr. ʿAlī Muḥyī al-Dīn al-Qaradāghī, the secretary-general of the International Union for Muslim Scholars the vice-president of the European Council for Fatwā and Research ; translated by Dr. Hossam Sabry. First English edition. – Doha, Qatar : Hamad Bin Khalifa University Press, 2021.

pages ; cm
ISBN 978-992-715-513-0

Includes bibliographical references (pages 287-295).

1. Bioethics -- Religious aspects -- Islam. 2. Islamic ethics. 3. Medical ethics.
4. Muslims -- Conduct of life. I. Sabry, Hossam, translator. II. Title

R725.Q27125 2021
174.957 – dc 23 202128104651

CONTENTS

INTRODUCTION 7
Study Methodology *10*
Targeted Audience *10*
Non-Medical Applicability *10*
Inclusiveness *11*

FRAMEWORK OF THREE CLUSTERS OF PRINCIPLES OF ISLAMIC BIOETHICS *13*
Theory Outline *14*
Source of Obligation *14*
Standard-Based Regulation *15*

CHAPTER ONE: TERMINOLOGY & INTRODUCTORY REMARKS *17*
1.1 Naẓarīyah (Theory) *17*
1.2 al-Ṭibb *17*
1.3 al-Ḥayawī *18*
1.4 Maqāṣid *18*
1.5 Maqāṣid in Medicine *21*
1.6 Akhlāq (Ethics) *45*
1.7 Cardinal Ethics *58*
1.8 Governing Principles of Biomedical Ethics *60*

CHAPTER TWO: CONTRIBUTIONS TO MEDICAL ETHICS DELINEATION *61*
2.1 Earlier Contributions to Medical Ethics *61*
2.2 Critical Review of the Four-Principle Approach *74*

CHAPTER THREE: TOWARDS AN ISLAMIC THEORY OF UNIVERSAL PRINCIPLES OF BIOMEDICAL ETHICS *93*
3.1 Universal Biomedical Principles from an Islamic Perspective *93*

APPENDIX: THE ISLAMIC CODE FOR MEDICAL AND HEALTH ETHICS 255
Chapter One: Physician Ethics 255
Chapter Two: The Physician's Duties Towards the Patient 255
Chapter three: Medical Confidentiality 265
Chapter Four: Physician Duties Towards Society 269
Chapter Five: Social Issues 270
Chapter Six: Advertisement and the Media 276
Chapter Seven: Physician Duties Towards the Establishment He Works at 278
Chapter Eight: Relations with Colleagues 278
Chapter Nine: Physician Rights 281
Chapter Ten: Physician Duties Towards His Profession 283

BIBLIOGRAPHY 287

INTRODUCTION

In the name of God, Most Gracious, Most Merciful.

Praise is due to God, the Lord of all worlds. May peace and blessings be upon our master and beloved ideal Muḥammad, who was sent as a mercy to all worlds, and upon his brothers of the prophets and messengers; his noble family; blessed companions and those who follow them righteously up to the Day of Judgment!

This study tackles two of the most important topics from an Islamic and human perspective. The first subject is medicine, which centers on human beings and the appropriate methods to maintain their physical and mental health, preserve progeny and provide the suitable treatment. Fulfilling this objective necessarily contributes to protecting property and wealth. Actually, both medicine and religion provide healing and mercy; however, religion is distinguished by a broader and more inclusive share of such mercy and healing. The Qurʾān reads: "We send down the Qurʾān as healing and mercy to those who believe".(1)

Based on this, some scholars reduced the scope of *Maqāṣid* (General objectives of *Sharīʿa*) into only two holistic objectives; namely, the preservation of religion and the preservation of people's souls or bodies. In his commentary on the Qurʾānic verse stating that "It is He who shows you [people] His signs and sends water down from the sky to sustain you, though only those who turn to

(1) Sūrat al-Isrāʾ (17:82). Unless otherwise stated, the translation of the Qurʾān used in this book is based on the translations provided by M.A.S. Abdel Haleem, Muḥammad Maḥmūd Ghâlī, and SAHIH INTERNATIONAL. Some translations used "Allah" instead of "God" which is modified here for the purpose of consistency.

God will take heed"[1], Imām al-Rāzī notes that: "The most important task is to maintain the interests of religions as well as those of human bodies. In terms of people's interests, God protects them by revealing signs and clear proofs, while He protects the interests of people's bodies by providing them with sustenance. Proofs for religions are comparable to sustenance for bodies. When both are provided, the act of Godly blessing comes in its perfect form by all measures and considerations."[2] Similarly, Imām al-Shāfi'ī limits scholarship and knowledge into two sciences, explaining that "Knowledge is all about two sciences: science of religion and that of body".[3]

The second subject is ethics, which represent the core of Islam, its spirit, its behavioral manifestations, its purposes and the original intent behind sending down the Scripture and messengers. God (May He be exalted) says: "We sent Our messengers with clear signs, the Scripture and the Balance, so that people could uphold justice".[4] In another verse God says: "It was only as a mercy that We sent you [Prophet] to all people".[5] Verily, the two morals, i.e., justice and mercy, represent the core of morality, the origin of virtues, the highest rank of behaviors and the noblest of ethics.

This study attempts to provide scholars and experts of *fiqh*, ethics, and medicine with a thorough investigation of the universal principles of bioethics based on the general objectives of the noble Islamic *Sharī'a*. Evidently, it is not

(1) Ghāfir (40: 13).

(2) al-Rāzī, Fakhr al-Dīn Muḥammad, *Mafātiḥ al-ghayb* (Beirut: Dār al-Kutub al-''Ilmīyah, 1421 A.H.), vol. 27, p. 38.

(3) *Ādāb al-Shāfi'ī*, vol. 2, p. 321; Abū Nu'aym al-Iṣfahānī, *Ḥilyat al-awliyā'*, vol. 9, p. 142; al-Ḥamawī, *al-aḥkām al-nabawīyah fī al-ṣinā'ah al-ṭibbīyah*, ed. Aḥmad al-Jamal (Beirut: Dār Ibn Ḥazm), p. 221.

(4) al-Ḥadīd (27: 25).

(5) al- Anbiyā' (21: 107).

an easy undertaking to write for a select group of prominent scholars with proven scholarly expertise to whom people turn to seek knowledge, look for guidance and rely upon their approach and methods. The present study comes in response to a request from the Research Center for Islamic Legislation and Ethics (CILE) to expand my contribution to CILE's first specialized seminar on bioethics and its relation to *Maqāṣid*. It is an honor and privilege to cordially respond to their kind request. I ask God, glory be to Him, to grant me success in this endeavor in order to be able to present a work befitting this great religion and those eminent scholars. I hope my work will provide an enlightened thought, a solid argumentation, a proper extrapolation and a holistic theorization of linking bioethics to the general objectives of Islamic *Sharīʿa*. I try my best to formulate an inclusive theory, taking into consideration the requirements of accuracy and standardization, and highlighting the means, aims, consequences and substantial formalities, so that this theory is presented, as much as possible, in its finest form and in a perfect fashion.

In line with the recommendations of CILE's first seminar, this study attempts to present the highlights of a complete theory of biomedical ethics based on *Maqāṣid* within a framework that has two parts: the first of which links biomedical ethical principles to the five or six universal necessities of *Sharīʿa*, while the second is premised on my notion of the eight principles of *maqāṣid*. It is not of primary concern here whether my eight-principle approach will be sanctioned or not. Rather, the priority is given to the success of a project based on a thorough Islamic theory of bioethics and linking the principles of biomedical ethics to the higher objectives of *Sharīʿa* so that such biomedical principles are reformulated under the umbrella of *Sharīʿa*.

STUDY METHODOLOGY

The present study employs a particular methodology which is not limited to exposition and simplification; rather it is based on argumentation, theorization, categorization, establishing foundation and standaradization in a simplified fashion that is easy to understand by non-*fiqh* medical specialists. It attempts to categorize subsidiary medical ethics under three holistic universal principles, highlighting their ancillary branches, their origins, as well as their source of obligation and motives while linking them to the general principle of legal interests (*maṣāliḥ*). Hopefully, adopting this approach contributes to the development of a comprehensive theory.

I think it will be more appropriate to draw the link between these ethical principles and the entire *maqāṣid* ecosystem, not only the higher objectives of *Sharīʿa*. By "ecosystem" I mean those objectives related to creation in general and specifically creation of human beings in addition to other objectives pertaining to medicine, physicians and non-physicians, and *fiqh* of consequences and blocking the means to evil.

TARGETED AUDIENCE

This theory is principally targeted at Muslim medical staff and secondarily at non-Muslim personel. Taking this as a point of departure, the study is expected to dwell on the issues of revelation, Islamic law, and religious moral behaviors. However, it also attempts to build on an alternative value system for non-Muslims.

NON-MEDICAL APPLICABILITY

This theory, though formulated speficically to provide moral regulations in the field of medicine, is still applicable to all professions and professionals.

INCLUSIVENESS

I will try my best to include physcians, medical professionals, life-related research, patients along with their guardians, and veterinarians in the three-principle approach that links bioethis to *maqāṣid*.

May God guide us to the truth and save us from slips and mistakes in beliefs, words and deeds! He alone is our source of providence and protection; the Best Lord, Patron and Guide to Success.

Prof. Dr. ʿAlī Muḥyī al-Dīn al-Qaradāghī

Framework of Three Clusters of Principles of Islamic Bioethics

Respect for Human Dignity	Beneficence	Justice
• Respect for autonomy (a principle requiring respect for the decision-making capacities of autonomous persons except for the cases of infectious disease)	• Continous creativity in provision of benefits for others	• Maintaining justice by governments
• Respect for man, whether dead or alive	• Perfectibility and quality	• Maintaining justice by medical, pharmaceutical and research institutions
• Maintaining confidentiality	• Removing harm and Avoiding causing harm to others	• Maintaining justice by physicians (all officials)
• Human rights	• Advancing benefits for people and institutions	
	• Showing mercy towards people, animals and environment	
	• Piety and God fearing (feeling responsibility, observing God's commandments, compliance with legal dicta	

NB. Decision-taking process is based on *fiqh* of balances in addition to certain clear-cut criteria.

THEORY OUTLINE

This theory consists of three main components:

First: the scientific aspect (Three universal principles of Islamic bioethics, namely: respect for dignity, beneficence and justice).

Second: Entity entitled to apply it (any natural or legal person required to put these principles into force). This includes: physicians, pharmacists, biomedical researchers, therapists, etc. This means all professionals in health care, pharmaceutical industry, and biomedical research on humans, animals, or environment. It also encompasses institutions providing treatment services including cell and gene therapy, pharmaceutical companies, biomedical research labs, and research institutes involving human and non-human subjects, whether natural or legal persons (each in proportion to relevant principles). Other professional institutions could be included in this component.

Third: Human subjects or patients subject to treatment or any kind of medical intervention.

SOURCE OF OBLIGATION

The source of obligation lies in three things:

1. *Sharīʿa* in its crystal-clear provisions demanding compliance with such principles in addition to sound instinct and intellect, live conscience and public interests.
2. Any contractual agreement regulating the relationship between different parties. This agreement with its terms, conditions, and provisions, represents the main source of obligation. God says, "You who believe, fulfil your obligations,"[1] and "Honor your pledges:

(1) al-Mā'idah (7:1)

you will be questioned about your pledges."[1] There are a lot of textual proofs of the Qur'ān and the Sunnah but there is no room here to cite all of them. However, in the presence of a contractual agreement, compliance with these principles, whether stipulated or not, becomes a legal and ethical obligation.

3. Laws and regulations, whether enforced by states or institutions, as will be shown later in some detail.

STANDARD-BASED REGULATION

The present study attempts to regulate the ethical principles based on certain criteria and standards as will be discussed later.

(1) al-Iisrā' (17:34)

CHAPTER ONE:
TERMINOLOGY & INTRODUCTORY REMARKS

This preliminary chapter attempts to clarify the meanings of some important terms before dwelling on the proposed theory.

1.1 *NAẒARĪYAH* (THEORY)

Linguistically speaking, the Arabic word *naẓarīyah* is etymologically taken from *naẓar* denoting vision, reflection, contemplation, etc.(1) In our present-day context, *naẓarīyah* is used to express a holistic abstract conception of general principles that govern the individual particulars and rulings.(2)

1.2 *AL-ṬIBB*

As the Arabic equivalent of medicine, al-*Ṭibb* is the treatment of human body and souls. In its Arabic linguistic sense, it connotes skillfulness, proficiency, and sagacity. A person whose profession is to treat people is called *Ṭabīb* (physician). Given the linguistic meaning, the word '*Ṭabīb*' can also refer to a skillful talented person, a kind smart one and a sage.(3)

---

(1) For detailed information about *naẓar,* see*: Lisān al-ʿArab*, *al-Qāmūs al-Muḥīṭ*, *al-Muʿjam al-Wasīṭ*.

(2) Jamāl al-Dīn ʿAṭīyah, *al-Tanẓīr al-Fiqhī* (Cairo: Maṭbaʿat al-madīnah), p. 9.

(3) *Lisān al-ʿArab*, *al-Qāmūs al-Muḥīṭ*, *al-Muʿjam al-Wasīṭ*, (entry: *Ṭibb*).

1.3 *AL-HAYAWĪ*

This word is the Arabic equivalent of 'bio' meaning life.(1) Based on this, the term '*al-Ṭibb al-Ḥayawī*' means biomedicine. It can relate to many categories including conventional medicine, veterinary medicine along with any medical disciplines and areas of specialty that typically study human beings such as biochemistry, biology, embryology, histology, anatomy, genetics, genetic engineering, pharmacology, zoology, etc.(2)

1.4 *MAQĀṢID*

The term '*maqṣid*' (plural: *maqāṣid*) is a verbal noun derived from the verb *qaṣada* that conveys several meanings, including determination, direction, straightness of path, justice, and moderation.(3) Technically, *maqāṣid al-Sharīʿa* is the deeper meanings and inner aspects of wisdom considered by the Lawgiver in all or most of the areas and circumstances of legislation without being confined to a particular type of *Sharīʿa* commands.(4) It may be also defined as the objectives and intents set by *Sharīʿa* to secure people's interests (*maṣāliḥ*).(5) Generally speaking, the general objectives of *Sharīʿa*, from my point of view, lie in the preservation of eight necessities; namely, religion, soul, mind, wealth, progeny, honor, societal and environmental security, and security of a just state.(6) A thorough inductive

(1) Ibid., (*Ḥayy)*.

(2) See *Wikipedia* (biomedicine).

(3) *Lisān al-ʿArab, al-Qāmūs al-Muḥīṭ, al-Muʿjam al-Wasīṭ*, (see: Qaṣad).

(4) Ibn ʿĀshūr, *Maqāṣid al-sharīʿah al-Islāmīyah*, ed. Mohamed El Tahir El Mesawi (Jordan: Dār al-Nafā'is, 1421 AH)), p. 251.

(5) Aḥmad al-Raysūnī, *Naẓarīyat al-maqāṣid ʿinda al-Imām al-Shāṭibī* (London; Washington: International Institute of Islamic Thought, 2005), p. 7.

(6) al-Qaradāghī, "Naẓarāt fī anwāʿ al-maqāṣid wa-tanawwuʿihā bi-tanawwuʿi maḥillihā: Hal hiya dalīl aw maslak aw manhaj? " in *Mawsūʿat Maqāṣid al-sharīʿah.*

investigation of scriptural texts reveals that the main intent of *Sharīʿa* is to fulfill certain universal interests of people in terms of three 'levels of necessity,' which are necessities (*ḍarūrāt*), needs (*ḥājīyāt*), and embellishments (*taḥsīnīyāt*). Those three levels are proportionally pertinent to one's faith, soul, mind, wealth, progeny according to the majority opinion, and honor in the view of some scholars.(1) Additionally, they apply to the protection of political, social and economic security of society and fighting banditry (*ḥirābah*) and corruption within society and the environment in addition to maintaining state security by preventing armed opposition and rebellion (*baghy*).(2)

It is not of primary concern here whether my eight-principle approach of *maqāṣid* will be sanctioned or not. Rather, the priority is given to delineating a link between ethics and *maqāṣid.* Actually, each of these higher objectives has two sides of protection; the positive side refers to the preservation and fulfilment of interests whereas the negative one refers to warding off all evils and harm. The eight universal objectives can be subsumed under three main categories:

1. Universal objectives (necessities, needs, embellishments) pertaining to individuals in terms of:
    a. Religion by means of preservation and protection against any kind of aggression in addition to consolidation and strengthening through sound proofs and righteous deeds. (This includes both sides of protection).
    b. Mind by means of preservation and protection against any harm in addition to development and cultivation through creativity and reasonable thinking.

---

(1) al-Shāṭibī, *al-al-Muwāfaqāt*, vol.3, p. 14.

(2) al-Qaradāghī, "Naẓarāt fī anwāʿ al-maqāṣid wa-tanawwuʿihā bi-tanawwuʿi maḥillihā".

c. Wealth by protecting it against any violations and increasing it through investment.
d. Honor (in terms of both sides of protection).

2. Universal objectives pertaining to the whole society with regard to both sides of protection, i.e. maintaining its security and stability and fending off evils of all kinds.

   The security of society includes protection of the environment and of animals. Talking about the crime of *ḥirābah* (banditry) and defiance of God, the Qur'ān highlights the act of spreading corruption in this world including society and surrounding environment. God says, "When he [a kind of human being] leaves, he sets out to spread corruption in the land, destroying crops and livestock – God does not like corruption."(1) It is known that *ḥirābah* is wreaking havoc and causing corruption in this world. God says, "On account of [his deed], We decreed to the Children of Israel that if anyone kills a person – unless in retribution for murder or spreading corruption in the land – it is as if he killed all mankind, while if any saves a life it is as if he saved the life of all mankind. Our messengers came to them with clear signs, but many of them continued to commit excesses in the land."(2) Contemplating how the Qur'ān approaches social issues, it becomes clear that they have been given special attention by God as indicated in the verses tackling spoils, booty, fair loans, etc.
3. Universal objectives pertaining to the legitimate state in terms of protecting its security and stability, defending it against any kind of aggression, and

(1) al-Baqarah (2: 205).
(2) al-Mā'idah (5: 33).

abiding by its laws and regulations (taken from *Sharīʿa* on the basis of clear-cut textual proofs or deduction).

1.5 *MAQĀṢID* IN MEDICINE

The general objectives of *Sharīʿa* in the field of medicine can be summarized in the following points:

First: Protecting souls, bodies, human organs as necessities.

The most important purpose of *Sharīʿa* in this specific field of medicine is the preservation of human body (organs, physical parts, systems and overall health) and protecting it against any harm and detriments. Consequently, it is not allowed to deal with human body in any way endangering it, causing any harm to human organs or souls, except in compliance with the teachings of God, the Wise Creator Who molded man and breathed into him of His Spirit.

Second: Warding off evils and harm

Warding off harm and evils, avoiding causes of illness and blocking the means to vulnerability are among the most significant purposes of *Sharīʿa*. To fulfill this purpose, God sanctioned the good things, and prohibited the wicked and evil ones. In enumerating the traits of the Prophet as mentioned in the Torah and the Gospel, the Qurʾān reads, "who follow the Messenger – the unlettered prophet they find described in the Torah that is with them, and in the Gospel – who commands them to do right and forbids them to do wrong, who makes good things lawful to them and bad things unlawful, and relieves them of their burdens, and the iron collars that were on them. So it is those who believe him, honor and help him, and who follow the light which has been sent down with him, who will succeed."(1)

(1) al-ʾAʿrāf (7: 157).

Moreover, the Prophet (PBUH) prohibited anything that could cause harm, evil or mischief. He was quoted as saying, “There should be neither harming nor reciprocating harm.”(1) In certain cases, prohibition was premised on the underlying harm and mischief. This is crystal clear in the following verse pinpointing the prohibition of consuming wine: “They ask you [Prophet] about intoxicants and gambling: say, ‘There is great sin in both, and some benefit for people: the sin is greater than the benefit.”(2) The aforementioned *ḥadīth* represents a general precept of Islam and a universal legal maxim of *Sharīʿa*. al-Suyūṭī, while commenting on the legal maxim of ‘harm must be eliminated,’ states that it has its provenance in the Prophetic *ḥadīth*, “There should be neither harming nor reciprocating harm.” He adds that many chapters of *fiqh* are premised on this specific legal maxim which gave rise to a number of additional maxims such as “Necessities render prohibited things permissible,” “Necessity is measured in accordance with its true proportions,” “Harm may not be eliminated by its equivalent” and “Need is ranked as necessity, be it public or private”.(3) Since Islam is a heavenly religion from God, The Ever-Wise, The Ever-Cognizant, who created human beings and knows their needs, it sanctioned everything that can secure their religious and worldly benefits. The Qurʾān reads, “How could He who created not know His own creation, when He is the Most Subtle, the All Aware?”(4)

---

(1) Reported by Mālik in al-Muwaṭṭaʾ, al-Shāfiʿī in his Musnad (1/324), Aḥmad in Musnad (1/313, 5/326); al-Ḥākim in al-Mustadrak (2/66) commenting that it is an authentic *ḥadīth* based on the conditions set by Muslim. The same is held by al-Dhahabī. It is also reported by al-Bayhaqī in Sunan (6/69) al-Dāraquṭnī (2/77). See: Majmaʿ al-ʾzawāʾid (4/204) and Miṣbāḥ al-zujājah by al-Kattānī (3/48).

(2) al-Baqarah (2: 219).

(3) See: al-Suyūṭī, *al-Ashbāh wa-al-naẓāʾir* (Beirut: Dār al-Kitāb al-ʿʿArabī, 1407 AH), pp. 173-81.

(4) al-Mulk (67: 14).

Islam adopts balanced legislations in different aspects of human life to enable people fulfill their mission in this world, i.e. vicegerency and positive construction of the earth. Thus, its legislations strike a balance between spiritual and material aspects, taking into consideration the needs of soul and body. The Prophet (PBUH) says, "Fast for a few days and give up fasting for a few days because your body has a right on you, and your eye has a right on you, and your guest has a right on you, and your wife has a right on you."[1] Similarly, it was reported that the Prophet (PBUH) made a bond of brotherhood between Salmān and Abū al-Dardā'. Salmān paid a visit to Abū al-Dardā' and found Umm al-Dardā' (his wife) dressed in shabby clothes and asked her why she was in that state. She replied: "Your brother Abū al-Dardā' is not interested in (the luxuries of) this world. In the meantime, Abū al-Dardā' came in and prepared a meal for Salmān. The latter requested Abū al-Dardā' to eat (with him) but Abū al-Dardā' said: "I am fasting." Salmān said: "I am not going to eat unless you eat." So, Abū al-Dardā' ate with him. When it was night and (a part of the night passed), Abū al-Dardā' got up (to offer the night prayer) but Salmān asked him to sleep and Abū al-Dardā' slept. After some time Abū al-Dardā' again got up but Salmān asked him to sleep. When it was the last hours of the night, Salmān asked him to get up and both of them offered (*Tahajjud*) prayer. Then Salmān told Abū al-Dardā': "You owe a duty to your Lord; you owe a duty to your body; you owe a duty to your family; so, you should give to everyone his due. Abū al-Dardā' came to the Prophet (PBUH) and reported the whole story. The Prophet (PBUH) said, "Salmān is right".[2]

(1) Reported by al-Bukhārī (4/182, 184 and 10/443).
(2) Reported by al-Bukhārī (4/182, 184 and 10/443).

Third: Preservation of health & Seeking Medical Treatment

The general objectives of *Sharīʿa* in the field of medicine include seeking medical treatment to maintain health and well-being, ensure the ability to work, produce, perform ritual acts of worship and positively contribute to the development of earth. In order to meet this objective, God commanded people to seek medication. It was reported by Aḥmad, al-Ḥākim, Abū Dāwūd and Ibn Mājah on the authority of Usāmah b. Sharīk who said, "I came to the Prophet (PBUH) while his Companions were sitting as if they had birds on their heads. I saluted and sat down. The desert Arabs then came from here and there. They asked: Messenger of God, should we make use of medical treatment? He replied: Make use of medical treatment, for God has not made a disease without appointing a remedy for it, with the exception of one disease, namely old age."(1)

In the same vein, Islam urges people to have a fit body, a firm belief and an avid soul. The Prophet (PBUH) says, "A strong believer is better and dearer to God than a weak one."(2) Islam dispels all myths in terms of diseases and remedies and disapproves any role for spirits, jinn and devils in this regard. Illness and health are decreed by God. However, there are certain causes and means for each. The Qurʾān reads, "Say, 'Only what God has decreed will happen to us."(3) In other verses, the Qurʾān tells us what the Prophet Ibrāhīm (Abraham) said, "He [God] who gives me food and drink; He who cures me when I am ill; He who will make me

---

(1) Aḥmad in Musnad (4/278), no. 18366; al-Tirmidhī, no. 2039; al-Ḥākim in al-Mustadrak (1/208, 4/422, 442, 456); Ibn Ḥibbān in his Ṣaḥīḥ, book of medicine (13/426); al-Bayhaqī in al-Sunan al-Kubrā (4/2, 368 and 9/343); Abū Dāwūd in al-Sunan, no. 3855; and Ibn Mājah, no. 3436. See: ʿAbd al-Malik b. Duhaysh, al-Aḥādīth al-mukhtārah (Mecca, 1410 AH), vol. 4, p. 169; al-Istidhkār (8/414); al-Muḥallá (4/176) Tahdhīb al-Āthār (1/499) and al-Muṣannaf by Ibn Abī Shaybah (5/31).

(2) Reported by Muslim, *ḥadīth* no. 2664.

(3) At-Tawbah (9: 52).

die and then give me life again."[1] Indeed, food is a required means to get rid of hunger; similarly, health and illness have their causes and means, but all are given by God. Therefore, Islam has abolished pessimism, prohibited hanging amulets and resorting to charlatans and sorcerers and relying upon them for good luck or warding off evil.[2] Alternatively, God commanded people to seek medication as part of believing in His divine decree and predestination.[3]

Fourth: Empowering man to fulfil role of vicegerent

It is well-known that man is entrusted with the task of vicegerency and positive construction of earth in line with God's teachings. This task requires a physically fit and strong person able to work, think and act. Fulfilling these requirements requires good health conditions, well-being and medication. That is to say, the general objectives of *Sharīʿa* in terms of vicegerency entail seeking medication in order for people to fulfil their mission.

Medicine Significance & Legal Ruling

Given the nature of medicine and its impacts and outcomes, we can conclude that this science touches on all aspects of human beings. When a person gets sick, his body weakens, his intellectual faculties are affected, and his ability to observe devotional acts is diminished. If his condition worsens, he will no longer be able to positively contribute to society and civilization. Indeed, a sound mind is in a sound body. Unlike healthy people, such a person will be preoccupied with his health condition and will give it priority over anything else. His contribution is in no way comparable to those enjoying health and vigor.

(1) al-Shuʿarāʾ (26: 79-81).

(2) See: al-Qaraḍāwī, *al-ḥalāl wa-al-ḥarām* (Beirut: al-Maktab al-Islāmī, 1405 AH), p. 219ff.

(3) See: *Mawārid al-ẓamʾān* (1/339).

Taking this into consideration, prudent scholars hold that the profession of medicine belongs to the category of collective obligations; if totally neglected, the community as a whole would be liable. al-Ghazālī, for example, stated that the collective duty is any science which is indispensable for the maintenance of this world, like medicine, which is necessary for the preservation of bodies. If a certain town has no physicians, destruction will hasten to befall its people, who will be put to critical situation by becoming victims of ruin. Verily, He, who has created the ailment, has created its medicine and guided the people to the way of using it and the causes of having it. For this reason, it is not permissible to cause oneself to be vulnerable to destruction by neglecting such medicine.(1) Similarly, al-Shāfi'ī limited scholarship and knowledge into two sciences, explaining that "Knowledge is all about two sciences: science of religion and that of body".(2) Limiting the scope of knowledge to these sciences is intended to emphasize their paramount significance. al-Ghazālī, during the phase of seclusion, severely criticized those scholars who afford little attention to medicine, scolding them for neglecting this duty. He reproached them for indulging in polemics of dialecticians at the expense of medical sciences to the extent that almost all physicians were non-Muslims.(3)

Based on the foregoing discussion, learning medicine is a communal obligation in principle. However, when this obligation is adequately met, it becomes recommended for those willing to serve people or at least legalized for the laity. In case of ill-intention or illegal methods, it could

(1) al-Ghazālī, *Iḥyā' 'ulūm al-dīn* (Cairo: 'Īsá al-Bābī al-Ḥalabī), vol. 1, p. 17, adapted.

(2) *Ādāb al-Shāfi'ī*, vol. 2, p. 321; Abū Nu'aym al-Iṣfahānī, *Ḥilyat al-awliyā'*, vol. 9, p. 142; al-Ḥamawī, *al-aḥkām al-nabawīyah fī al-ṣinā'ah al-ṭibbīyah*, ed. Aḥmed al-Jamal (Beirut: Dār Ibn Ḥazm), p. 221.

(3) Ibid.

be rendered forbidden. In other cases, learning medicine becomes an individual obligation when there is only one person who can shoulder this responsibility. To sum up, the five legal rulings are applicable to learning medicine; it could be obligatory, recommended, permissible, reprehensible, or prohibited. The same holds true for the categories of declaratory legal rulings (*al-ḥukm al-waḍʿī*), i.e. cause, condition, impediment, validity and invalidity. A medical treatment may be a cause of liability in case of negligence or malpractice on the part of the physician. Still, a legal ruling could be conditioned and premised on a given medical decision.

Interplay Between *Fiqh* and Medicine

In various respects, there is a close relationship between *fiqh* and medicine.

First: The laws of Islamic *Sharīʿa* govern different issues related to medicine in terms of permissibility, impermissibility and the necessary ethics and etiquette.

The Muslim physician needs Islamic *fiqh* to distinguish between permissible and impermissible medical interventions, including medication, plastic surgery, organ transplantation, etc. Moreover, *fiqh* is needed to delineate etiquette and morals of physicians, the legal guiding principles, and any liability for their actions. Furthermore, patients also need *fiqh* to learn the legal rulings pertaining to ritual purity, acts of worship, dispositions in case of terminal illness where the person is not entitled to donate more than half of his wealth.

Second: *Fiqh* depends on medicine in construing legal rulings for medical affairs. Actually, passing a judgment on something is dependent on having a proper conception thereof. A jurist cannot decide the correct legal ruling of a medical issue without adequate information provided by a competent physician or a general investigation of the relevant medical resources. This is a requisite condition for the validity of *ijtihād* and realization of a proper legal ruling. Any *fatwā* issued without thorough knowledge and deep understanding and conception is assailable and useless. The person practicing such *ijtihād* or issuing this baseless *fatwā* commits a grave sin. Such a *muftī* deserves the punishment promised to ignorant judges in the following *ḥadīth* in which the Prophet (PBUH) says, "Judges are of three types, one of whom will go to Paradise and two to Hell. The one who will go to Paradise is a man who knows what is right and gives judgment accordingly; but a man who knows what is right and acts tyrannically in his judgment will go to Hell; and a man who gives judgment for people when he is ignorant will go to Hell." Commenting on this *ḥadīth*, Abū Dāwūd said: this is the soundest tradition on this subject.(1) Another narration by Ibn Mājah states that "One who judges while not knowing, ruining the rights of the people, so he is in the Fire."(2)

Furthermore, jurists need medicine in the following cases:

1. To determine whether a certain thing is harmful. If the potential harm is serious, such a thing will be prohibited. If it is minor harm, the legal ruling will be reduced to reprehensibility. For instance, in tackling the legal ruling of performing ablution with water heated by the sun in utensils made of materials other than gold and silver, al-Shāfi'ī stipulated that reprehensibility is to be decided on the basis of a medical dictum.(3)

---

(1) This *ḥadīth* is reported by Abū Dāwūd in al-Sunan (no. 3102), al-Tirmidhī (no. 21244), Ibn Mājah (2306).

(2) Reported by Ibn Mājah in Sunan, no. 2306.

(3) See al-Shāfi'ī, *al-Umm* (Beirut: Dār al-Ma'rifah), vol. 1, p. 3; al-Nawawī, *al-Majmū'* (Cairo: Sharikat al-'ulamā'), vol. 1, p. 78.

2. To determine whether a patient should be given the legal concessions and mitigation (*al-Rukhaṣ*) in acts of worship including ritual purity, prayers, pilgrimage, fasting, etc. Moreover, medicine is resorted to in order to decide a person's mental competence and the resultant limitation of legal capacity.
3. It is employed in verification of lineage and paternity in certain cases.
4. Forensic medicine as a mechanism of establishing evidence of crimes.
5. In certain issues of marriage to prove defects that annul the contract such as impotence.

There are many other aspects where the medical dictum plays a decisive role in deciding the legal ruling. Given this importance, some classical jurists reproached their contemporary scholars for not paying due attention to medicine as a collective obligation.

In sum, there has to be a sort of collaboration between jurists and physicians in order to construe the legal rulings for the new medical incidents. The physicians play an informative role to expound the nature and details of a given issue while jurists employ such information to find the appropriate legal ruling. In this way, epistemological collaboration and meticulous investigation can materialize. In his book titled *Adab al-Ṭabīb,* Isḥāq b. 'Alī al-Rahāwī recommended this complementarity. He commented that there are certain things one is urged to seek before it is too late. Those things come under two categories; the first category fulfills all interests and moralities of self. This category can be secured through certain resources including religious compendiums which combine ethics and perfect morals. This is the first thing to seek; you and your offspring should learn them by rote memorization from eminent scholars, and attentively reflect over terms and underlying meanings in order to acquire such morals. The second category fulfills the interests of one's body and its individual organs. This knowledge is derived from the science of medicine. To get such knowledge, one needs to study hard the relevant books and learn from the competent professionals while he is still young. Such knowledge can be honed and refined by helping them in their medical practice. By so doing, this will contribute to developing and reforming one's self and complement the fruit reaped from religious books. People of medicine are characterized by justice, chastity, courage, compassion, modesty, and fairness. They opt for truthfulness, abhor lies, and distance themselves from the unlawful. Any fair, chaste, well-mannered and noble person is expected to hold them in high esteem and admit the sublime position of medicine and medical professionals.(1)

Juridical Opinions on Seeking Medical Treatment

Jurists hold different views concerning the permissibility of pursuing medical treatment. If medical treatement is ruled to be obligatory, then the person neglecting it is sinful and worthy of punishment; if it is ruled to be recommended, then a person pursuing it will be rewarded with no punishment for the one who neglects it. The juristic debate examines suchc rulings. Is it neutrally permissible with no reward or punishment? Or is it prohibited and the person seeking it is sinful? Alternatively, is it reprehensible and seeking it is blameworthy? In answering these questions, various juristic views were developed.

The first view, permissibility of medical treatment, is adopted

(1) This is cited from the speech given by his excellency Dr. Muḥammad al-Ḥabīb b. al-Khawjah, the Secretary General of Jeddah-based Fiqh Academy, during a symposium on the Islamic vision of some medical practices, organized in Casablanca, Morocco, on 14-17 June 1997. See: Islamic Organization for Medical Sciences Publication Series, 2nd volume, p. 48.

by the majority of jurists. However, some of them opt for permissibility with preference for avoiding it.(1) Ibn Taymīyah points out that a lot of righteous and knowledgeable people preferred to avoid medical treatment and this is the opinion attributed to Aḥmad. However, some of Aḥmad's disciples and companions opted for obligation or recommendation.(2) The second view, recommendation of medical treatment, is adopted by the Shafī'īs, Ḥanafīs, and the majority of Malikīs, in addition to a group of the pious predecessors and later scholars.(3) The third view maintains the obligation of medical treatment when it is available. This view is adopted by a group of Shafī'īs and Ḥanbalīs especially when the efficacy of treatment is likely to be ascertained. According to some Ḥanafī jurists, the obligation is limited to the case of definitive efficacy of medical treatment where it becomes analogous to using food to defeat hunger or water for thirst.(4) The fourth view advocating the impermissibility of medical treatment is attributed to some extreme mystics. This view is only mentioned for the sake of argumentation. It is totally ignored by some well-versed scholars who report unanimous agreement on permissibility. al-Ḥamawī states that "Jurists are in agreement on the permissibility of seeking medical treatment. They only debated whether it is preferable to avoid it or seek it."(5)

---

(1) For details, see al-Ghazālī, *Iḥyā' 'ulūm al-dīn,* op. cit., vol. 4, p. 279; Ibn Taymīyah, *Majmū' al-Fatāwá*, vol. 21, p. 564; al-Nawawī, *al-Majmū'*, vol. 5, p. 96; *Tuḥfat al-aḥwadhī, ḥadīth* no. 1961; *Kashshāf al-qinā'*, vol. 2, p. 76; al-Nawawī, *Sharḥ Muslim*, vol. 3, p. 90; al-Ḥamawī, *al-Aḥkām al-Nabawīyah*, p. 325. See also papers written by 'Alī'Alī al-Muḥammadī, Muḥammad 'Alī al-Bār, Muḥammad 'Adnān Ṣaqqāl, and 'Abd Allāh Muḥammad 'Abd Allāh on Medical Treatment in *Journal of Fiqh Academy*, 3 (7) 563-727.

(2) Ibn Taymīyah, *Majmū' al-Fatāwá*, vol. 21, p. 564.

(3) See, in addition to the previous references, al- *Fatāwá al-Hindiyya, vol. 5, p. 354;* Sharḥ al-Zurqānī 'alá al-Muwaṭṭa', vol. 4, p. 329.

(4) Ibn Mufliḥ al-Maqdisī, *al-Ādāb al-shar'īyah*, vol. 2, p. 361; Ibn Taymīyah, *Majmū' al-Fatāwá*, vol. 21, p. 564 & vol. 24, p. 269.

(5) al-Ḥamawī, *al-Aḥkām al-Nabawīyah*, p. 325.

The view of reprehensibility (or impermissibility if any) is based on the argument that seeking medical treatment conflicts with trusting God and putting one's faith in His healing power. For example, one report includes reference to those entering paradise without questioning. According to this tradition, they do not resort to incantation, evil omen or cauterization but they instead place their trust in God.[1] It was reported that some companions visited Abū Bakr while lying on his deathbed and suggested to invite a physician to see him. He said, "My physician [God] has already seen me and said, 'I do whatever I like to do'". Similarly, Abū al-Dardā' was asked in his terminal illness, "What is your complaint? "My sins," he answered. His visitors asked, "What do you wish?" He replied, "God's mercy." They said, "Shall we invite a physician?" He responded, "The physician has made me ill."[2] A group of righteous people once visited their ill friend. One of them asked him, "Shall we call a physician?" He did not answer, so they repeated the question. He thereupon replied with few lines of poetry telling them that a physician will not be able to do anything with a predestined fate. Even a physician dies when his life comes to an end.

A physician with medicine and prescription,
cannot provide cure or protection.
Strangely he dies of the same affliction,
sadly, unable to take any action.

When asked about seeking medical treatment, Aḥmad b. Ḥanbal went for permissibility, with a preference for avoiding it.

(1) Abū Nuʿaym al-Iṣfahānī, *Ḥilyat al-awliyāʾ*, vol. 1, p. 34; *Muṣannaf ʿAbd al-Razzāq*, vol. 13, p. 262.

(2) Abū Nuʿaym al-Iṣfahānī, *Ḥilyat al-awliyāʾ*, vol. 2, p. 218; *Muṣannaf ʿAbd al-Razzāq*, vol. 13, p. 309.

On the other hand, al-Ḥamawī maintained that pursuing medical treatment does not necessarily conflict with putting one›s faith in God. True reliance on God and belief in Divine power call for respecting, rather than, neglecting, the causes that God tied to certain cases. When a person is adept at medicine and takes the suitable procedures while putting his faith in God and asking Him for healing, in such a case he resembles a peasant ploughing his land, planting seeds and asking God to send down rain and protect this plant. Trust in God is not detached from seeking the necessary means. That is why God says, "O you who have believed, take your wary (precautions)".(1) When a Bedouin man asked the Prophet, "O Messenger of God! Shall I tie my camel and rely (upon God), or leave it loose and put my trust in God?" He said: "Tie your camel first, then put your trust in God."(2) Moreover, the Prophet (PBUH) urged people to take whatever necessary precautions. In one narration, he requested them to lock up their doors.(3) In fact, true reliance on God is not antithetical to consideration of causal connections. That is why the Prophet (PBUH) resorted to a cave in the course of his migration from Mecca. Disregarding causes and causal connection is incongruent with both reason and revelation.

As to the cases in which seeking medical treatment was disregarded, they could be explained as follows: the person

---

(1) al-Nisā' (5: 71).

(2) Reported by al-Tirmidhī, chapters on the description of the Day of Judgement, no. 2522. He commented that it is an authentic strange *ḥadīth*. al-Manāwī said, this *ḥadīth* is reported by Ibn Ḥibbān in his Ṣaḥīḥ with an authentic chain of narrators (2/382) (see: Fayḍ al-Qadīr 2/8). Moreover, this *ḥadīth* is also reported by al-Haythamī in Mawārid al-ẓam'ān, no. 2549, Ibn Ḥajar in Fatḥ al-bārī (10/212), al-Zabīdī in Itḥāf al-sādah al-muttaqīn (9/57), al-Hindī, Kanz al-'ummāl, no. 5667 and Abū Nu'aym al-Iṣfahānī, *Ḥilyat al-awliyā'* (8/390).

(3) Reported by al-Bukhārī, Book of Beginning of Creation, Chapter of the best possession of a Muslim will be a herd of sheep; Muslim, Book of Drinks, Chapter: It is recommended to cover vessels, tie up water skins, close doors; Aḥmad in *Musnad* (3/386, 395); al-Bayhaqī in al-Sunan al-Kubrā (1/275); al-Bukhārī, *al-Adab al-mufrad*, no. 122; al-Baghawī, *Sharḥ al-sunnah* (11/389).

may have initially sought treatment; the person said this out of belief in God's predestination with no conflict with the necessity of treatment; the person believes, on the basis of gnostic knowledge, that his life term has come to an end; the person is so occupied by his spiritual condition and concern for salvation in the hereafter; the person suffers from a chronic disease with no certain cure. Such reasons and causes explain the stance of some righteous people and the view held by Aḥmad b. Ḥanbal. Actually, a person is legally required to do one's best to obtain benefits, taking into consideration all possible means and the connection between causes and their ensuing effects.(1)

The view of obligation is based on some Prophetic dicta expressed in the form of categorical command which denotes obligation. Moreover, this view comes in conformity with the ultimate objectives and necessities of *Sharīʿa* which demand the observation of soul and body.

Preponderant Opinion

Considering the bulk of available legal evidence and the higher objectives of *Sharīʿa*, it can be concluded that the five legal rulings may apply to medical treatment. It could be obligatory when negligence leads to intentionally killing oneself or harming any bodily organ as testified by competent physicians. This is based on the fact that the preservation of soul and body is one of the five necessities of *Sharīʿa*.(2) Likewise, medical treatment is accentuated and urgently required in case of infectious diseases such as pulmonary tuberculosis, diphtheria, typhoid and cholera.(3)

---

(1) See: Aḥkām al-Nabawīyah fī al-ṣināʿah al-ṭibbīyah, pp. 327-30.

(2) See ʿAlī ʿAlī al-Muḥammadī, "Ḥukm al-tadāwī fī al-Islam» in *Journal of Fiqh Academy*, 3 (7), p. 570.

(3) Muḥammad ʿAlī al-Bār, "al-ʿilāj al-ṭibbī» in *Journal of Fiqh Academy*, 3 (7), p. 602.

A raft of textual proofs can be cited in support of the necessity of warding off evil. One of the main legal maxims states that there should be neither harming nor reciprocating harm.[1] A group of jurists, including some of Shafīʻīs and Ḥanbalīs,[2] adopt the view that pursuing medical treatment is generally obligatory, while some others limit such obligation to the cases of likely efficacy. According to some Ḥanafī jurists,[3] the obligation is restricted to the case of definitive efficacy of medical treatment. It is analogous to eating bread in order to defeat hunger or drinking water to quench thirst; neglecting this is prohibited if there is a possible risk of death. The same holds true for medical treatment; consequently, any negligence of a definitive medication is in conflict with true reliance on God as elaborated in *al-Fatāwá al-Hindiyya*.

Those jurists based their argument on various textual proofs from the Qur'ān and the Sunnah. For example, the Qur'ān says "Do not contribute to your destruction with your own hands,"[4] and "Do not kill each other, for God is merciful to you."[5] In addition, Usāmah b. Sharīk said that, I came to the Prophet (PBUH) and his Companions were sitting as if they had birds on their heads. I saluted and sat down. The desert Arabs then came from here and there. They asked: Messenger of God, should we make use of medical treatment? He replied: Make use of medical treatment, for God has not made a disease without appointing a remedy for

(1) Based on a Prophetic tradition reported by Reported by Mālik in al-Muwaṭṭa', p. 464; Aḥmad in Musnad (1/313, 5/326); Ibn Mājah (2/784). It is declared authentic by many scholars including al-Albānī in Irwā› al-ghalīl, no. 896.

(2) Ibn Taymīyah, *Majmū' al-Fatāwá*, vol. 21, p. 564 & vol. 24, p. 269; al-Ghazālī, *Iḥyā' 'ulūm al-dīn*, op. cit., vol. 4, p.279; Ibn Mufliḥ al-Maqdisī, *al-Ādāb al-shar'īyah*, vol. 2, p. 361.

(3) See: *al-Fatāwá al-Hindiyya*, vol. 5, p. 355.

(4) al-Baqarah (2: 195).

(5) al-Nisā' (4: 29).

it, with the exception of one disease, namely old age.(1) On the authority of Abū al-Dardā', the Prophet (PBUH) said: God has sent down both the disease and the cure, and He has appointed a cure for every disease, so treat yourselves medically, but use nothing unlawful.(2) Accordingly, if seeking medical treatment is obligatory, it becomes prohibited to ignore it especially in case of contagious diseases or risks of serious harm or even death. Jābir narrated that: We set out on a journey. One of our people was hurt by a stone, that injured his head. He then had a sexual dream. He asked his fellow travelers: Do you find a concession for me to perform *tayammum* (dry ablution)? They said: We do not find any concession for you while you can use water. He took a bath and died. When we came to the Prophet (PBUH), the incident was reported to him. He said: They killed him; may God kill them! Could they not ask when they did not know? The cure for ignorance is inquiry.(3)

Seeking medical treatment could be recommended in case of speculative efficacy.(4) This is supported by the practice and sayings of the Prophet (PBUH).(5) Alternatively, medication is permissible in other cases according to the

---

(1) Reported by Abū Dāwūd in al-Sunan, along with *'Awn al-ma'būd* (10/334); al-Tirmidhī declared this *ḥadīth* to be *ḥasan ṣaḥiḥ* (Lit. Good authentic narration). See: *Tuḥfat al-aḥwadhī* (6/190). It is also reported by Ibn Mājah, al-Nasā'ī and al-Ḥākim.

(2) Reported by Abū Dāwūd in al-Sunan, along with *'Awn al-ma'būd* (10/351).

(3) Reported by Abū Dāwūd, al-Dāraquṭnī (69), al-Bayhaqī (1/228). The narration on the authority of Ibn 'Abbās was reported by Abū Dāwūd, al-Bayhaqī, Ibn Ḥibbān, al-Ḥākim, Abū Nu'aym in Ḥilyat al-awliyā' (3/317). al-Ḥāfiẓ Ibn Ḥajar commented in Bulūgh al-marām with Subul al-salām (1/161), "This tradition is reported by Abū Dāwūd with a weak chain of narrators." However, this narration is corroborated by various ways of transmission, that is why Ibn al-Sakan declared it as an authentic (*ṣaḥiḥ*) and it was reported by Ibn Khuzaymah in his Ṣaḥīḥ (1/138), Ibn Ḥibbān in Ṣaḥīḥ (2/304), al-Ḥākim in al-Mustadrak (1/165).

(4) See: *al-Fatāwá al-Hindiyya*, vol. 5, p. 355.

(5) See: Abū Dāwūd in al-Sunan, along with *'Awn al-ma'būd* (10/339, 41, 49); *Fatḥ al-bārī* (10/147, 150) where al-Bukhārī reported that the Prophet (PBUH) made use of cupping.

majority of jurists.(1) al-Ghazālī notes that a countless number of righteous predecessors sough medical treatment; however, a group of prominent companions avoided it. On the other hand, the Prophet (PBUH) pursued medical treatment. If it was not preferred, he would not have sought it. Indeed, his reliance on God is in no way less perfect than others.(2)

al-Ghazālī refutes the claim of conflict between pursuing medical treatment and reliance on God on the basis that the Prophet resorted to it and commanded people to do so. It is, he argues, like eating food or drinking water to defeat hunger or thirst. They are causes for ensuing effects as decreed by God. He cites as supporting evidence the report of plague that took place during the caliphate of 'Umar. The caliph went out to visit Sham but he got the news of plague. There was a difference of opinion whether they should proceed further or retreat to their homes. Those who wanted to proceed based their opinion on putting faith in God. They did not want to run away from death and the Divine decree. The Qur'ān relates a story of people doing so; God says, "Consider those people who abandoned their homeland in fear of death, even though there were thousands of them."(3) Finally, 'Umar decided to go back. Some of the companions asked him "Are you going to run away from the Divine Decree?" He answered, we are running from the Divine Decree to the Divine Decree. 'Abd al-Raḥmān b. 'Auf told him that God's Messenger (PBUH) said, "If you hear that this plague has broken out in a land, do

(1) See: *al-Fawākih al-dawānī*, vol. 2, p. 442; al-Qurṭubī, *al-Jāmiʿ li-aḥkām al-Qurʾān,* vol. 10, p. 199. ʿAlīʿAlī al-Muḥammadī, "Ḥukm al-tadāwī fī al-Islam» in *Journal of Fiqh Academy*, 3 (7), p. 570

(2) al-Ghazālī, *Iḥyāʾ ʿulūm al-dīn*, op. cit, vol. 4, p. 283.

(3) al-Baqarah (2: 243).

not go to it; but if it breaks out in a land where you are present, do not go out escaping from it."[4]

Based on the forgoing discussion, it is crystal clear that seeking medical treatment reflects observation of the causal connection. This treatment is a cause to be respected and utilized. Neglecting it could amount to prohibition if it brings about any harm. This view is emphasized by Ibn al-Qayyim who elaborated on the causal connection between medical treatment and healing in his book entitled *al-ṭibb al-Nabawī*. In this book, he presents medical treatment as consistent with God's Divine decree and universal rules. On the other hand, ignoring medication may be permissible if there is no use of it. al-Ghazālī listed five reasons for avoiding medical treatment, including the case when a person suffers from a chronic disease with no known or definitive cure.[5]

Considering the special nature and possible consequences of genetic therapy, there has to be a particular ruling for each of its different forms based on a thorough understanding. Indeed, issuing a judgment on something is dependent on having a proper conception thereof. I discussed the different legal rulings of this kind of medical intervention in a previous work. Generally speaking, permissibility is conditioned on taking necessary precautions and avoiding any harmful consequences.[6]

Besides the previous proofs, the following general rules and legal precepts govern medical treatment.

1. Objectives of *Sharīʿa* in terms of preservation of necessities (*ḍarūrāt*), needs (*ḥājīyāt*), and embellishments (*taḥsīnīyāt*) in addition to weighing

(4) Reported by al-Bukhārī and Muslim. See: *Fatḥ al-bārī* (10/179) and *Ṣaḥīḥ* of Muslim (4/1740) no. 2219.

(5) al-Ghazālī, *Iḥyā' 'ulūm al-dīn*, op. cit, vol. 4, p. 279.

(6) al-Qaradāghī, ʿAlīʿAlī al-Muḥammadī, *Fiqh al-Qaḍāyā al-Ṭibbīyah al-Muʿāṣirah* (Beirut: Dār al-Bashā'ir al-Islāmīyah, 2nd ed., 2008) pp. 301-36.

interests against evils. There are some relevant rules and legal maxims in this regard including: "Warding off harm should always take priority over the accruement of benefit"; "Minor damage will be endured to get rid of major damage"; "Harm is to be removed as much as possible"; "Harm may not be eliminated by its equivalent"; "Necessities render prohibited things permissible"; "Necessity is measured in accordance with its true proportions"; "Private harm is tolerated in order to ward off a public one"; "In the presence of two evils, the one whose harm is greater is to be avoided by the commission of the lesser"; "The lesser of the two evils is tolerated"; "Harm is to be warded off as much as possible"; "Need is ranked as necessity, be it public or private"; "Necessity does not invalidate the right of others"; "Hardship begets facilitation"; "Relaxation should be afforded in the case of difficulty"; and "There should be neither harming nor reciprocating harm."(1)

2. Consideration of means and methods. A prohibited means does not justify a noble end. Consequently, it is not allowed to use a prohibited means in medical treatment except in cases of dire necessities which render prohibited things permissible, or needs which are ranked as necessity.(2) Ibn al-Qayyim considered the principle of blocking means to evil as constituting a fourth of religion and Islamic *fiqh*.(3)
3. Consideration of consequences, ends, outcomes and effects of treatment. al-Shāṭibī points out that heeding

---

(1) Cited above.

(2) al- Shāṭibī explained that such a means in fact exploits a given benefit only to get a prohibited thing. (See: *al-Muwāfaqāt*, vol. 4, p. 556).

(3) Ibn al-Qayyim, *I'lām al-muwaqqi'*īn *'an* Rabb al-'Ālamīn, ed. Ṭaha *'Abd* al-Ra*'ūf* Sa'd (Cairo: Dār al-nahḍah al-jadīdah), vol. 3, pp. 134-59.

the outcomes of actions is consistent with the higher objectives of the law, whether the actions concerned are in accordance with the law or in violation thereof. Therefore, the *mujtahid* is not to judge a human action, be it one of commission or omission, until he has given careful thought to the consequences to which the action will lead. A given action may be intended to acquire certain benefit or prevent some sort of evil, however, it may result in an opposite outcome. If generally permitted, the action intended to secure a benefit may lead to an equal or greater evil. In this specific case, this permissibility cannot be accepted. The same is true for the action intended to ward off an evil as it may lead to even a greater one.[1] A lot of legal maxims are based on this principle of consideration of consequences.[2]

IIFA Resolution

The International Islamic *Fiqh* Academy (IIFA) issued its resolution no. 67/5/7 concerning medical treatment as follows.

First: Seeking Medical Treatment

The basic rule on medical treatment is that it is permissible in *Sharīʿa* by virtue of the mentions made about it in the Holy Qurʾān and in both the verbal and the actual Sunnah, and in view of its contribution to "self-preservation", one of the objectives of legislation. Rulings on medical treatment vary according to the situations and persons involved:

A. It is obligatory if ignoring it may result in the person's self-destruction, loss of an organ or

(1) al- Shāṭibī, *al-Muwāfaqāt*, vol. 4, pp. 552-53.
(2) Ibid., vol. 4, p. 556.

disability, or if the illness can spread to others as in the case of contagious diseases.

B. It is desirable if ignoring it may weaken the body without entailing the consequences mentioned in the first case above.

C. It is permissible if not covered by the preceding two cases.

D. It is undesirable if there is a risk that the action to be taken may provoke complications that are worse than the illness to be removed.

Second: Treatment of Desperate Cases

A. According to the Islamic faith: illness and cure are in the hands of Almighty God; medical treatment is a way of adopting the means laid down by Almighty God in the universe; and it is impermissible to despair of God's mercy but necessary to maintain the hope of recovery by the leave of God. Doctors and patient's relatives should raise the morale of the patient and continue to look after him and alleviate his psychological and physical suffering regardless of the chances of recovery or lack thereof.

B. The determination of whether a case is clinically desperate depends on the assessment of physicians, the available medical possibilities in time and space, and the patient's circumstances.

Third: The Patient's Permission

A. The patient's permission for treatment is essential if the patient is in full legal capacity to give it. If he is not, the permission of his (or her) legal guardian shall be sought according to the order of guardianship in *Sharīʿa*, and in conformity with its provisions which limit the scope of the guardian's action to the benefit and interest of the person under guardianship as well as to removing harm from him (or her). If the guardian, however, resolves not to give permission, his decision shall not be taken into consideration if it is clearly detrimental to the person under guardianship. The right of permission shall then be transferred to the next guardian and ultimately to the ruler.

B. The ruler shall order the medical treatment when deemed appropriate in cases of contagious diseases and preventive immunities.

C. In emergency cases, when the life of the victim is in danger, medical treatment shall not depend on permission.

D. In carrying out medical research, it is imperative to obtain the agreement of the subject if he is totally fit in a way that is devoid of coercion (as in the case of jailed people) and financial enrichment (as in the case of the poor). Moreover, the research to be undertaken must not involve any harm. It is not permissible to carry out medical research on persons that are incapacitated or those of diminished capacity, even with the permission of their guardians.[1]

Using Prohibited Medicine

Considering the bulk of textual indicants and thorough investigation, it is established that Islamic *Sharīʿa* was sent as a mercy for all mankind. Thus, all of its provisions and

(1) *Journal of Fiqh Academy*, 3 (7) 731-33. This translation is quoted, with slight modification, from Resolutions and Recommendations of the Council of the Islamic Fiqh Academy 1985-2000 (Jeddah: Islamic Development Bank, 2000), p. 139ff.

regulations intend to fulfil people's interests and protect them against any evils. Accordingly, anything declared prohibited necessarily involves a sort of evil and harm, either to body, mind, wealth, or religion. Taking this as a point of departure, we can safely state that anything definitely deemed unlawful based on a textual proof never can be a source of healing; rather it is a cause of ailment. It was reported that a man asked the Prophet (PBUH) about liquor, thereupon the latter expounded that it is prohibited. But the person explained that he prepares it as a medicine, whereupon the Prophet (PBUH) said: It is not medicine, but an ailment.(1) Commenting on this report, al-Nawawī argues that this proves the prohibition of acquiring liquor and making use of it. It is clearly stated that liquor can never be a medicine; therefore, it is not allowed to use it in medical treatment.(2) Similarly, Ibn Ḥajar notes that this report is cited as supporting evidence for prohibition of using illegal ingredients as liquor in medical treatment.(3) Prevention of using liquor as a remedy is established by a textual indicant which differentiates it from other items.(4)

IFC Resolution

The Islamic *Fiqh* Council (IFC) affiliated to the Muslim World League deliberated over the issue of medicines containing alcohol and drugs in its 16th session held in Mecca in 21-26/10/1424 AH corresponding to 5-10/1/2002 and issued its decision no. 6/16 which stated:

After deliberating and discussing this issue, reviewing

(1) Reported by Muslim in his Ṣaḥīḥ, no. 3670; Ibn Mājah, no 3491; Aḥmad in Musnad, no. 18036, 18107, 21646.

(2) See sharḥ al-Nawawī of Ṣaḥīḥ Muslim, book of drinks, no. 3670.

(3) *Fatḥ al-bārī*, discussion of *ḥadīth* no. 6744.

(4) See: al-Qaraḍāwī, *al-ḥalāl wa-al-ḥarām*, op. cit., p. 74.

all papers, and taking into consideration the principles of necessity, removing hardship, warding off evils and choosing the lesser of two evils, the Islamic *Fiqh* Council resolves that:

1. It is not permissible to use liquor as a medicine in any way based on the following Prophetic traditions: "God did not make your cure in what He made unlawful to you (Related by al-Bukhārī)", "God has sent down both the disease and the cure, and He has appointed a cure for every disease, so treat yourselves medically, but use nothing unlawful " (Narrated by Abū Dāwūd in al-Sunan, Ibn al-Sunnī and Abū Nuʿaym). When Ṭāriq b. Suwaid asked the Prophet (PBUH) about liquor, he answered that, "It is no medicine, but an ailment." (Reported by Ibn Mājah and Abū Nuʿaym).
2. It is permissible to use medicines containing alcohol in small quantities that are essential in the pharmacological industry, provided that such medicines are prescribed by a competent doctor. It is also permissible to use alcohol externally on wounds as a cleansing agent, killer of germs and in creams and ointments that are used externally.
3. The Islamic *Fiqh* Council urges pharmaceutical companies and pharmacists in Muslim countries and importers of medicines to do their best to reduce the use of alcohol in medicines to the absolute minimum, and to use substitutes wherever possible.
4. The Council urges doctors to reduce the prescription of alcohol-containing medicines to the minimum. May God grant us success!

1.6. *AKHLĀQ* (ETHICS)

Linguistically, *akhlāq* in Arabic is the plural form of *khuluq* (ethic).[1] In philology, both *khalq* (creation) and *khuluq* share the same root, however, the former is related to physical shapes and figures to be seen by naked eyes while the latter is dedicated to traits and characteristics discerned by the intellect.[2] As for the technical meaning of *akhlāq*, al-Māwardī defines it as "internal dispositions which naturally surface but are forcibly suppressed."[3] al-Ghazālī defines it as "Existing capabilities in the soul (of someone) that enable him to easily perform various actions without requiring deep thinking and contemplation."[4] In my view, *khuluq* can be defined as a conduct that is based on internal will, yielding goodness when naturally inclined to the good, or badness if inclined to the bad. Taking into consideration its motives, *khuluq* can still be defined as a group of values and principles that govern human conducts and behaviors. In terms of its outcomes and effects, *khuluq* may be defined as a set of, accepted or rejected, conducts and behaviors. Ethics represent the good or bad traits and qualities emanating from the heart and psyche. Such traits could be a natural disposition for some people, while for others, they can be acquired by disciplining, cultivating and nurturing.[5] Simply put, some people are instinctively characterized by noble inborn ethics maintained by sound upbringing and virtuous milieu. This can be understood from the Prophet's (PBUH) remarks to al-Mundhir al-Ashajj in which he said,

(1) *Lisān al-ʿArab*, *al-Qāmūs al-Muḥīṭ*, *al-Muʿjam al-Wasīṭ* (entry: Khuluq).

(2) *Lisān al-ʿArab,* vol.10, p. 86; al-Jurjānī, *al-taʿrīfāt,* p. 104.

(3) al-Jurjānī, *al-taʿrīfāt, p. 104.*

(4) al-Ghazālī, *Iḥyāʾ ʿulūm al-dīn*, vol. 3, p. 53.

(5) *Tahdhīb al-akhlāq*, p. 12; Muḥammad ʿAbd Allāh Darāz, *Dustūr al-akhlāq fī al-Qurʾān*, trans. ʿAbd al-Ṣabūr Shāhīn (Beirut: Muʾassasat alrisāla, 1416), p. 35; Abd al-Raḥmān Ḥabannakah, al-Akhlāq al-Islāmīyah wa- ususuhā, vol.1, p. 33.

"You have two characteristics which God likes: gentleness and deliberation." He asked: Have I acquired them or has God created (them) in my nature? He replied: No, God has created (them) in your nature. al-Ashajj then said: Praise be to God Who has created in my nature two characteristics which He and His Apostle like.(1) Based on this report, Ibn al-Qayyim argues that some ethics represent a natural disposition while others can be acquired and developed.(2) There are other ethics which can be inculcated and developed. This can be gleaned from the following tradition where the Prophet (PBUH) says, "And (know) that he who refrains from begging others (or doing prohibited deeds), God will make him contented and not in need of others; and he who remains patient, God will bestow patience upon him, and he who is satisfied with what he has, God will make him self-sufficient. And there is no gift better and more vast (that you may be given) than patience."(3)

Ethics in Islam: An Overarching Purpose, Not a Means

As one explores the *Sharīʿa* texts, ranging from those related to creed and the revelation of divine books, sending prophets, worship, and rituals to those concerned with interpersonal relationships, economics, legal punishments, family affairs, politics, and *jihād*, it becomes evident that the primary focus is on attaining virtue, reinforcing noble values, and maintaining excellent behavior so as to enable society to lead a happy life. Ethics is not a separate branch of Islam but is rather a fundamental objective that pervades

---

(1) Reported by Aḥmad (4/205), Abū Dāwūd as expounded by al-Albānī in the authentic reports by Abū Dāwūd, *ḥadīth* no. 5225. The first part of this *ḥadīth* is reported by Muslim, no. 17, 18, 25.

(2) Madārij al-sālikīn, vol. 3, p. 315.

(3) Reported by al-Bukhārī in Ṣaḥīḥ, no. 1449; Muslim in Ṣaḥīḥ, no. 1053; Abū Dāwūd as expounded by al-Albānī in the authentic reports by Abū Dāwūd, *ḥadīth* no. 1644.

all elements of life. Ethics is essential to a person's survival just as a soul is to human life, blood is to a human body, or water is to the life of plants. In this sense, the Noble Qur'ān summarizes the objectives of sending the Prophet Muhammad (PBUH) by referring to the concept of mercy — namely a mercy for all humans, animals, and inanimate creatures — and he is considered the epitome of ethics and values. God says, "And in no way have We sent you except as a mercy to the worlds."(1) The Prophet (PBUH) said, "I have been sent to perfect the noble traits of character."(2) When God praised the Prophet, He mentioned his noble character. The Qur'ān reads, "And surely you are indeed of a magnificent character."(3)

Another indication of the great significance of ethics lies in the fact that God described Himself with the noble traits, including mercy, compassion, generosity, truthfulness, justice, etc. Moreover, God considers injustice as a basis for disbelief and all kinds of corruption. God states, "Surely associating (others with Allah) is indeed a monstrous injustice."(4) According to the Qur'ān, injustice is a cause of destroying tyrants, God says, "Say, 'Think: if the punishment of God should come to you, by surprise or openly, would anyone but the evildoers [the unjust] be destroyed?'"(5), "Sure it is (that) the unjust will not

---

(1) al- Anbiyā' (21: 107).

(2) Reported by Mālik, al-Bukhārī, *al-Adab al-mufrad.* al-Albānī included it in the authentic collection, *ḥadīth* no. 45. Another narration of the same *ḥadīth* states that the Prophet said, I have been sent to perfect the virtuous traits of character." This narration is reported by al-Bukhārī, *al-Adab al-mufrad* and declared authentic by al-Albānī in commenting on *al-Adab al-mufrad*, no. 207. A third narration uses the phrase *ḥasan al-akhlāq* (good traits of character) as narrated in Mishkāt al-Maṣābīḥ and declared as a *ḥasan* (good) *ḥadīth* by al-Albānī, no. 5023.

(3) al-Qalam (68: 4).

(4) Luqmān (31: 13).

(5) al-'An'ām (6: 47).

prosper”,[1] “And in no way would We be causing towns to perish except that their populations are unjust”.[2] Dozens of Qur᾽ānic verses condemn injustice and praise justice and urge people to stick to it in all cases. For instance, God says, “Do not let hatred of others lead you away from justice, but adhere to justice, for that is closer to awareness of God.”[3] Moreover, an inclusive verse of ethics, which is regularly recited in Friday sermon, states that, “God commands justice, doing good [*iḥsān*], and generosity towards relatives and He forbids what is shameful [obscenity], blameworthy [maleficence], and oppressive. He teaches you, so that you may take heed.”[4] When the Qur᾽ān lists the personal traits of righteous people, it begins with the noble manners, in terms of acts and sayings. God says, “The servants of the Lord of Mercy are those who walk humbly on the earth, and who, when the foolish address them, reply, ‘Peace’.”[5] Then, it mentions other traits such as moderation in spending, avoidance of any aggression, etc. Talking about pious people who deserve to be admitted into paradise, the Qur᾽ān highlights in Sūrat al-Dhāriyāt (Q: 51) their beneficence and kindness toward the poor and needy. At the beginning of Sūrat al-Mu’uminūn (Q: 23), the traits of the true believers are listed. They are the ones who are submissive to God, show mercy toward the poor, pay heed to their deposits and their covenants, and veer away from idle talk and vices. One of the most important objectives of belief in God and the Last Day is for the believer to attain a level of God-consciousness enabling him to abstain from immoral behavior. The Qur᾽ān

(1) al-᾽An῾ām (6: 21).
(2) al-Qaṣaṣ (28: 59).
(3) al-Mā᾽idah (5: 8).
(4) al-Naḥl (16: 90).
(5) al-Furqān (25: 63).

includes a multitude of examples highlighting the effects of faith on behaviors. One prominent example is the story of Yusuf (Joseph) and the wife of the chief minister of Egypt. God says, "The woman in whose house he was living tried to seduce him: she bolted the doors and said, 'Come to me,' and he replied, 'God forbid! My master has been good to me; wrongdoers never prosper.'"[(1)] Such effects are evident in the humanitarian field. God says, "They give food to the poor, the orphan, and the captive, though they love it themselves, saying, 'We feed you for the sake of God alone: We seek neither recompense nor thanks from you. We fear the Day of our Lord—a woefully grim Day.'"[(2)] On the other hand, the Qur'ān explains how disbelief affects people's behaviors and lead them to cruelty, greed and avarice. God says, "Have you seen him who cries lies to the Doom? That is the one who repulses the orphan. And does not urge the (offering) of food to the indigent."[(3)]

In fact, all acts of worship are somehow related to ethics and noble manners. In terms of ritual prayers and remembrance of God, the Qur'ān states, "Prayer restrains outrageous and unacceptable behavior. Remembering God is greater."[(4)] As for zakāt (alms giving), God says, "Take of their riches a donation to purify them and to cleanse them thereby; and pray for them; surely your prayer is sereneness (i.e., tranquility) for them; and God is Ever-Hearing, Ever-Knowing."[(5)] In terms of fasting, the Qur'ān states, "You who believe, fasting is prescribed for you, as it was prescribed for those before you, so that you

(1) Yusuf (12: 23).
(2) al-Insān (76: 8-10).
(3) al-Mā`ūn (107: 1-3).
(4) al-`Ankabūt (29: 45).
(5) al-Tawbah (9: 103).

may be mindful of God."(1) Concerning pilgrimage, God says, "The pilgrimage takes place during the prescribed months. There should be no indecent speech, misbehavior, or quarrelling for anyone undertaking the pilgrimage."(2) Additionally, God lays great emphasis on rectifying hearts. The Qur᾽ān confirms that, "It is neither their meat nor their blood that reaches God but your piety."(3) In the field of politics, the Qur᾽ān focuses on fulfilling covenants and trusts, maintaining justice, and doing good. God says, "God commands you [people] to return things entrusted to you to their rightful owners, and, if you judge between people, to do so with justice: God's instructions to you are excellent, for He hears and sees everything."(4) It is not possible here to dwell on all legislations that are related to ethics. However, it can be stated that all such legislations are intended to fulfill the interests of people and protect them against any potential harm and evils. Indeed, God is in no need of people. The Qur᾽ān affirms that "God is the Ever-Affluent, (Literally: Ever-Rich) and you are the poor ones,"(5) "If you are ungrateful, remember God has no need of you."(6) Therefore, He commands such legislations, acts of worship and beliefs for people to be righteous and just; consequently, they can positively contribute to this universe on the basis of justice, mercy and equality. The glorious Qur᾽ān affords utmost attention to ethics and noble manners in hundreds of verses as indicated above. Prof. Muḥammad ʻAbd Allāh Darāz wrote an in-depth analysis and study in this regard titled, *Dustūr al-akhlāq fī al-Qur᾽ān*. By this

---

(1) al-Baqarah (2: 183).
(2) al-Baqarah (2: 197).
(3) al-Ḥajj (22: 37).
(4) al-Nisā᾽ (4: 58).
(5) Muḥammad (47: 38).
(6) al-Zumar (39: 7).

study, Darāz presented a unique contribution to the field of ethics and ethical philosophy.

Likewise, the Sunnah, including the Prophet's (PBUH) sayings, deeds and tacit approvals, deals in great detail with ethics. In this sense, it represents an inclusive encyclopedia and a detailed resource exemplifying the noble teachings of the Qur'ān and the sublime qualities of the Prophet (PBUH) as mercy from God Who says, "And in no way have We sent you except as a mercy to the worlds."[1] Evidently, the Prophetic Sunnah includes a raft of chapters dedicated to ethics and noble character. A quick glimpse of al- Nawawī's *Riyāḍ al-ṣāliḥīn* testifies to this fact. Though it is a small book, it is crammed with 180 chapters on positive ethics in addition to another 115 ones dealing with negative qualities. Here is a list of some important chapters and sections:

> Devotion, sincerity and intention, repentance, patience, truthfulness, self-accountability, piety, certitude and reliance, uprightness, reflecting the perfect creatures of God, struggling against one's soul, doing good deeds increasingly in old age, multiplicity of ways to good deeds, moderation in worship, persistent observation of good deeds, acting upon Sunnah, properly accepting God's decree, forbidding heresies and baseless religious practices, reviving an act of Sunnah, guiding others to good deeds, cooperation for noble deeds, giving advice, enjoining good and forbidding evil, severity of punishment for those enjoining good but doing evil, repaying deposits, forbiddance of injustice, inviolability of Muslim's honors and rights, veiling the defects of Muslims, satisfying Muslim's needs, intercession, reconciliation and establishing peace

(1) al- Anbiyā' (21: 107).

among people, supreme status of weak Muslims, kind treatment of orphans, daughters, poor persons and the needy, treating women kindly, husband's rights on his wife, spending on family, spending legitimate earnings, urging family to obey God, maintaining neighbor's right, dutifulness and kindness toward parents, forbiddance of being undutiful to parents, virtue of being dutiful to parent's friends, revering Prophet's (PBUH) kin, revering people of knowledge and righteous ones, visiting and accompanying of righteous people, virtue of love for the sake of God, signs of God's love for devotees, warning against harming righteous people, judging people according to apparent behavior, fearing God, longing for God's forgiveness, virtue of hope, combining between fear and hope, weeping out of fearing God, abstention from worldly delights, leading an austere life, contentment of simple life and spending moderately, lawful earning, earning one's livelihood, virtue of generosity and spending, forbiddance of miserliness and greed, altruism and helping others, competing in deeds for the Hereafter, noble status of thankful wealthy persons, desirability of frequenting to graveyards, dislike of hoping for death due to afflictions, God-fearingness and avoiding doubtful matters, modesty and leniency, forbiddance of arrogance and haughtiness, good character and noble manners, forbearance and tolerance, pardoning and tolerating people, bearing harm, refusal of violating God's orders, advising people in authority, noble status of just rulers, avoidance of pursuing positions of authority, virtue of chastity and modesty, keeping secrets, fulfilling promises, continuing to do good, using kind words and smiling, clear articulation of speech, attentive listening, moderate admonition of others, tranquility and calmness, attending prayers and knowledge sessions, entertaining a guest, desirability of giving glad tidings, bidding farewell to friends, consultation, avoidance of criticizing food, etiquette of eating, visiting the sick, escorting the dead to graves and performing funeral prayer, curbing one's tongue and avoidance of backbiting, forbiddance of listening to backbiting, forms of permissible backbiting, avoidance of gossip, malicious reporting, prohibition of telling lies, reproaching double-dealing, permissible forms of lying, maintaining accuracy in narration, strict forbiddance of perjury, avoidance of cursing, permissibility of cursing indefinite sinful persons, avoidance of calling names and insulting Muslims, avoidance of mentioning the dead unfairly, prevention of causing harm, avoidance of mutual detest and antagonism, forbidding envy, prohibition of spying and eavesdropping, avoidance of thinking ill of Muslims, prohibition of despising Muslims, forbiddance of schadenfreude, prohibition of slandering people's lineage, prohibition of fraudulence and cheating, forbiddance of betrayal, or hurting others by obliging and reproach, forbiddance of boasting and aggression, on quarrelling and hostility, avoidance of secret conversation in presence of a third party, avoidance of exaggeration in punishing one's beast, slave, or son, prohibition of torturing by fire, prohibition of intentional delay of debts by wealthy persons, undesirability of withdrawing a gift, forbiddance of taking orphan's wealth unlawfully, prohibition of usury, prohibition of hypocrisy and showing off, forbiddance of looking at a non-Maḥram woman, prohibition of staying in private with a non-Maḥram woman, forbiddance of twig, tattooing and splitting teeth, avoidance of mannerism and theatricality, avoidance of bewailing loudly the dead, prohibition of consulting soothsayers, avoidance of believing in bad omen, prohibition of intentional false oath, avoidance of cursing fever, dislike of cursing wind, avoidance of cursing roosters, forbiddance of insolence and obscene language, avoidance of speaking gutturally, warning against saying, "my soul is evil", forbiddance of describing a woman's beauty to men except for legal causes, prohibition of defecation on roadways, forbiddance of urination into stagnant water, avoidance of gifting some sons to the exclusion of others, forbidding women to mourn over the dead for more than three days, undesirability of sale in which the dweller of the town sells for the Bedouin, forbiddance of wasting money, forbiddance of brandishing a weapon at a Muslim jokingly, dislike of going out of the Mosque after delivering the call to prayer, dislike of reclining from accepting sweet basil, undesirability of praising one in his presence, dislike of coming out of a town in case of the plague, strict forbiddance of sorcery, forbiddance of using gold and silver utensils, forbiddance of wearing saffron-dyed clothes for men, forbiddance of keeping silent for a whole day.

Other books of Ḥadīth collections are replete with traditions on ethics and noble manners. This confirms the great significance and wide scope of ethics in Islam. That is why a lot of Muslim scholars paid special attention to this specific field, such as al-Ghazālī in *Iḥyā' 'ulūm al-dīn*, Ibn al-Qayyim in *Minhāj al-qāṣidīn*, and Ibn al-Jawzī in most of his works, just to name a few.

Delineating Ethics According to their Origins

Islamic ethics and values are abundant. An investigation of the books of Prophetic traditions will unequivocally reveal hundreds of chapters that address ethics directly or indirectly.(1) One perspective through which ethics may be delineated involves linking them to the eight higher objectives of *Sharīʿa* as indicated above. A second perspective involves associating them with the following moralities:

1. A positive relationship between a person and his Lord.
2. A positive relationship between a person and other people.
3. A positive relationship between a person and animals.
4. A positive relationship between a person and the environment.

These ethics, values, virtues, and ideals can also be delineated from a third perspective, which involves ranking them in terms of strength, outcomes, impacts, and associated punishment. For instance:

1. Islam categorizes some ethics as obligations and duties whereby their violation entails legislative action and punitive measures.
2. There are other ethics that have been ordained by God, but worldly punishments were not set for those who violate them.
3. Ethics such as altruism are categorized in Islam as virtues and ideals to which one should aspire.

Based on the forgoing discussion, ethics in Islam are closely related to doctrines, rituals, and legislations. Put differently, ethics permeate all aspects of religion. God,

---

(1) See the books of Ḥadīth, especially Ṣaḥīḥ of al-Bukhārī, Ṣaḥīḥ of Muslim, the four collections of al-Sunan, al-muwaṭṭa', and Sunan of al-Dārimī; where hundreds of sections on ethics can be found.

glory be to Him, praised the Prophet (PBUH), saying, "And surely you are indeed of a magnificent character."(1) Commenting on this verse, al-Ṭabarī explains that God addresses His Prophet (PBUH) saying, you are characterized by noble manners; namely, the manners of the Qur'ān as educated by God. Those manners typify Islam and its legislations.(2) The same meaning is expressed by 'Ā'isha (May Allah be pleased with her). She was once asked about the character of the Prophet. She answered, "His character was the Qur'ān."(3) It may be appropriate here to briefly mention some of those noble manners. They include:

> Belief in God and His oneness, devotion and sincerity, patience, truthfulness, modesty, timely self-accountability, piety, certitude and reliance, uprightness, beneficence, keeping good relations with one's kin, repelling evil with good, doing good, cooperation in doing good, giving advice, warding off evil, accruement of benefit, fulfilling covenants and trusts, justice, prevention of injustice, helping the oppressed, honoring human rights and dignity, veiling people's defects, avoidance of spreading vices, fulfilling people's needs, kind intercession and reconciliation among people, taking care of the elders, the weak, the poor and the needy, courage, generosity, fulfilling the rights of parents, offspring, relatives and neighbors, respecting people of knowledge and elders, true love, non-maleficence, asceticism, abstention from worldly delights, leading an austere life, contentment of simple life and spending moderately, altruism,

---

(1) al-Qalam (68: 4).

(2) al-Ṭabarī, Jāmi' al-bayān, vol. 23, p. 528.

(3) Reported by al-Bukhārī, *al-Adab al-mufrad* and declared authentic due to external factors by al-Albānī in commenting on *al-Adab al-mufrad*, no. 234. He also included it in Ṣaḥīḥ al-jāmi', no. 4811.

forbearance, kindness, forgiveness, avoiding nasty people, self-discipline, keeping secrets, using kind words, cheerfulness, attentive listening, tranquility and calmness, entertaining a guest, avoidance of criticizing food, visiting patients, escorting the dead to graveyards, avoidance of telling lies, having good thoughts of people, avoiding backbiting, avoiding perjury, avoidance of cursing others, be dead or alive, avoidance of despising others, avoiding a grudge and envy, avoidance of spying and eavesdropping, avoiding schadenfreude, avoidance of slandering people's lineage, avoidance of boasting, transparency and avoiding cheating and deception, fulfilling promises, avoidance of betrayal, avoidance of hurting others by obliging and reproach, avoidance of quarrelling and hostility, avoidance of secret conversation in presence of a third party, avoidance of showing off, avoiding mannerism and theatricality, avoidance of frequent swearing by God, avoidance of consulting soothsayers and believing in bad omen, avoidance of cursing fever, diseases and the wind, avoidance of insolence and obscene language, avoidance of speaking gutturally, the removal of harmful object from the road, maintaining equality, etc.[(1)]

In terms of medical ethics, Jamāl al-Dīn al-Subkī listed some moral principles to be observed by physicians. These include giving sincere advice; showing beneficence and kindness toward the patients; advising the patient to write his will if he believes that he is likely to die soon; adequately understanding the nature of disease before giving any prescription; taking time in deciding the suitable treatment;

(1) See chapters of noble character and moralities in *Riyāḍ al-ṣāliḥīn*, collections of Sunnah, and *Iḥyā' 'ulūm al-dīn.*

taking into consideration the mood of the patient; to be well-versed in his profession; and to believe that healing is given by God.[1] Furthermore, a physician needs to have the adequate professional knowledge and expertise. It was reported that the Prophet (PBUH) asked two physicians who attended a sick person, "which of you is the better physician?"[2] A lot of early Muslim physicians firmly warned against practicing medicine without having the necessary qualifications. al-Rāzī argued that thieves and bandits are far better than those practicing medicine without being physicians.[3] In our present-day world, it is agreed by all countries to outlaw practicing medicine without a license.[4] Of primary concern in this regard is the ethic of self-accountability and God-consciousness. It is the basic principle upon which all other ethics are based. Equally important, ethics include humbleness, sincerity, truthfulness, honesty, secrecy and confidentiality, and honoring people's dignity.[5]

Actually, Islam commands people to stick to noble ethics and avoid bad manners. The Qur᾽ān presents ethics in the form of commands and prohibitions taking into consideration the varying levels of each category.

1.7 CARDINAL ETHICS

They represent the foundations of all particular and ancillary ethics. Scholars have attempted to include such numerous ancillary morals under certain cardinal virtues. For instance, al-Ghazālī reduces them into four fundamentals. According to him, all branches of human traits can be categorized

(1) See: *Mu'īd al-ni'am wa-mubīd al-niqam*, p. 20.

(2) Reported by Mālik in al-Muwaṭṭa', vol. 4, p. 328; Ibn 'Abd al-Barr, al-Tamhīd, vol. 5, p. 263.

(3) al-Rāzī, Adab al-ṭabīb, p. 81.

(4) al-Qaradāghī, 'Alī'Alī al-Muḥammadī, *Fiqh al-Qaḍāyā al-Ṭibbīyah al-Mu'āṣirah,* op. cit., pp. 110-13; Ibn Abī Uṣaybi'ah, *'Uyūn al-anbā' fī ṭabaqāt al-aṭibbā'*, p. 17.

(5) Ibid.

under four virtues; namely, wisdom, courage, temperance and justice. Wisdom represents the virtue of rational faculty, while courage is the virtue of irascible faculty. On the other hand, temperance embodies the concupiscent faculty while justice is the perfection of all other virtues respectively. According to some people it is on justice that the ordering of heaven and earth is centered. al-Ghazālī explains that there are four virtues of the psyche. These are: the intellect whose perfect status is knowledge; temperance with God-fearingness as its perfect status; courage and its perfect status is striving (*mujāhadah*); and justice whose perfect status is fairness and equitability. They represent the true fundamentals of religion.(1)

In like manner, Miskawayh included sub-virtues under the above-mentioned four fundamentals.(2) By contrast, vices are derived from these four; they are ignorance, injustice, evil and cowardice. Besides these cardinal vices, al-Ghazālī along with other scholars numerated some fundamental vices such as: greed as the source of humiliation, lust, stinginess and grief; envy as the cause of all evils, wars, disputes, and annihilation; grudge, hatred and arrogance as begetting tyranny and despisement. Tackling the concept of the mother virtue, Muḥammad ʻAbd Allāh Darāz argues that all ethics and virtues are derived from piety and God-consciousness (*Taqwā*).(3) Aḥmad al-Raysūnī adopted the same view in his august paper submitted to the first seminar organized by the Research Center for Islamic Legislation and Ethics (CILE). However, he maintained that there is another virtue to be added to God-consciousness; it is mercy or compassion.(4)

---

(1) al-Ghazālī, Mīzān al-ʻamal, p. 27.

(2) *Tahdhīb al-akhlāq*, p. 19.

(3) Muḥammad ʻAbd Allāh Darāz, *Dustūr al-akhlāq fī al-Qurʾān*, p. 87.

(4) al-Raysūnī, "al-akhlāq fī al-ṭibb", a paper presented to *CILE's first seminar on Islamic Bioethics*, January 5-7, 2013.

1.8 GOVERNING PRINCIPLES OF BIOMEDICAL ETHICS

They are the universal principles that constitute the normative framework of ethics. Put differently, they represent the standard code against which behaviors and professional practices are benchmarked and liability is established. In *Principles of Biomedical Ethics*, Tom L. Beauchamp and James F. Childress present the four-principle approach to biomedical ethics. According to them, the principles in this framework are grouped under four general categories: (1) respect for autonomy (a principle requiring respect for the decision-making capacities of autonomous persons), (2) non-maleficence, (3) beneficence, and (4) justice. This theory was thoroughly investigated by CILE first seminar in which Tom Beauchamp participated. During this seminar, I presented a critical review of two papers independently submitted by Beauchamp and Muḥammad ʻAlī al-Bārr. Unfortunately, there is no room here to reflect on this review. The said seminar concluded that it is necessary to study these ethical principles in light of Islamic values and beliefs and link them to the framework of *Maqāṣid*. This specific conclusion is the aim of the present study.

CHAPTER TWO:
CONTRIBUTIONS TO MEDICAL ETHICS DELINEATION

This chapter consists of two main sections; the first deals with earlier contributions to medical ethics with special reference to the declaration of Helsinki and the Islamic charter of medical and health ethics. The second presents a critical review of the four-principle approach of bioethics.

2.1 EARLIER CONTRIBUTIONS TO MEDICAL ETHICS

All heavenly books such as Torah, Gospel, and the Qur᾽ān focus on nurturing ethics and disciplining souls and hearts in order to instill the best standards of conduct. Special attention has been paid to medical ethics. Historical Records show that all civilizations have done so. For instance, the ancient Egyptian civilization and the Greek one through its Hippocratic Oath developed a wide group of excellent medical ethics as will be discussed later. Similarly, a lot of modern contributions and systems attempt to delineate medical ethics; it is to that subject that we now turn.

1. The Council for International Organizations of Medical Sciences (CIOMS)

A non-governmental organization established jointly by WHO and UNESCO in 1949, the Council for International Organizations of Medical Sciences significantly contributed to medical ethics. Those contributions led to the publication of the Helsinki declaration in 1964 and the revised version of 1975 in addition to CIOMS's international ethical guidelines.[1]

2. Helsinki Declaration of 1983 & 1989

This declaration has been revised several times including the revisions of 1983 and 1989. Some revisions were undertaken by CIOMS. The outcome was the issuance of two sets of guidelines: International Guidelines for Ethical Review of Epidemiological Studies in 1991, and International Ethical Guidelines for Biomedical Research Involving Human Subjects in 1993. The second set of guidelines were later revised in December 1998, 1999, and 2000. In January 2001, a formal committee of eight members was convened to redraft the ethical guidelines. The committee members came from Africa, Latin America, USA and the CIOMS Secretariat. The consequent draft was posted on the CIOMS website in in June 2001.

3. CIOMS Conference in 2002

Attended by a select group of experts from all over the world, the CIOMS Conference was convened in 2002 to draft a new text. The 2002 text consists of a statement of general ethical principles, a preamble and 21 guidelines, with an introduction and a brief account of earlier declarations and guidelines.

4. Nuremberg Code

Nuremberg code was created as a result of the Doctors' Trial in 1947 in which some physicians were tried for crimes against humanity for the atrocious experiments they carried out on unwilling prisoners of war.

---

(1) See: ʿAbd al-Raḥmān al-ʿAwaḍī and Aḥmad al-Jundī (eds.), *al-Mīthāq al-Islāmī al-ʿālamī li al-akhlāqīyāt al-ṭibīyah wa al-ṣiḥḥīyah* (Kuwait: Islamic Organization for Medical Sciences, 1426 AH), p. 138; see also the paper presented by Muḥammad ʿAlī al-Bār.

5. UN Universal Declaration of Human Rights in 1948 & International Covenant on Civil and Political Rights in 1966

The adoption of the UN's Universal Declaration of Human Rights in 1948 and International Covenant of Civil and Political Rights in 1966, has imparted legal force to the rights of patients to ensure protection of their dignity, will and autonomy.

6. Directive 2001/20/EC of the Council of the European Union on Clinical Trials

The council of the European Union adopted the directive 2001/20/EC on the clinical trials on human subjects. This directive was put in force in 2004.

7. Council of Europe Protocol on Biomedical Research

With its 44 European member countries, the Council of Europe prepared a protocol on biomedical research to be implemented all over Europe.

8. The four principles of biomedical ethics by Tom L. Beauchamp and James F. Childress

A later section is specifically dedicated to reviewing this four-principle approach.

9. Contributions by Islamic Organization for Medical Sciences

The Islamic Organization for Medical Sciences (IOMS) assumes a very important role in the field of medical research and ethics. This organization, founded by Dr. ʿAbd al-Raḥmān al-ʿAwaḍī, actively works in two directions:

First: Clarifying the Islamic point of view on certain

medical issues. To this end, it organizes several seminars and conferences which bring together jurists, physicians and professional experts to collectively discuss contemporary issues and construe the proper legal rulings based on correct perception and deep understanding of the given questions. The IOMS has already issued many important legal verdicts in this specific field.

Second: The organization published an Islamic document on the code of medical and health professions in 1982. The Islamic Code consists of 108 articles characterized by comprehensiveness and accuracy. Due to its great importance, I highlight its articles in a separate appendix at the end of this study.

al-ʿAwaḍī explains that the IOMS was established with a view to examining a given issue in a thorough way in order to delineate the foundations and rules to be followed, the framework to be adopted, and the ethics to be observed. It pinpoints the medical obligations and ethical principles in an attempt to revive the once-dominating Islamic medicine and give due respect to the medical profession and professionals.(1) In addition, Dr. Aḥmad al-Jundī, Assistant Secretary General, stresses that the publication of the Islamic Code for Medical and Health Ethics marks a milestone for IOMS both regionally and internationally. This code is unique in its content and represents a historic development in medical thought.(2) It was released in 2005.

Expanding the Scope of Medical Ethics

The ethical principles discussed here shall be applicable to research and medical trials on humans, animals and

---

(1) See: ʿAbd al-Raḥmān al-ʿAwaḍī and Aḥmad al-Jundī (eds.), *al-Mīthāq al-Islāmī al-ʿālamī li al-akhlāqīyāt al-ṭibīyah wa al-ṣiḥḥīyah*, op. cit., pp. 11-12.

(2) Ibid, p. 17.

environment. The same holds true for the governing rules employed in resolving any conflict between benefits and harm. In this sense, these trials are allowed only to fulfill certain benefits or prevent harm; otherwise, they will be a kind of transgression, unacceptable even against animals. Taking necessary precautions is accentuated in case of human subjects. Furthermore, every means leading to the goal has to be lawful as noble goals do not justify prohibited means. There has to be a good chance of success for trials on human subjects. A legal maxim states that any act that is no longer fit to fulfill an intended objective may be rendered null and void.(1) Helsinki Declaration stipulates that medical research involving human subjects must conform to generally accepted scientific principles, be based on a thorough knowledge of the scientific literature, other relevant sources of information, and adequate laboratory and, as appropriate, animal experimentation. Competence and sincerity are prerequisites for those physicians, researchers, or professionals undertaking the medical trials.(2) They have to be sincere, honest, and straight; they are expected to avoid any kind of cheating and deception.

Given the great significant of this matter, the present section dwells on the ethical principles of the Helsinki Declaration for regulating medical research involving human subjects. The declaration goes as follows:(3)

> Adopted by the 18th WMA General Assembly, Helsinki, Finland, June 1964 and amended by the:
>
> 29th WMA General Assembly, Tokyo, Japan, October 1975

---

(1) See: ʻIzz al-Dīn b. ʻAbd al-Salām, *al-Qawāʻid al-kubrá*, vol. 2, p. 249.

(2) ʻAbd al-Raḥmān al-ʻAwaḍī and Aḥmad al-Jundī (eds.), *al-Mīthāq al-Islāmī al-ʻālamī li al-akhlāqīyāt al-ṭibīyah wa al-ṣiḥḥīyah*, op. cit., p. 166.

(3) Quoted in Arabic in: ʻAbd al-Raḥmān al-ʻAwaḍī and Aḥmad al-Jundī (eds.), *al-Mīthāq al-Islāmī al-ʻālamī li al-akhlāqīyāt al-ṭibīyah wa al-ṣiḥḥīyah*, op. cit., pp. 305-14.

35th WMA General Assembly, Venice, Italy, October 1983

41st WMA General Assembly, Hong Kong, September 1989

48th WMA General Assembly, Somerset West, Republic of South Africa, October 1996

52nd WMA General Assembly, Edinburgh, Scotland, October 2000

A) Introduction

1. The World Medical Association has developed the Declaration of Helsinki as a statement of ethical principles to provide guidance to physicians and other participants in medical research involving human subjects. Medical research involving human subjects includes research on identifiable human material or identifiable data.
2. It is the duty of the physician to promote and safeguard the health of the people. The physician's knowledge and conscience are dedicated to the fulfillment of this duty.
3. The Declaration of Geneva of the World Medical Association binds the physician with the words, "The health of my patient will be my first consideration," and the International Code of Medical Ethics declares that, "A physician shall act only in the patient's interest when providing medical care which might have the effect of weakening the physical and mental condition of the patient."
4. Medical progress is based on research which ultimately must rest in part on experimentation involving human subjects.

5. In medical research on human subjects, considerations related to the well-being of the human subject should take precedence over the interests of science and society.
6. The primary purpose of medical research involving human subjects is to improve prophylactic, diagnostic and therapeutic procedures and the understanding of the etiology and pathogenesis of disease. Even the best proven prophylactic, diagnostic, and therapeutic methods must continuously be challenged through research for their effectiveness, efficiency, accessibility and quality.
7. In current medical practice and in medical research, most prophylactic, diagnostic and therapeutic procedures involve risks and burdens.
8. Medical research is subject to ethical standards that promote respect for all human beings and protect their health and rights. Some research populations are vulnerable and need special protection. The particular needs of the economically and medically disadvantaged must be recognized. Special attention is also required for those who cannot give or refuse consent for themselves, for those who may be subject to giving consent under duress, for those who will not benefit personally from the research and for those for whom the research is combined with care.
9. Research Investigators should be aware of the ethical, legal and regulatory requirements for research on human subjects in their own countries as well as applicable international requirements. No national ethical, legal or regulatory requirement should be allowed to reduce or eliminate any of the protections for human subjects set forth in this Declaration.

B) Basic Principles for all Medical Research

10. It is the duty of the physician in medical research to protect the life, health, privacy, and dignity of the human subject.
11. Medical research involving human subjects must conform to generally accepted scientific principles, be based on a thorough knowledge of the scientific literature, other relevant sources of information, and on adequate laboratory and, where appropriate, animal experimentation.
12. Appropriate caution must be exercised in the conduct of research which may affect the environment, and the welfare of animals used for research must be respected.
13. The design and performance of each experimental procedure involving human subjects should be clearly formulated in an experimental protocol. This protocol should be submitted for consideration, comment, guidance, and where appropriate, approval to a specially appointed ethical review committee, which must be independent of the investigator, the sponsor or any other kind of undue influence. This independent committee should be in conformity with the laws and regulations of the country in which the research experiment is performed. The committee has the right to monitor ongoing trials. The researcher has the obligation to provide monitoring information to the committee, especially any serious adverse events. The researcher should also submit to the committee, for review, information regarding funding, sponsors, institutional affiliations, other potential conflicts of interest and incentives for subjects.

14. The research protocol should always contain a statement of the ethical considerations involved and should indicate that there is compliance with the principles enunciated in this Declaration.
15. Medical research involving human subjects should be conducted only by scientifically qualified persons and under the supervision of a clinically competent medical person. The responsibility for the human subject must always rest with a medically qualified person and never rest on the subject of the research, even though the subject has given consent.
16. Every medical research project involving human subjects should be preceded by careful assessment of predictable risks and burdens in comparison with foreseeable benefits to the subject or to others. This does not preclude the participation of healthy volunteers in medical research. The design of all studies should be publicly available.
17. Physicians should abstain from engaging in research projects involving human subjects unless they are confident that the risks involved have been adequately assessed and can be satisfactorily managed. Physicians should cease any investigation if the risks are found to outweigh the potential benefits or if there is conclusive proof of positive and beneficial results.
18. Medical research involving human subjects should only be conducted if the importance of the objective outweighs the inherent risks and burdens to the subject. This is especially important when the human subjects are healthy volunteers.
19. Medical research is only justified if there is a reasonable likelihood that the populations in which

the research is carried out stand to benefit from the results of the research.

20. The subjects must be volunteers and informed participants in the research project.
21. The right of research subjects to safeguard their integrity must always be respected. Every precaution should be taken to respect the privacy of the subject, the confidentiality of the patient's information and to minimize the impact of the study on the subject's physical and mental integrity and on the personality of the subject.
22. In any research on human beings, each potential subject must be adequately informed of the aims, methods, sources of funding, any possible conflicts of interest, institutional affiliations of the researcher, the anticipated benefits and potential risks of the study and the discomfort it may entail. The subject should be informed of the right to abstain from participation in the study or to withdraw consent to participate at any time without reprisal. After ensuring that the subject has understood the information, the physician should then obtain the subject's freely-given informed consent, preferably in writing. If the consent cannot be obtained in writing, the non-written consent must be formally documented and witnessed.
23. When obtaining informed consent for the research project the physician should be particularly cautious if the subject is in a dependent relationship with the physician or may consent under duress. In that case the informed consent should be obtained by a well-informed physician who is not engaged in the investigation and who is completely independent of this relationship.

24. For a research subject who is legally incompetent, physically or mentally incapable of giving consent or is a legally incompetent minor, the investigator must obtain informed consent from the legally authorized representative in accordance with applicable law. These groups should not be included in research unless the research is necessary to promote the health of the population represented and this research cannot instead be performed on legally competent persons.
25. When a subject deemed legally incompetent, such as a minor child, is able to give assent to decisions about participation in research, the investigator must obtain that assent in addition to the consent of the legally authorized representative.
26. Research on individuals from whom it is not possible to obtain consent, including proxy or advance consent, should be done only if the physical/mental condition that prevents obtaining informed consent is a necessary characteristic of the research population. The specific reasons for involving research subjects with a condition that renders them unable to give informed consent should be stated in the experimental protocol for consideration and approval of the review committee. The protocol should state that consent to remain in the research should be obtained as soon as possible from the individual or a legally authorized surrogate.
27. Both authors and publishers have ethical obligations. In publication of the results of research, the investigators are obliged to preserve the accuracy of the results. Negative as well as positive results should be published or otherwise publicly available. Sources of funding, institutional affiliations and

any possible conflicts of interest should be declared in the publication. Reports of experimentation not in accordance with the principles laid down in this Declaration should not be accepted for publication.

C) Additional Principles for Medical Research Combined with Medical Care

28. The physician may combine medical research with medical care, only to the extent that the research is justified by its potential prophylactic, diagnostic or therapeutic value. When medical research is combined with medical care, additional standards apply to protect the patients who are research subjects.
29. The benefits, risks, burdens and effectiveness of a new method should be tested against those of the best current prophylactic, diagnostic, and therapeutic methods. This does not exclude the use of placebo, or no treatment, in studies where no proven prophylactic, diagnostic or therapeutic method exists.
30. At the conclusion of the study, every patient entered into the study should be assured of access to the best proven prophylactic, diagnostic and therapeutic methods identified by the study.
31. The physician should fully inform the patient which aspects of the care are related to the research. The refusal of a patient to participate in a study must never interfere with the patient-physician relationship.
32. In the treatment of a patient, where proven prophylactic, diagnostic and therapeutic methods do not exist or have been ineffective, the physician, with informed consent from the patient, must be free to use unproven or new prophylactic, diagnostic and therapeutic measures, if in the physician's judgement

it offers hope of saving life, re-establishing health or alleviating suffering. Where possible, these measures should be made the object of research, designed to evaluate their safety and efficacy. In all cases, new information should be recorded and, where appropriate, published. The other relevant guidelines of this Declaration should be followed.

Note of Clarification on Paragraph 29

The WMA is concerned that paragraph 29 of the revised Declaration of Helsinki (October 2000) has led to diverse interpretations and possible confusion. It hereby reaffirms its position that extreme care must be taken in making use of a placebo-controlled trial and that in general this methodology should only be used in the absence of existing proven therapy. However, a placebo-controlled trial may be ethically acceptable, even if proven therapy is available, under the following circumstances:

1. Where for compelling and scientifically sound methodological reasons it is necessary to determine the efficacy or safety of a prophylactic, diagnostic or therapeutic method; or
2. Where a prophylactic, diagnostic or therapeutic method is being investigated for a minor condition and the patients who receive placebo will not be subject to any additional risk of serious or irreversible harm.

All other provisions of the Declaration of Helsinki must be adhered to, especially the need for appropriate ethical and scientific review.(1)

---

(1) The translation is available on the website of World Medical Association. See also: ʿAbd al-Raḥmān al-ʿAwaḍī and Aḥmad al-Jundī (eds.), *al-Mīthāq al-Islāmī al-ʿālamī li al-akhlāqīyāt al-ṭibīyah wa al-ṣiḥḥīyah*, op. cit., pp. 305-14.

A Commentary on the Declaration of Helsinki

As for the principles set forth in this declaration, they do not conflict with the rules and provisions of Islamic *Sharīʿa*. Rather, they are in agreement with the established proofs and sources of legislation including the Qurʾān, the Sunnah, *ijmāʿ* (Juridical Consensus) in addition to the legal objectives of preserving benefits and fending off evils. It is beyond the scope of this study to highlight the legal evidence in support of each principle. Consequently, there is no problem in adopting this declaration.

2.2 CRITICAL REVIEW OF THE FOUR-PRINCIPLE APPROACH

Introduction

This section deals with the four principles of biomedical ethics as enunciated by Tom Beauchamp in his paper presented to CILE's first specialized seminar on bioethics in 2012. Beauchamp investigates the nature and sources of principles in recent biomedical ethics and provides an analysis of the four-principles framework. He explains the central role played in the four-principles account by the theory of common morality, which is comprised not only of principles (and rules), but also of virtues, ideals, and rights. In addition, he shows how universal principles are fashioned into particular moralities and the circumstances under which moral pluralism is coherent with universal morality. Finally, he shows how principles are made practical for particular moralities through specification. Finally, he shows the relevance of principles for discussions of human rights, multiculturalism, and cultural imperialism.(1) The four principles of biomedical ethics according to Beauchamp are:

1. Respect for Autonomy

This principle is concerned with the patient. It is defined as a person's free will and freedom of choice without any interference from other persons. Beauchamp outlines two conditions for autonomy: "liberty (the absence of controlling influences)" and "agency (self-initiated intentional action)." It means that the patient is free to accept or refuse certain medication and requires that a physician respects the requests made by the patient, if he is able to, or by his family on his behalf. Despite the ethical issues that arise in situations where a patient refuses a necessary medical intervention, the principlist approach prioritizes respect for autonomy over other ethical principles. However, Beauchamp states that this prioritization may be dismissed in certain cases. He explains, "Many kinds of competing moral considerations can validly override respect for autonomy under conditions of a contingent conflict of norms. For example, if our choices endanger the public health, potentially harm innocent others, or require a scarce and unfunded resource, exercises of autonomy can justifiably be restrained or overridden."(2)

Given this clarification, it becomes clear that this is not an absolute principle applicable in all cases. Rather, it is more of a general rule that is susceptible to exceptions that also require clearly defined guidelines. The guidelines for these exceptional cases were outlined by the International Islamic *Fiqh* Academy (IIFA), affiliated with the Organization of

---

(1) Tom Beauchamp, "The Principles of Biomedical Ethics as Universal Principles," a paper presented to *CILE's first seminar on Islamic Bioethics*, 2012.

(2) Ibid., p. 3.

Islamic Cooperation (OIC), in its resolution no. 69/5/7. The exceptional cases as identified by the resolution are: infectious diseases, caesarian operations for saving the life of a newborn baby even if the mother and her husband refuse the operation, and accidents during which a patient has lost consciousness. The IIFA resolution states that:

First: The Patient's Permission

A. The patient's permission of the treatment is essential if the patient is in full legal capacity to give it. If he is not, the permission of his (or her) legal guardian shall be sought according to the order of guardianship in *Sharīʿa*, and in conformity with its provisions which limit the scope of the guardian's action to the benefit and interest of the person under guardianship as well as to removing harm from him (or her). If the guardian, however, resolves not to give permission, his decision shall not be taken into consideration if it is clearly detrimental to the person under guardianship. The right of permission shall then be transferred to the next guardian and ultimately to the ruler.

B. The ruler shall order the medical treatment when deemed appropriate as in case of contagious diseases and preventive immunities.

C. In emergency cases, when the life of the victim is in danger, medical treatment shall not depend on permission.

D. In carrying out medical research, it is imperative to obtain the agreement of the subject if he is totally fit in a way that is devoid of coercion (as in the case of jailed people) and financial enrichment (as in the case of the poor). Moreover, the research to be undertaken must not involve any harm. It is not permissible to carry out medical research on persons that are incapacitated or those of diminished capacity, even with the permission of their guardians.(1)

2. Non-maleficence

This principle refers to the prevention of harm and injury and is associated with the Hippocratic medical ethics according to the mandate, "Above all [or first] do no harm." This principle is also included in the Hippocratic Oath. The principle of non-maleficence establishes a variety of specific ethical rules, among which are:

(i) "Don't kill."

(ii) "Don't cause pain or suffering to others."

(iii) "Don't incapacitate others."

In this regard, Beauchamp quotes the British physician Thomas Percival, who asserted that, "a principle of non-maleficence fixes the physician's primary obligations and triumphs even over respect for the patient's autonomy in a circumstance of potential harm to patients."(2)

3. Beneficence

This principle refers to the promotion of good. Beauchamp acknowledges that the line between that which is demanded under the principle of beneficence and that which is not is undoubtedly difficult to draw. In fact, it is deemed impossible to draw a precise line under this principle

(1) *Journal of Fiqh Academy*, 3 (7) 731-33. This translation is quoted, with slight modification, from Resolutions and Recommendations of the Council of the Islamic Fiqh Academy 1985-2000 (Jeddah: Islamic Development Bank, 2000), p. 139ff.

(2) Tom Beauchamp, "The Principles of Biomedical Ethics as Universal Principles," op. cit., p. 3.

without considering the particulars of different contexts.[1] There have been many contentious debates arguing for the sufficiency of the principle of non-maleficence and the possibility of it replacing the principle of beneficence. However, Beauchamp rejects this proposition, arguing that a physician's commitment to preventing harm cannot be merged with his commitment to providing them with care. An example of the first would be preventing murder or disablement while the latter involves advancing the interests of people.[2] On the other hand, one can argue that the principle of beneficence implies that of non-maleficence and preventing harm, as will be discussed later.

4. Justice

Justice in this context refers to the fair distribution of health care and its costs within societies. It also refers to the fair opportunity principle.[3] Given this understanding, this principle primarily addresses governments rather than physicians.

After reviewing each of these points, I can honestly say that this is a very well-written research paper serving to elaborate on the four principles of biomedical ethics as developed by Tom Beauchamp and James Childress since 1976 and to this day. There is no exaggeration in stating that it is invaluable research. Therefore, I merely have a few clarifying points to add with the purpose of providing an Islamic foundation to these principles which will lead to the development of a comprehensive theory that is compatible with Islamic values and principles.

---

(1) Ibid., pp. 3-4.

(2) Ibid.

(3) Ibid., p. 5.

1. A Historical Perspective

In introducing the origin of biomedical ethics, Dr. Beauchamp states, "Principles that can be understood with relative ease by the members of various disciplines figured prominently in the early developments in the history of biomedical ethics during the 1970s and early 1980s."(4) In this regard, I believe Dr. Beauchamp is referring specifically to the emergence of these four principles as a structured framework and the appearance of writings that focused on interpreting, explaining, and connecting them. However, the history of ethics (including medical ethics) is rather ancient and can be traced back to the ethical values taught by the heavenly religions, namely Judaism, Christianity, and Islam, notwithstanding slight discrepancies in details, foundations, and terminology. Moreover, the presence of general ethical principles can be found across several ancient civilizations, such as the Pharaonic Civilization, Hammurabi's Code of Laws, ancient Greek philosophy, as well as Buddhist and Hindu civilizations. For example, in the Ancient Egyptian civilization, the Book of the Dead mentions that a dead person is brought to stand in front of the God Osiris. The dead person then justifies his actions saying, "I come to you my lord in submission to witness your magnificence; I come bearing truth and abandoning dishonesty, for I have never been unjust towards another and have avoided the path of those gone astray." He then accounts that he was never disobedient, nor a liar, nor harmful to others, nor committed or assisted with murder, nor a thief, nor committed adultery or embezzlement, nor violated the sanctity of death, nor cheated in trade. He then states, "I am pure, I am pure, I am pure, and as long as I am innocent

(4) Ibid., p. 1.

of sin, place me amongst the victorious my Lord."[1] In Hammurabi Code there are some articles comprising a set of general ethical principles in addition to some medical ethics. This code focused on the principles of beneficence, non-maleficence, justice and equity. It also paid great attention to health, cleanliness, and a proper drainage system for dirty and soiled waters. It was considered a crime to throw dirt in canals and potable water.[2]

Moreover, the Buddhist, Indian and ancient Chinese civilizations laid great emphasis on promoting good and avoiding evils. The Greek philosophers paid special attention to beneficence and non-maleficence. The Hippocratic Oath (350-460 B.C) established those principles making use of Pythagorean Cult which paid due attention to the religious ethics, sciences, medicine, and philosophy that prevailed in that era. The Hippocratic Oath stressed loyalty to the teacher and his posterity, and the necessity to keep the profession of medicine secret except to those who deserve it based on their character, or to the children of previous physicians. It also emphasized being virtuous, keeping secrets, beneficence, non-maleficence, modesty, sobriety, patience, promptness and piety. The physician must be upright and pure in character, diligent, and conscientious in caring for the sick. Moreover, the physician in Hippocratic Oath is like a parent in their relationship with the patient, as if the pateint is his son or daughter trying his best to benefit him/her and prevent any harm that would befall him/her, and keeping all his/her secrets.[3]

---

(1) See; Muḥammad ʿAlī al-Bār, *al-akhlāq: uṣūluhā al-dīnīyah wa-judhūruhā al-falsafīyah*, (kunūz al-maʿārif, 2010), p. 62ff.

(2) Encyclopedia Britannica, 15th ed., 1982, vol. 4, p. 878.

(3) Ibn Abī Uṣaybiʿa, *ʿUyūn al-anbāʾ fī ṭabaqāt al-aṭibbāʾ* (Beirut: Maktabat al-ḥayāh, 1965), p. 45ff; Muḥammad ʿAlī al-Bār, "The 4 Principles of Biomedical Ethics", a paper presented to CILE, pp.11-12.

Similarly, the heavenly religions emphasize in their scriptures those four principles and other moralities. In the Old Testament, the Ten Commandments (Exodus 20/1-7) starts by "Worship no God but Me", monotheism, observing the Sabbath and then "Respect your father and your mother. Do not commit murder (thou shall not kill). Do not commit adultery. Do not steal. Do not accuse anyone falsely and do not desire another man's house; do not desire his wife, his slaves, his cattle, his donkeys or anything that he owns". There is also a mention of treatment of slaves who should be treated fairly. (Exodus 15/12-15).(4) We also find in the New Testament, (Mathew 5/3-12): "Happy are those who are humble...Happy are those who are merciful to others... Happy are the pure in heart...Happy are those who work for peace," (Mathew 5/43): "Love your enemies and pray for those who persecute you," "If anyone slaps you on the right cheek, let him slap you on the left cheek too."(5) Actually, Islam pays due attention to morality in general and medical ethics in particular. It deals with moral principles in a detailed fashion as will be discussed later.

2. The Source and Authority of Ethics

The argument for the importance of ethics in general, and that of medical ethics in particular, is eloquently presented by Dr. Beauchamp. He explains, "If some principles were dropped from the framework, the demands of the moral life would not be what we know those demands to be, just as a landscape would not be the same landscape if certain rocks, trees, or plants were removed from it."(6) He also adds,

---

(4) Unfortunately, Jews do not follow those teachings and we witness how they treat Palestinians with cruelty and brutality.

(5) See: New Testament, esp. Mathew 5: 3-12, 19: 16-26.

(6) Tom Beauchamp, "The Principles of Biomedical Ethics as Universal Principles," op. cit., p. 1.

"From centuries of experience we have learned that the human condition ends to deteriorate into misery, confusion, violence, and distrust unless certain principles are enforced through a public system of norms. Everyone living a moral life in any society is aware of the fundamental importance of moral standards such as not lying, not stealing others' property, keeping promises, respecting the rights of others, and not killing or causing harm to others. When complied with, these shared norms lessen human misery and foster cooperation. These norms may not be necessary for the survival of a society, as some have maintained, but it is not too much to claim that these norms are necessary to ameliorate or counteract the tendency for the quality of people's lives to worsen or for social relationships to disintegrate."(1)

While Dr. Beauchamp emphasized the importance of ethics as well as the four principles, he considered ethics to be the source from which adherence to the four principles emerges. In this regard he wrote, "All principles can in some contexts be justifiably overridden by other moral norms with which they come into contingent conflict."(2) I argue that the practice and impact of morality will be undermined if commitment to moral principles is contingent merely on ethical obligation. In fact, the foundational commitment to these principles as presented in Beauchamp's paper appears weak and fragile. The reason for this lies in the fact that Beauchamp, as well as other moral philosophers, founded their moral theory on utilitarianism without taking religious aspects into consideration. This means that in situations where ethics conflict with certain economic interests

(1) Ibid., p. 5.
(2) Ibid., p. 1.

prohibited by Islam and other religions (such as alcohol), priority is given to those interests over religion despite their negative social impact outweighing their benefits. As God explains, "They ask you [Prophet] about intoxicants and gambling: say, 'There is great sin in both, and some benefit for people: the sin is greater than the benefit.'"(1)

Dr. Muḥammad *'Alī* al-Bār says: "Despite all these codes and regulations medical research is replete with horrendous stories of cheating, maiming and even killing many innocent persons, both before and after the Nuremberg Code. The Nuremberg trials of the Nazi physicians opened the eyes on what was happening both in the democratic countries of the West and the heinous experiments of Nazi Germany."(2)

It is well known that the most resolute commitments arise from religious obligation and legislation. Otherwise, we would have to rely on the integrity of a person's conscience, which can be rather volatile. Generally, if a person is not driven by fear of God and hope for His reward, he will easily be tempted to pursue his own personal interests and will most likely prioritize his own interests over the interests of others. It is quite likely that he will surrender to his whims, desires, and individualistic perspective, which, as often seen, has led to the strangest outcomes due to people's lack of piety, fear of God, and negligence of the Day of Judgment.

2.1 Violations Associated with the "Active Conscience" Slogan

Below are examples demonstrating that conscience alone is insufficient to ensure moral commitment and that strong religious endorsement and legislation are necessary.

(1) al-Baqarah (2: 219).

(2) Muḥammad 'Alī al-Bār, "The 4 Principles of Biomedical ethics", a paper presented to CILE, p. 22.

1. Beauchamp and Childress emphasize in their book Principles of Biomedical Ethics the fact that African-Americans suffering from hypertension should not be treated in a hospital's Casualty Department if they do not have medical insurance. They argue that several researchers have found that poor patients with such circumstances will be unable to continue or follow-up their medication due to the absence of a family physician or their lack of medical insurance. Hence, they consider treating them to be a waste of time, effort and money.(1) As stated by Dr. Muḥammad *'Alī* al-Bār, both Beauchamp and Childress agree, without explicitly stating so, that these patients should be left to suffer and die from their hypertension or its sequela e.g. strokes, heart attacks, heart failure, and kidney failure.(2) If this is the view supported by the authors of Principles of Biomedical Ethics, what is to be expected from those who do not concern themselves with writing about ethics? Rather, what was expected from these two ethicists was a criticism of the unjust American healthcare system that excludes 50 million citizens from the right to medical treatment, especially given that America was not suffering from a financial crisis at that time and, in fact, was one of the world's richest countries. It is truly intriguing, on the other hand, to find that Cuba, America's poorer neighbor, provides free medical insurance not only to its citizens, but also to those visiting Cuba.(3)

---

(1) Beauchamp, T and Childress, J: Principles of Biomedical Ethics (note. 8), pp 347-348.

(2) Muḥammad ʿAlī al-Bār, "The 4 Principles of Biomedical ethics", a paper presented to CILE, p. 12.

(3) Ibid.

2. In 1915 the U.S. Public Health produced Pellagra in 12 Mississippi inmates to find a cure for the disease. In 1935, after millions died from the disease, the director of the U.S. Public Health Office said that they had known Niacin is a cure for this disease for some time, but withheld it as it affected "negroes", as he called them.
3. In 1941 doctors gave 800 poor pregnant women radioactive iron, to investigate its effect on pregnancy.
4. In 1945 Col. Safford Warren, of the University of Rochester, injected plutonium into patients of the University Hospital without their knowledge. Three patients at the University of Chicago's Billings Hospital were similarly injected with plutonium.
5. In 1950 Dr. Josef Strokes of Pennsylvania infected 200 female prisoners with viral hepatitis.
6. In 1945-1947, CIA and U.S. Navy trials on LSD, Scopolamine and Mescaline involved military and civilians who were given these hallucinating drugs without their knowledge. The army released chemical clouds on six American and Canadian cities that resulted in increase of respiratory illness.

In 1953, U.S. Atomic Energy Commission gave 200 pregnant women high doses of I-131 and then aborted them at different stages to learn at what stages the serious effect occurs. Ohio State Prison inmates were injected with live cancer cells to study the progress of the disease by Dr. Chester Southam of Sloan-Kettering Institute. Moreover, mostly African American cancer patients with lower than average intelligence were exposed to large doses of radiation in Cincinnati Radiation Experiments (1960-1972). None of the patients consented to the experiment or had any idea of the potential side effects. These experiments were sponsored by the United States Military. Subjects experienced severe burns and some died as a direct result of the experiments.

7. The Jewish Chronic Disease Hospital in 1963 injected 22 chronically ill and debilitated non-cancer patients with live human cancer cells. Patients were not told of the cancer injection. This hospital covered up the lack of consent and tried to fraudulently obtain consent. Two years after the investigation, the American Cancer Society appointed the principle investigator of this experiment as a Vice President.
8. In 1996 Pfizer used eleven Nigerian children as guinea pigs in non-consensual unlicensed trial which resulted in their death. The company agreed to pay 75 million dollars as compensation for their death. This company was ordered to pay 2.3 billion dollars to resolve criminal and civil allegations of illegally promoting some drugs.
9. In 2012, the British drug maker GlaxoSmith Kline was ordered to pay $3 billion in fines for criminal and civil violations involving ten drugs that are taken by millions of people.

The above examples and many others cited by Dr. Muḥammad 'Alī al-Bār[1] show that live conscience failed to act, which proves that conscience will be mostly effective if it is linked to belief in God and the Day of Judgment. One of the best examples in this regard is the story of the young girl whose mother used to mix milk with water before selling it to people. When the young girl saw her mother doing this, she objected and said the commander of the faithful, namely 'Umar b. al-Khaṭṭāb, forbade this. Her mother said: "'Umar does not see us". The girl replied: "If 'Umar does not see

(1) Muḥammad 'Alī al-Bār, "The 4 Principles of Biomedical ethics", op. cit., pp. 22-3.

us, surely the Creator and Lord of 'Umar sees us and knows everything." That is the same meaning that Luqman taught his son: "My son, if even the weight of a mustard seed were hidden in a rock or anywhere in the heavens or earth, God would bring it [to light], for He is all subtle and all aware"(1)

Sincere belief (īmān), on the other hand, establishes God-consciousness (*taqwá*), fear of God, a desire for His reward, and constant awareness of God's watchfulness in all situations. This belief serves as a genuine internal incentive for a person to observe good deeds and avoid harming others. It is described as a state of *iḥsān*, which follows the stages of īmān (sincere belief) and Islam as explained by the Prophet (PBUH) in the authentic tradition, "*Iḥsān* is to worship God as if you see Him, and if you do not achieve this state of devotion, then (take it for granted that) God sees you." (2)

3. Are the Four Principles All-inclusive and Restrictive?

The four principles of biomedical ethics are not representative of all common morality and not based on complete induction. Rather, they form a part of a larger moral framework. Beauchamp acknowledges this (as does Childress in their coauthored book), stating in his research, "Some critics think that Childress and I hold that the four principles constitute the full set of universal norms. However, we claim far less. We claim only that these principles we have identified and put in the form of a framework for biomedical ethics are a part of universal morality. We selectively draw these principles from the common morality in order to construct a normative framework for biomedical ethics."(3) Therefore,

(1) Luqmān (31:16).

(2) Reported by al-Bukhārī, no. 4777 and Muslim, no. 9.

(3) Tom Beauchamp, "The Principles of Biomedical Ethics as Universal Principles," op. cit., p. 6.

these principles are neither comprehensive nor precursory. Instead, they are founded on this larger framework whose very structure is debatable. For instance, whereas justice is included as one of the four principles, the question arises as to why equal treatment of all patients is not included as a principle. Equality is arguably a significant principle serving to prevent discrimination based on aspects such as wealth, race, etc. Likewise, there are other countless ethical principles that may be considered worthy of inclusion in the framework of biomedical principles. These include principles such as loyalty towards a physician's teachers and mentors — as included in the Hippocratic and Islamic Oath — and honesty, transparency, keeping promises, and upholding contracts. It is worth noting that, as acknowledged by both Beauchamp and Childress, these principles are merely an attempt at constructing a normative framework for biomedical ethics and are not intended to encompass all morals, values, and ideals. Nonetheless, these are truly admirable efforts leading to a positive attempt, although there remains a need for further discussion and critique.

3.1 The Distinction between Principles and Common Morality

Prior to discussing this topic, it must be noted that Beauchamp differentiates between the four principles and common morality. He defines the four principles as the normative framework for biomedical ethics and common morality as that which encompasses several other rules and values such as: "(i) Do not kill; (ii) Do not cause pain or suffering to others; (iii) Prevent evil or harm from occurring; (iv) Rescue persons in danger; (v) Tell the truth; (vi) Nurture the young and dependent; (vii) Keep your promises; (viii) Do not steal; (ix) Do not punish the innocent; and (x) Obey the law."[1] Given this distinction, we can confidently say that the four principles do not cover the range of morals, values, and religious and human ideals. In fact, the method through which certain ethics are categorized as principles while others are not is in itself debatable and subject to ongoing discussion.

On a different note, it may be acceptable to conflate non-maleficence and beneficence under the single principle of beneficence, which is defined as promoting good. This definition implies one's avoidance of causing harm to others. In regard to this issue, some scholars of Islamic jurisprudence have indeed categorized preventing harm under the principle of interests (*maṣlaḥah*) since this prevention is in itself a benefit and seeks to advance interests. In turn, the two principles are considered synonymous.

4. Physician's Internal Morality

The four principles afford little attention to the development of the physician's internal morality. As demonstrated earlier, their concern is primarily with external actions and behaviors. Needless to say, it is the physician in particular, and people in general, around which all these principles and actions revolve and through which they come to fruition. Therefore, in order to ensure the practice of these principles, it is necessary that morals and values be ingrained within all individuals in the field of medicine, ranging from the physician to the custodian. It is a known fact that the process of moral development begins from early childhood and continues on through higher education taking place at home and in other institutions. However, this moral development can only be firmly ingrained through

(1) Ibid., p. 5.

associating it with God-consciousness and belief in God and the Day of Judgment. It is perhaps this negligence of the element of faith, which started during the Renaissance era, that has resulted in today's European and Western reality. In my opinion, this argument is one that is perhaps embraced by all individuals who believe in God and the Last Day, whether they are Jewish, Christian, or Muslim or belong to any other religion that is based on the belief in a person's accountability to an Omniscient God.

The connection between morality and faith is a central issue in Islam and is pervasive throughout its creed, worship practices, and rituals, all of which are intended to affect a person's actions and behavior. For example, a person who, believes that God sees him in all situations will be wary of disobeying God's commandments or committing any sins. He believes that God is Omnipotent over His creation. In turn, he holds a firm conviction that if he commits any injustice, harm, or betrayal towards another person or practices any other type of wrongdoing and does not suffer consequences in this world, he will undoubtedly be held accountable for these actions and will suffer due punishment on the Day of Judgment. On the other hand, if he obeys God's orders and maintains positive conduct, he will be rewarded accordingly and will enter Paradise in the Hereafter. As with belief, Islam emphasizes a strong connection between worship practices and their impact on a person's behavior. For instance, with regard to prayer, God says, "… prayer restrains outrageous and unacceptable …".[1] With regard to fasting, God says, "You who believe, fasting is prescribed for you, as it was prescribed for those before you, so that you may be mindful

(1) al-`Ankabūt (29: 45).

of God".[1] Similarly, in reference to almsgiving (*zakāh*), God says, "In order to cleanse and purify them [Prophet], accept a gift out of their property [to make amends] and pray for them– your prayer will be a comfort to them. God is all hearing, all knowing."[2] In other words, it is intended to purify their hearts from greed, selfishness, and other evils of the heart and simultaneously enable them to rise to noble character. In fact, prior to prayer, God described good moral behavior and noble character as a form of worship in His saying, "The servants of the Lord of Mercy are those who walk humbly on the earth, and who, when the foolish address them, reply, 'Peace'."[3]

Indeed, all religions founded on the belief in God and the Last Day have a profound effect on their followers and establish a strong commitment to ethics and moral behavior. This element of faith should not be neglected, especially within environments characterized with a strong religiosity. For societies lacking this religious element, morality should be nurtured in accordance with the natural disposition that all humans are born with.

A final issue that I would like to address is the correlation between the principles of beneficence and utilitarianism. There has been a great deal of controversy around this issue by those critics doubting the applicability of beneficence as a foundation for making ethical decisions. In her paper "Applying the Four Principles," professor R. Macklin describes a study that was designed to determine the economic and health impacts of selling a kidney. The study's participants comprised 305 individuals from Chennai, India who had sold their kidneys. According to the results of the

(1) al-Baqarah (2: 183).
(2) At-Tawbah (9: 103).
(3) Sūrat al-Furqān (25:63).

study, 96 percent of the participants had sold their kidneys to pay off debts, and the average price of a kidney was $1,070. Most of the money received was spent on debts, food, and clothing. The study also revealed that the effects of undergoing a nephrectomy included a one-third decrease in the average family income of participants, and 86 percent of participants reported deterioration in their health. Further, 97 percent of the participants did not recommend for others to sell their kidneys. Although this is one study that took place in one country, it nonetheless highlights a critical issue that remains contentious to this day. That is, how can the negative social, economic, and health impacts be balanced with the benefits received by those who purchase the kidneys?[1] According to Macklin one anthropological study found that the predominant reason behind people selling kidneys was their need to pay off high interest debts to local moneylenders. In addition, it found that most of the money from selling a kidney ended up with organ brokers, while only a small portion was paid to the sellers themselves.

(1) See Ruth Macklin (2003). Applying the four principles. Journal of Medical Ethics 29(5): 275–280.

CHAPTER THREE:

TOWARDS AN ISLAMIC THEORY OF UNIVERSAL PRINCIPLES OF BIOMEDICAL ETHICS

This chapter explains the Islamic perspective on the universal principles of bioethics in terms of their structure, source, authority, motives, and the outline of the proposed theory.

3.1 UNIVERSAL BIOMEDICAL PRINCIPLES FROM AN ISLAMIC PERSPECTIVE

The subject of ethics and ethical principles has been my concern for more than a quarter of a century. During my participation in a public lecture in Britain in 1988, I was asked about the possibility of organizing the multitude of Islamic moralities and virtues under one group of inclusive and universal foundations and principles similar to the western codes of conduct. At that time, I answered the question very briefly, however, this subject has kept occurring to my mind. Later on, I was entrusted with the academic supervision of a post-graduate student where I suggested the possibility of organizing the different moralities in light of four kinds of relationships. Those four relationships include: a positive relationship between a person and his Lord; a positive relationship between a person and other people; a positive relationship between a person and animals; a positive relationship between a person and the environment. Though important, this categorization is not an easy undertaking. A while later, I was asked by CILE to write a response to two papers presented by Tom Beauchamp and Muḥammad ʻAlī al-Bārr. In my response, I attempted to link the four-principles approach of bioethics to the principles of *maqāṣid*, whether they are five, six, or eight objectives. The participant scholars found my paper appealing. Thereupon, CILE requested me to expand my paper; consequently, I devoted a lot of effort and time to this subject and finally I could come up with a holistic theory, building on previous scholarly contributions.

According to this theory, the universal principles and all-inclusive foundations of biomedical ethics can be summed up in three principles, namely, *iḥsān* (beneficence), dignity (honoring human dignity), and justice. All biomedical ethics, be they primary or secondary, can be traced back to these three principles. They cover the aforementioned four principles of bioethics and ensure normativity, accuracy and structuring. Moreover, these principles fulfill the positive aspects of utilitarianism and deontology. The great emphasis laid on these principles in the Qurʾān proves their universality. Actually, the Qurʾān pays due attention to them both in the Meccan and Medinan chapters. The most comprehensive Qurʾānic verse reads as following, "God commands justice, doing good [*iḥsān*], and generosity towards relatives and He forbids what is shameful [obscenity], blameworthy [maleficence], and oppressive. He teaches you, so that you may take heed."[1] This verse highlights two important principles, i.e., justice in contrast with injustice and transgression, and beneficence as opposed to maleficence, wrongdoing and obscenity. The principle of honoring human dignity is accentuated in many verses including those pertaining to the creation of Adam and

(1) Sūrat al-Naḥl (16: 90).

the dignified status of his offspring as will be shown later in some detail.

3.1.1 Beneficence (*Iḥsān*)

Etymologically speaking, *iḥsān* means to do what is good, or to perfect something. Both connotations are used in the Qur'ān. God says, "If you do good (*aḥsantum*), you do good for yourselves,"[1] "...and formed you and perfected (*aḥsana*) your forms".[2] The Arabic term *iḥsān* refers to a variety of meanings which revolve around the idea of perfection, beautification, and being pleasant and favorable.[3]

The root *ḥasana* and its relevant derivatives have about 200 mentions, of which *ḥasuna* (i.e. to excel and improve) occurs only once: "And *ḥasuna* (how excellent) these companions are".[4] This verb occurs 12 times in the forms of simple past tense, the present tense, and the imperative mood, as God (May He be exalted) says: "He is my master, he *aḥsana* (i.e. perfected) my living state".[5] It also occurs 36 times in the superlative degree of comparison *aḥsana.* The derivative *muḥsin* occurs 40 times in singular and plural forms. The term *iḥsān* itself has 12 mentions. In an attempt to articulate a comprehensive definition of this term reflecting its different uses and meanings, al-Rāghib al-Aṣfahānī explains that *al-ḥasan* refers to everything that is desirable, favorable and pleasant. This desirability is decided by three things; intellect, whim, and sense. The word *ḥasanah* is used to denote any pleasing thing or good fortune as opposed to *sayyi'ah* or misfortune. God says, "When good fortune

(1) Sūrat al-'Isrā' (17: 7). This translation is provided by SAHIH INTERNATIONAL.
(2) Sūrat Ghāfir (40: 64), as per SAHIH INTERNATIONAL.
(3) *Lisān al-'Arab, al-Qāmūs al-Muḥīṭ, al-Mu'jam al-Wasīṭ,* (entry: *Ḥassan*).
(4) (al-Qur'ān, 4:69).
(5) (al-Qur'ān, 12:23).

comes their way, they say, 'This is from God,' but when harm befalls them, they say, 'This is from you [Prophet],'"[1] "Anything good that happens to you [Prophet] is from God; anything bad is [ultimately] from yourself."[2] al-Aṣfahānī adds that *iḥsān* is materialized in two forms: being beneficent toward others, and being beneficent in one's own deeds. In this vein, we may understand the saying of 'Alī b. Abī Ṭālib that "People are known by their deeds"; that is to say they are known for what they know or do well. In fact, beneficence is broader than doing good to others… It is even superior to justice as the latter means to get one's due rights and fulfill duties, while beneficence is to do more than required. In other words, maintaining justice is obligatory while beneficence is recommended. Those meaning are used in the Qur'ān. God says, "Who could be better in religion than those who direct themselves wholly to God, do good,"[3] "and the culprit shall pay what is due in a good way,"[4] "…but do good, for God loves those who do good"[5] and "… there is no reason to reproach those who do good".[6] From my point of view, *iḥsān* is used more broadly in the Qur'ān. The same holds true for the Sunnah. Some Prophetic traditions will be cited later to highlight its unique meanings.[7] In one notable tradition, the Prophet answers a question about *iḥsān* as "to worship God as if you see Him, and if you do not achieve this state of devotion, then (take it for granted that) God sees you."[8]

(1) al-Nisā' (4: 78).
(2) al-Nisā' (4: 79).
(3) al-Nisā' (4: 125).
(4) al-Baqarah (2: 178).
(5) al-Baqarah (2: 195).
(6) al-Tawbah (9: 17)
(7) See: *Mu'jam Alfāẓ al-Sunnah; al-mufradāt fī gharīb al-Qur'ān*, pp. 118-19.
(8) Reported by al-Bukhārī, Book of belief (1/114), Muslim, Book of belief (1/40), Aḥmad in Musnad (1/27, 51, 52; 2/107, 436; 4/139, 164).

Iḥsān according to Ibn Ḥajar means to perfect something or do good to someone. The first meaning is intended in the above ḥadīth as it refers to perfection in terms of worship. However, this does not preclude the second meaning because the person by perfecting worship is doing good to oneself. *Iḥsān* in worship is fulfilled by sincerity, devotion, full preoccupation and being mindful of God. The answer given in the above-mentioned ḥadīth stresses two states; firstly, a state when the heart is fully attached to God so this person worships God as if he sees Him. The other state in which the person firmly believes that God sees him and knows all his acts. The two states are reached only through God-consciousness. al-Nawawī argues that the underlying meaning of this tradition goes as follows, "You need to be persistent in worship even if you cannot see God as He already sees you". In his point of view, this specific part of the *ḥadīth* represents an important foundation and principle for Muslims; it is the main intent, noble aim and customary practice of the truthful and righteous people; it is a concise but comprehensive expression full of meanings.(1) In another narration reported by Muslim, the Prophet answered that *iḥsān* implies that you fear God as if you are seeing Him.(2)

Actually, the Sunnah attaches some meaning to *iḥsān*. Based on some traditions, *iḥsān* amounts to obligation, not mere recommendation. For instance, the Prophet (PBUH) says, "Verily God has prescribed *iḥsān* (perfection) for everything. So, when you kill, you must make the killing in the best manner; when you slaughter, make your slaughter in the best manner...".(3) al-Nawawī comments that this is

(1) Fatḥ al-bārī (1/120).

(2) Reported by Muslim in Ṣaḥīḥ, book of faith, ḥadīth no. 10 (1/40).

(3) Reported by Muslim in Ṣaḥīḥ, book of hunting and slaughtering, no. 1955 (edition of Abū Ḥayyān, 7/118-19); Abū Dāwūd in al-Sunan, along with *'Awn al-ma'būd* (8/10); Ibn Mājah (2/3170).

a universally applicable *ḥadīth* that encompasses a lot of Islamic rules and foundations.[1] The wording of this *ḥadīth* clearly shows the obligation of *iḥsān* as a way of perfection because the Arabic word '*Kutiba*' translated here as prescribed is used in the Qur'ān and the Sunnah to denote obligation. The Qur'ān (2: 183) uses the same word which could be translated as follows, "You who believe, fasting is prescribed for you, as it was prescribed for those before you."[2] In my view, the meaning of *iḥsān* as explained by the Prophet (PBUH) takes into consideration means and causes. Fearing God and believing that He watches us lead to real perfection in everything.

Relationship between Justice and Beneficence

The Qur'ān mentions justice and beneficence separately, which indicates that they are not synonymous. God says, "God commands justice, doing good [*iḥsān*], and generosity towards relatives and He forbids what is shameful [obscenity], blameworthy [maleficence], and oppressive. He teaches you, so that you may take heed."[3] Consequently, Muslim scholars held different views in this regard. al-Ṭabarī, for instance, listed different interpretations for justice and beneficence. According to Ibn 'Abbās, justice in this verse is to testify the oneness of God while *iḥsān* is to observe the obligatory acts of worship. Others maintain that justice is fairness while *iḥsān* is performing acts of worship. Still, some scholars understand *iḥsān* as patience and persistence in worship, both in cases of distress and prosperity, or hardship and ease; this is to observe the

(1) Sharḥ al-Nawawī 'alá Ṣaḥīḥ Muslim (7/119).

(2) Tafsīr al-Māwardī: *al-nukat wa-al-'uyūn*, ed. of Kuwait, vol.1, p. 196; al-Aṣfahānī, *al-Mufradāt*, p. 423.

(3) al-Naḥl (16: 90).

obligatory acts of worship.[1] Ibn Kathīr reports that Sufyān b. 'Uyaynah explains justice as having equal inward and outward righteous conditions, while *iḥsān* means to be more righteous inwardly. However, Ibn Kathīr understands justice as fairness and balance.[2] Likewise, al-Māwardī lists the same meanings but adds that justice is to judge fairly while *iḥsān* is to bestow favor.[3] Ibn al-ʿArabī sees justice as a mediation between two extremes; it is opposed to injustice. God has created this world in duality and justice is established by striking balance between the two opposing sides. On the other hand, *iḥsān* can materialize in terms of knowledge and deeds; you need to know that your self is imperfect while God is absolutely perfect; *iḥsān* in deeds is mirrored in God's orders... Based on this, a person is responsible for the care and well-being of a pet bird in their possession.[4]

In addition, Imām al-Rāzī discusses this issue in some detail where he presents a suitable methodology to be adopted in case of multiple interpretations. He argues that there is a multitude of prohibitions and obligations. To better understand the suitable meaning of a given term, it is necessary to find a reasonable connection. If not, the meaning is undoubtedly false. If we are to interpret justice and *iḥsān* as different terms with different meanings, we need to delineate this connection between the term and its given meaning. When such a connection is not explained, then giving priority to a certain interpretation is arbitrary and baseless. In commenting on the aforementioned Qurʾānic verse, al-Rāzī explains that God commands three

(1) al-Ṭabarī, *Jāmiʿ al-bayān*, ed., Ahmad Shākir, edition of Dār Ibn Ḥazm (8/198).
(2) Tafsīr Ibn Kathīr, Dār Ibn Ḥazm, vol. 2, p. 1648.
(3) Tafsīr al-Māwardī, op. cit., vol. 2, p. 408.
(4) Ibn al-ʿArabī, Aḥkām al-Qurʾān (Beirut: Dār al-Maʿrifah), vol. 3, p. 1172.

things, namely, justice, *iḥsān*, and generosity towards relatives. On the other hand, God forbids another three things; obscenity, maleficence, and oppression. Those things are different. Justice is a sort of mediation and moderation between two extremes, which is to be observed in all cases. Obligations include beliefs and deeds; there has to be moderation in terms of beliefs. As far as *iḥsān* is concerned, it could sometimes be praiseworthy or even blameworthy to do more than what justice and moderation dictate. For instance, justice entails doing the required acts of worship, however, *iḥsān* materializes when a person does more than required. In sum, to increase your acts of worship in terms of quality and quantity is an act of *iḥsān*. In this vein, we can understand the *ḥadīth* of Jibril (Gabriel) when he asked the Prophet (PBUH) about *iḥsān*. If someone asks about the reason for such an interpretation of *iḥsān,* we may answer that: by persistent obedience and increasing acts of worship a person is doing *iḥsān* to oneself. In this sense, justice is to suffice oneself with doing the required while *iḥsān* is to do more in terms of quality and quantity. *Iḥsān* in this sense includes honoring God's commandments and showing compassion to people.(1)

For some contemporary scholars, justice is to tell the truth and decisively act in accordance with this truth. *Iḥsān*, they argue, is to be tolerant, increase your acts of worship and do not content yourself with doing obligations only. Accordingly, *iḥsān* is broader in its scope. Every good act is included in *iḥsān*. To command *iḥsān* entails every good deed, kind treatment and healthy relationship, whether with God, family, society, or all people.(2) Other scholars maintain

---

(1) al-Rāzī, al-Tafsīr al-kabīr, Dār Iḥyā' al-turāth al-'Arabī, vol. 20, pp. 101-04.

(2) Sayyid Quṭb, *Fī ẓilāl al-Qur'ān* (Cairo: Dār al-Shurūq), vol. 4, p. 2190.

that justice is all about fairness while *iḥsān* is perfection. The latter denotes observing more than obligatory acts of worship and doing the best in return for the good or the less in return for the evil.(1) As already mentioned, al-Rāghib al-Aṣfahānī states that *iḥsān* is superior to justice; seeking justice is obligatory while seeking *iḥsān* is praiseworthy.(2) In addition, some scholars including Ibn 'Aṭīyah hold the view that justice is to fulfill the obligations in terms of beliefs, legislations and trusts, while *iḥsān* pertains to commendable things.(3)

Preponderant Opinion

The preponderant meaning of *iḥsān* from my point of view includes everything dictated by Islamic noble manners and spiritual values. It is not confined to justice only; it covers toleration as evidenced by the glorious Qur'ān where God says, "Hurry towards your Lord's forgiveness and a Garden as wide as the heavens and earth prepared for the righteous, who give, both in prosperity and adversity, who restrain their anger and pardon people – God loves those who do good."(4) Restraining anger and pardoning people are acts of *iḥsān*, not justice. Metaphorically speaking, the scales of justice represent equal rights and responsibilities while in *iḥsān* the tray of responsibilities is weightier than that of rights as the person is expected to tolerate and waive some of his rights. Justice is based on firmness and decisiveness as opposed to *iḥsān* which is based on forgiveness, toleration and waiving rights. In this light, *iḥsān* is not limited to the category of commendable acts; rather, it may encompass some obligations as well.

---

(1) Wahbah al-Zuḥaylī, *al-Tafsīr al-Munīr* (Damascus: Dār al-Fikr), vol. 4, p. 212.

(2) al-Rāghib al-Aṣfahānī, *al-mufradāt fī gharīb al-Qur'ān*, pp. 118-19.

(3) Tafsīr Ibn 'Aṭīyah, edition of Qatar (8/493); *al-Baḥr al-muḥīṭ* (5/529).

(4) 'Āl 'Imrān (3: 133-34).

Summary & Analysis

Based on a deliberate analysis of the different uses of *iḥsān* in the Qur'ān, the Sunnah, exegesis, and philology, it is possible to highlight six meanings:

1. To do good and whatever advances interests and benefits for others;
2. To avoid any kind of maleficence and harm;
3. Perfection;
4. To do what is best and pay due attention to premium quality to reach the level of creativity;
5. To worship God as if you see Him (God-consciousness);
6. Mercy.

The first meaning of *iḥsān* is to say/do good and whatever advances interests and benefits. *Iḥsān* in this sense covers all noble manners and values. Such manners could be recommended or obligatory. In fact, ethics are an important element of faith;(1) thus, they are obligatory by default. However, there are certain cases in which some values are only recommended. Take for instance doing good towards parents; this kind of *iḥsān* is obligatory as indicated in many verses of Qur'ān. To sum up, *iḥsān* in the Qur'ān denotes all good things, be they obligatory or recommended; each kind has its due reward. The following verses can be cited in support of this argument. God says, "If you do good, you do good for yourselves,"(2) "[Those] who do good and remain conscious of God, will have a great reward,"(3) "Those who did well will have the best reward and more,"(4) "If you do good and are mindful of

---

(1) al- Bukhārī reports (1/51) that the Messenger of God says, "Īmān (faith) has over sixty branches; modesty is a branch of Imān".

(2) al-'Isrā' (17: 7). This translation is provided by SAHIH INTERNATIONAL.

(3) 'Āl 'Imrān (3: 172).

(4) Yūnus (10: 26).

God, He is well aware of all that you do,"(1) "Do good to others as God has done good to you".(2) There may be some indications supporting recommendation instead of obligation. For instance, the brothers of Yūsuf (Joseph) address him saying, "...take one of us in place of him. Indeed, we see you as a doer of good [*al-Muḥsinīn*]". Here they ask for something more than justice; they ask for *iḥsān*. The following verse can be understood in the same light. God says, "Who will give God a good [*ḥasan*] loan, which He will increase for him many times over? It is God who withholds and God who gives abundantly, and it is to Him that you will return."(3) This *ḥasan* loan is recommended. This also applies to doing favors to others. Generally, this meaning is more likely to be used with commendable acts, such as charities and endowments.

However, *iḥsān* is still applicable to certain kinds of obligatory almsgiving and maintenance such as *zakāt* and maintenance of wife and offspring. God says, "but make fair provision for them, the rich according to his means and the poor according to his– this is a duty for those who do good [*al-Muḥsinīn*]."(4) The majority of jurists concur that this maintenance is obligatory. In answering the argument of those maintaining the view of recommendation, Ibn al-ʿArabī explains that *taqwā* has different categories; some of which are obligatory.(5)

To conclude, using *iḥsān* in the sense of doing good (advancing interests) is oft-repeated in the Qurʾān. Here are some examples, God says, "God commands justice,

---

(1) al-Nisāʾ (4: 128).
(2) al-Qaṣaṣ (28:77).
(3) al-Baqarah (2: 245).
(4) al-Baqarah (2: 236).
(5) Ibn al-ʿArabī, Aḥkām al-Qurʾān, op. cit., vol. 1, p. 217.

doing good [*iḥsān*]";[1] "Shall the reward of good [*iḥsān*] be anything but good?";[2] "…and say, "Relieve us!" Then We" shall forgive you your sins and increase the rewards of those who do good [*al-Muḥsinīn*]"';[3] "…but do good, for God loves those who do good";[4] "For saying this, God has rewarded them with Gardens graced with flowing streams, and there they will stay: that is the reward of those who do good";[5] "This is how We reward those who do good";[6] "The mercy of God is close to those who do good";[7] "God never wastes the reward of those who do good";[8] "Give good news to those who do good";[9] "But We shall be sure to guide to Our ways those who strive hard for Our cause: God is with those who do good";[10] and "They will receive their Lord's gifts because of the good they did before."[11]

Based on the above-mentioned Qur'ānic verses, it can be concluded that:

1. The reward of good (*iḥsān*) is forgiveness and mercy. God will reward those people both in this worldly life and the hereafter.
2. *Iḥsān* is one of the commandments. The command form of address indicates obligation.
3. People are expected to do good in return for good.
4. Eternal life in gardens graced with flowing streams is the reward for those who constantly do good.

(1) al-Naḥl (16: 90).
(2) al-Raḥmān (55: 60).
(3) al-Baqarah (2: 245).
(4) al-Baqarah (2: 195).
(5) al-Mā'idah (5: 85).
(6) al-Ṣāffāt (37: 105).
(7) al-'A'rāf (7: 56).
(8) al-Tawbah (9: 120).
(9) al-Ḥajj (22: 37).
(10) al-'Ankabūt (29: 69).
(11) al-Dhāriyāt (51: 16).

5. God is pleased with those who do good.
6. Those doing good are close to God and more entitled to His mercy.
7. There are good tidings, both in this life and the hereafter, for those who do good.
8. God aids, supports and protects those who do good.
9. God guides those who do good to the straight path in this world and the life to come.
10. God blesses those who do good with righteous offspring and wealth.

As for the second meaning of *iḥsān*, it is non-maleficence. It is a principle requiring the avoidance of causing harm to others. This is inherently and inseparably linked to *iḥsān*; there can never be *iḥsān* in the presence of maleficence and harm. Based on this, some scholars of *uṣūl* (Islamic legal theory) conflate warding off harm with the principle of advancing interests. *Iḥsān*, in this sense, encompasses avoiding any kind of harm, be it minor or major. It includes other rules and principles such as: Do not kill; Do not cause pain or suffering to others; Prevent evil or harm from occurring. The principle of non-maleficence is the best example of a centuries-old principle in medical ethics since the era of Imhotep and Hippocrates. It has long been associated in Hippocratic medical ethics with the injunction: "Above all [or first] do no harm."(1) In our present-day world, the British physician Thomas Percival emphasizes that a principle of non-maleficence fixes the physician's primary obligations and triumphs even over respect for the patient's autonomy in a circumstance of potential harm to patients. Among these specific circumstances, the case when a patient makes inquiries which, if faithfully answered, might prove

(1) Tom Beauchamp, "The Principles of Biomedical Ethics as Universal Principles," op. cit., p. 3.

fatal to him; consequently, it would be a gross and unfeeling wrong to reveal the truth. His right to it is suspended, and even annihilated; because it would be deeply injurious to himself, to his family, and to the public. And he has the strongest claim, from the trust reposed in his physician, as well as from the common principles of humanity, to be guarded against whatever would be detrimental to him.[1]

There are countless proofs to support the necessity of preventing harm, abuse, maleficence, and mischief. There is no room here to discuss them in detail, but it may suffice to state that all prescribed penalties and disciplinary punishments are set in return for physical or moral harm. This harm is the effective cause of prohibition. God describes His Prophet (PBUH) as, "Making lawful for them the good things, and prohibiting for them the wicked things".[2] The wicked things refer to anything that causes harm, physically or morally. When God prohibited gambling and consumption of alcohol, He based this on their harmful effects. The Qur'ān reads, "They ask you [Prophet] about intoxicants and gambling: say, 'There is great sin in both, and some benefit for people: the sin is greater than the benefit.'"[3] There are other cases where the glorious Qur'ān prohibits a specific harm as in the following verses. God says, "Do not hold on to them with intent to harm them and commit aggression";[4] "No mother shall be made to suffer harm on account of her child";[5] "And let no harm be done to either scribe or witness";[6] and "Or debts, with no harm done to anyone."[7]

---

(1) Ibid.
(2) al-'A'rāf (7: 157).
(3) al-Baqarah (2: 219).
(4) al-Baqarah (2: 231).
(5) al-Baqarah (2: 233).
(6) al-Baqarah (2: 282).
(7) al-Nisā' (4: 12).

Similarly, the Sunnah is replete with a lot of traditions in support of this fact. For instance, the Prophet (PBUH) says, "There should be neither harming nor reciprocating harm."(1) Another narration states that "There should be neither harming in Islam nor reciprocating harm."(2) A third narration adds that "He who causes harm to a Muslim will be harmed by God, and he who acts in a hostile manner against a Muslim, will be punished in the same way by God." (3) Accordingly, it is not permissible in Islam for any Muslim to cause harm to others because a Muslim is expected to show mercy, blessing and love. It is evident that harm includes both moral and physical aspects. A Muslim, be a physician or not, shall not harm or cause harm to others. Moreover, rights are restricted if exercising them will lead to any kind of harm to others.

Relationship between Iḥsān and Rationality

There is a close relationship between *iḥsān* and rationality because declaring something as good or bad can be dependent on reason. The Islamic tradition is laden with a lengthy discussion of the theological issue of *al-Taḥsīn al-'aqlī* (i.e. determining what is good and what is detestable by reason). It is a point of contention among scholars, however. The preponderant view states that judgment and

(1) Reported by Ibn Mājah and al-Dāraquṭnī. Mālik narrated it in al-Muwaṭṭa' as a *mursal ḥadīth* with many corroborating ways of transmission; it was also reported by al-Ḥākim who comments that it is an authentic *ḥadīth* based on the conditions set by Muslim. Moreover, it is narrated in Sunan by al-Bayhaqī (6/69 & 70, 10/133), al-Istidhkār (6/196) and al-Tamhīd (20/157) by Ibn 'Abd al-Bar who states that the meaning of this *ḥadīth* is authentic. al-Nawawī mentions in *Bustān al-*'ārifīn that this is a *ḥasan ḥadīth* while Ibn Daqīq al-'Īd clarifies in his *al-Ilmām* that it is of a sound *isnād* even if al-Bukhārī and Muslim did not include it in their books of Ṣaḥīḥ. Ibn Rajab considers it authentic in *Jāmi' al-'ulūm wa-al-ḥikam* (2/211).

(2) Reported by al-Ṭabarānī and Abū Dāwūd in *Mursal ḥadīth*, no. 451.

(3) Related by al-Ḥākim in al-Mustadrak as an authentic *ḥadīth* based on the conditions set by Muslim.

legislation are fixed by God but notions of right and wrong are intuitively available to the human mind. Consequently, reason can decide that telling lies and injustice are detestable while truthfulness and justice are good. On the other hand, *iḥsān* as saying or doing good is included in the principle of unattested public interests (*al-Maṣāliḥ al-mursalah*) as elaborated by Muslim scholars. According to some scholars, this principle is one of the eight legal indicants of Islamic *fiqh*.[1]

Moreover, *iḥsān* could be included in the precept of appropriateness and suitability (*Munasib*) as a method of identifying the effective cause of analogy (*qiyās*). This appropriate attribute is used to establish a legal ruling which brings about a certain benefit. It is of two kinds; one pertaining to worldly interests and includes three categories, namely, necessities (*ḍarūrāt*), needs (*ḥājīyāt*), and embellishments (*taḥsīnīyāt*). The other kind relates to the hereafter such as purification of one's soul. This appropriate attribute could be effective, proper or unattested.[2] Based on the forgoing, *iḥsān* has something to do with the process of *ijtihād* where reason plays an important role in identifying it and its three categories of interests, i.e., necessities, needs and embellishments.

The third meaning of *iḥsān* is perfectibility: It is to work perfectly in the best manner and degree. It is to fulfill all the professional and technical conditions and standards in conformity with the legal regulations and functional criteria of the work in question. This meaning is reiterated in many verses and Prophetic traditions. *Iḥsān* in this sense

---

(1) See al-Shāṭibī, *al-al-Muwāfaqāt*, vol. 2, p. 8ff; al-Ghazālī, al-Mustaṣfá, vol. 1, p. 287; al-Rāzī, al-maḥṣūl, vol. 2/220); Ibn al-Najjār, Sharḥ al-Kawkab al-munīr, vol. 4, p. 159ff.

(2) al-Āmidī, *al-Iḥkām Fī Uṣūl al-Aḥkām* (3/396); al-Rāzī, *al-Maḥṣūl* (2/218); al-Ghazālī, *Shifā' al-ghalīl*, p. 169; Ibn al-Najjār, *Sharḥ al-Kawkab al-munīr* (4/159-76); al-Bazdawī, *Kashf al-asrār* (3/352).

(i.e. perfectibility), is either an obligatory ordainment or a recommended matter that is highly encouraged in accordance with the category of work. Perfectibility in domains of industries, occupations, and sciences is at least a collective duty, unless it proves an individual obligation in cases of necessity. The nation cannot cope with new serious challenges around the world in fields of sciences, technology, and industry without an increasing scale of perfectibility and creativity. It is included under the legal maxim: What is necessary to fulfill an obligation is also an obligation. The polymath sheikh al-Qaraḍāwī said, "Of the salient values in the field of production that comes next only to the value of work is the perfectibility and accuracy of work. For Islam, it is not only necessary to work but also to perfect the work. In other words, Islam requires to do work excellently and perform it perfectly in the highest quality. For Islam, this perfectibility is not a simple supererogatory or redundant or marginal matter, but it is a religious obligation ordained upon every Muslim."(1)

According to an authentic *ḥadith*, the Prophet (PBUH) said: "Verily God has prescribed *iḥsān* (perfection) for everything. So, when you kill, you must make the killing in the best manner; when you slaughter, make your slaughter in the best manner. Let one of you sharpen his knife and give ease to his animal (in order to reduce his pain)."(2) This *ḥadīth* uses the Arabic word '*Kutiba*' translated here as prescribed to denote obligation. The Qur'ān (2: 183) uses the same word which could be translated as following, "You who believe, fasting is prescribed for you, as it was

(1) See: al-Qaraḍāwī, *Dawr al-qiyam wa-l-akhlāq fī al-iqtiṣād al-Islāmī* (Cairo: Maktabat Wahbah, 1415 AH), pp. 151-52.

(2) Reported by Muslim in Ṣaḥīḥ, book of hunting and slaughtering, on the authority of Shaddad b. 'Aus no. 1955.

prescribed for those before you";[1] "You who believe, fair retribution is prescribed for you in cases of murder."[2] A person who works neglectfully is religiously condemned for overlooking a religious duty and violating God's ordainments on the believing servants. The Prophet (PBUH) says: "Surely, God loves that when anyone of you does a work, he should perfect it"[3] and,"God loves that when a person performs a work, he should perfect it." [4]

As to the fourth meaning of *iḥsān*, it is doing what is best, most excellent, and most beautiful. This requires exerting continuous efforts on the part of those in charge of any activity to achieve two purposes:

(a) The best quality of performance, work, and outcome along with keeping transparency and openness as well as endeavoring to have the best scenarios.

(b) Creativity in work, so the physician or the organization won't be a mere imitator but they should, each in their respected domain, carefully monitor and follow up in order to be creative in the relevant field and achieve the best and greatest ever possible service to humankind.

This meaning is repeated in several verses, for example, God says: "He may test you which of you is best in deed...".[5] The expression "*aḥsanu 'amala*" (i.e. best in deed), is formulated in this indefinite manner to convey relativity and puts no limit to creativity. It implies that the test of Muslims is not through simple actions or even good

(1) al-Baqarah (2: 183).

(2) al-Baqarah (2: 178).

(3) Related by al-Bayhaqī in *Shu'ab al-īmān* on the authority of 'Ā'isha. al-Albānī declared it as *ḥasan, ḥadīth* no. 1880.

(4) Repoeted by al-Bayhaqī on the authority of Kulayb and declared as *ḥasan* by al-Albānī in Ṣaḥīḥ al-Jāmi', no. 1891.

(5) al-Mulk (67: 2).

actions but through the production of the best in science, the best technology, the best activity, the best results, and the best care and service. The verse also points out that this excellence knows no limit and must continue progressively making today better than yesterday and tomorrow better than today in all areas of specialties and activities. Thus, God makes the superiority of Muslim nations conditional upon what services, benefits, and best-quality guidance in all fields the Muslims offer to humankind. God (May He be exalted) says: "You (true believers in Islam) are the best of peoples ever raised up for mankind."(1) *Li an-nās* (i.e. for mankind), the preposition "li" (i.e. "for") in the verse implies serving and befitting people through useful matters and bringing about their welfare. With respect to economic activities, the Qur᾿ān is not content with demanding (what is good), it requires to do (the best). This appears explicitly in the Qur᾿ānic command to grow and develop the orphan's wealth and the ban placed on approaching this wealth unless it be in the best manner, namely the best ways to keep the orphan's wealth and the best ways of investment to grow and increase it. God (May He be exalted) says: "And approach not the wealth of the orphan save with that which is better, till he reach maturity."(2) This commandment is emphasized in two chapters of the Qur᾿ān, al-An῾ām and al-Isrā᾿.(3) Since doing what is best is required in case of orphan's wealth, then doing what is best is greatly necessary in more serious activities such as taking care of patients. In this context, fair treatment is not enough, but the best treatment is a must.

With respect to the fifth meaning of *iḥsān*, it finds its

(1) ᾿Āl ῾Imrān (3: 110).

(2) al-᾿An῾ām (6: 152).

(3) al-Qur᾿ān (6: 152 & 17: 34). See: al-Qaraḍāwī, *Dawr al-qiyam wa-al-akhlāq fī al-iqtiṣād al-Islāmī*, op. cit., p. 152.

origin in the Prophetic tradition dealing with the same subject. The Prophet (PBUH) says, "Iḥsān is to worship God as if you see Him, and if you do not achieve this state of devotion, then (take it for granted that) God sees you."(1) In another version, the Prophet (PBUH) says, (*iḥsān* implies) that "you fear God as if you are seeing Him, and though you see Him not, verily He is seeing you. He (the inquirer) said: You (have) told the truth."(2) A third narration on the authority of Ibn Masʿūd quotes the Prophet (PBUH) as saying, "*Iḥsān* is to work for God as if you are seeing Him, and though you see Him not, verily He is seeing you."(3)

Pursuant to this meaning, *iḥsān* means that a human being must have a deep feeling and firm belief that God observes and sees him, so at times of worship or work, do your deeds as if you are in front of God Who sees you. Endeavor to the best of your ability to reach perfection, high quality, and creativeness. This degree of *iḥsān* is the utmost point man can get. However, other serious degrees are also there but a little bit less important than this highest degree, which is to know for sure that God sees you. This sight is another motive, not less than the first, to achieve good quality, perfection, and creativeness.

As far as the Islamic creed is concerned, it is well known that a Muslim who does not believe that God sees him is not a believer, as this is part and parcel of the Islamic creed.

---

(1) Reported by Muslim, Book of belief, no. 5, Abū Dāwūd in al-Sunan, no. 4695 and Ibn Mandah, book of belief, no. 9 where he comments that this tradition is authentic by consensus of opinion. It is also reported by Aḥmad (1/179) and al-Nasāʾī with an authentic chain of narrators as clarified by al-Albānī, *ḥadīth* no. 5005.

(2) Reported by Muslim in his Ṣaḥīḥ, no. 10.

(3) Tafsīr Ibn Kathīr (6/356). al-Haythamī reported this narration on the authority of Ibn ʿAbbās in Majmaʿ al-zawāʾid (1/44). He commented that its chain of narrators includes Shahr b. Ḥawshab. It is also reported by al-Bayhaqī in al-Sunan al-ṣaghīr (1/14) where he clarified that it is reported as per the condition set by Muslim.

The above-mentioned reports provide three interpretations for *iḥsān*: "to worship God", "to fear God", and "to work for God". Indeed, there is no conflict between them, for "to worship" includes two meanings: first, a general meaning equally applies to all good useful deeds devoted for the sake of God; second, a special meaning applies to religious rituals. The third interpretation, "to work for God", affirms the general meaning of "to worship", whereas the second meaning, "to fear God" is firmly associated with the deep belief that creates a sincere righteous human working on these two ranks. This interpretation, "to fear God", achieves the meanings of righteousness, piety, God-fearing, and careful observation of God's rules before work, at work, and after work. These due concerns are sources for plenty of good and welfare, strong motives for quality and perfection, and stimuli for being creative.

Evidently, the Prophet did not interpret *iḥsān* in this honorable authentic *ḥadīth* according to its familiar meaning, that is, to do what is good and act perfectly. Instead, he emphasized the motive behind these meanings, as this motive activates powers and only through it the sought purpose comes true. Worldly motives could sometimes achieve good perfection and even creativity, but the public welfare and commitments only come true when souls got purity through high discipline and association with the Creator. This is the proper intent behind the honorable *ḥadīth*. Very recently, fair economists have stated that the financial crisis from 2008 until now stemmed actually and essentially from the absence of ethics. The actual crisis is thus ethical and has led to a financial and economic crisis, which is an embodiment of the importance of *iḥsān* in this regard.

People are naturally inclined to love money and power.

God says, "He [man] is truly excessive in his love of wealth,"(1) "The love of desirable things is made alluring for men – women, children, gold and silver treasures piled up high, horses with fine markings, livestock, and farmland – these may be the joys of this life, but God has the best place to return to."(2) A man could only restrain his powerful desires through *taqwā* and *iḥsān* in this sense as would be later explained. This subconscious spiritual side that the Prophet (PBUH) mentioned in his interpretation of *iḥsān* requests a Muslim physician to rise to this level when dealing with the patient or the organization. He should do all his work perfectly as if doing it in the presence and observation of God Who watches him.

Imagine that a senior official or a minister of health is going to attend a surgery; undoubtedly, the physician will do his best, pay utmost care and spare no effort. Definitely, the Muslim physician shall feel an extra responsibility as God sees him. Acknowledging the great significance of this aspect, Islam affords utmost attention to purifying people's souls and rectifying innermost thoughts. Muslims are required to change themselves positively. The Qur'ān declares, "God does not change the condition of a people unless they change what is in themselves."(3) This is why God imposed the fasting of a complete month and made it one of the central obligatory foundations of Islam, connecting it with *taqwā* to attain the true meaning of self-observation and self-reformation. God says, "You who believe, fasting is prescribed for you, as it was prescribed for those before you, so that you may be mindful of God."(4)

---

(1) al-'Ādiyāt (100: 8).
(2) 'Āl 'Imrān (3: 14).
(3) al-Ra'd (13:11).
(4) al-Baqarah (2: 183).

This *taqwā* is the result of belief, sound doctrine, ritual acts of worship and constant remembrance of God. Attaining it is a primary objective of sending down revelations and messengers. God says, "It is He who raised a messenger, among the people who had no Scripture, to recite His revelations to them, to make them grow spiritually and teach them the Scripture and wisdom—before that they were clearly astray."(1)

The Qur'ān is clear on pinpointing the most important job of the Prophet (PBUH), which is to do his utmost to help human spirits be purified and lofty through reciting God's verses, disciplining one's soul and heart, clearing them from all diseases and filling them with the best virtues and moralities by means of continuous training. Furthermore, it is necessary to direct the mind to readings useful for the universe and humanity as well as to books presenting wisdom and means to public welfare to the whole humanity to achieve the mission of mercy to all creations.

The glorious Qur'ān uses the term *taqwā* and its derivatives 120 times. In addition, there are other related terms with the same linguistic meaning of protection and prevention of harm in this world and the hereafter. For instance, God says, "The pilgrimage takes place during the prescribed months. There should be no indecent speech, misbehavior, or quarrelling for anyone undertaking the pilgrimage – whatever good you do, God is well aware of it. Provide well for yourselves: the best provision is to be mindful of God [*taqwā*] – always be mindful of Me, you who have understanding."(2) This verse avers that *taqwā* prevents evil deeds and words; it provides protection from

(1) al-Jum'ah (62: 2).
(2) al-Baqarah (2: 197).

harm, even against animals and plants. Whenever this *taqwā* is deeply entrenched in hearts, people become so mindful of God and restrain their tongues and organs against inward and outward obscenities and mischief. The term '*taqwā*' has been repeatedly echoed concerning familial questions, particularly the good preservation of one's wife or else gentle separation on equitable manners. It also occurs on the relationship with parents and relatives, for *taqwā* helps to safeguard this relationship and to keep patience, forbearance, lenience, kindness, benevolence, and charitability. God says, "Be mindful of God, in whose name you make requests of one another. Beware of severing the ties of kinship: God is always watching over you."(1) In addition, the same term occurs in the context of testimony and justice. The Qur'ān reads, "You who believe, be steadfast in your devotion to God and bear witness impartially: do not let hatred of others lead you away from justice, but adhere to justice, for that is closer to awareness of God. Be mindful of God: God is well aware of all that you do."(2)

In fact, *taqwā* is used in all aspects of human activity including acts of worship, rites, dealings, and penalties. al-Rāghib al-Aṣfahānī notes that *taqwā* is to be on guard against all possible dangers that you fear. Fear and *taqwā* are interchangeably used in accordance with contexts in question. Moreover, Aḥmad al-Raysūnī explains that *taqwā* is technically used to express a moral, spiritual, cordial state that helps the person who gets it to show fine sense of responsibility and self-accountability, so he considers the anticipated consequences and effects of his actions and then acts independently whether the matter belongs to him

---

(1) al-Nisā' (4:1).

(2) al-Mā'idah (5:8).

privately, or pertains to his God or else concerns God's other beings.(1) In fact, *taqwā* is the self-control that could restrain a person from wrongdoings, so "Umar b. ʿAbd al-ʿAzīz said, "A person who has *taqwā* is self-restrained, not free to do all what he likes." (2) That is why 'Umar, the second caliph, objected to Jābir b. ʿAbdullah (may God be pleased with him): "Would you buy whatever you desire!" (3)

Tawqā signifies the watchful heart, the guiding insight, and the careful precaution. Literally, it is a prudent caution and careful safeguarding against what a human hates or fears.(4) It is also the self-blaming soul that reproaches a person when he does evil or neglects good; it motivates him to abandon harmful sins and expedite to good deeds. Islam associates *taqwā* with several supreme virtues such as guidance, righteousness, spiritual success and salvation, and winning God's Satisfaction, Garden, and even the Sublime Paradise as well as declaring it the best provision a person can keep in many verses. God says, "Believers, if you remain mindful of God, He will give you a criterion [to tell right from wrong] and wipe out your bad deeds, and forgive you: God's favor is great indeed."(5) Muslims are also required to cooperate for doing what helps to attain virtue and righteousness, God (May He be exalted) says: "Help one another to do what is right and good; do not help one another towards sin and hostility. Be mindful of God, for His punishment is severe."(6) The Holy Qurʾān is keen to introduce *taqwā* to help good marital relationship and good human and familial ties. We

(1) Aḥmad al-Raysūnī, "Ethics in Medicine" a paper presented to *CILE's first seminar on Islamic Bioethics.*

(2) Related by al-Bayhaqī in *Shuʿab al-īmān* (5/63).

(3) al-Ḥāfiẓ al-Mundhirī, al-Targhīb wa-al-tarhīb (4/150).

(4) see: *Lisān al-ʿArab, al-Qāmūs al-Muḥīṭ*, entry: *waqā*.

(5) al-ʾAnfāl (8: 22).

(6) al-Māʾidah (5: 2).

almost see no marital issue related to keeping the bond of marriage or to marital separation that is not formulated with, or followed by, the mention of *taqwā*. The same is true for the familial relationships whose discussion is beyond the scope of this research.(1)

The Sunnah provides an elaborate discussion on this issue as reported in many *ḥadīths*. For example, the Prophet (PBUH) says: "Fear God wherever you are, do good deeds after doing bad ones, the former will wipe out the latter, and behave decently towards people".(2) This perfect *ḥadīth* regulates the relationship between the human being and his lord as one that should depend on *taqwā* to provide an abundant source of all good for all God's creation. It ordains that human relationships should be based on morality and decency in all cases, God (May He be exalted) says: "Good and evil cannot be equal. [Prophet], repel evil with what is better and your enemy will become as close as an old and valued friend."(3) However, when a person commits a sin, he should speed up to do a good deed and repent to God with a broken heart and beseech Him for forgiveness. When a sin violates others' rights, a person should apologize for the wronged party, repay the violated rights or trusts, and restore natural status of things. *Taqwā* embodies human spiritual conscience and moral self-control; it prevents involvement in mischief and sins and restrains one's steps from abysses of lusts. It was *taqwā* that guarded Prophet Joseph (peace be upon him) when the wife of his master tried to seduce him: "The woman in whose house he was living tried to

---

(1) See entry (wafā) in Farīd Wajdī, *Mu'jam alfāẓ al-Qur'ān al-Karīm*; Wensink, *Mu'jam alfāẓ al-Sunnah*.

(2) Reported by al-Tirmidhī with a sound chain of transmission; See: ʿĀriḍat *al-Aḥwadhī* bi-*sharḥ Ṣaḥīḥ* al-*Tirmidhī* (4/349). It is declared in Ṣaḥīḥ al-Tirmidhī that this tradition is *ḥasan ṣaḥiḥ*.

(3) Fuṣṣilat (41:34).

seduce him: she bolted the doors and said, 'Come to me,' and he replied, 'God forbid! My master has been good to me; wrongdoers never prosper."[1] It was also *taqwā* that guaranteed the enforcement of the *Sharīʿa* – prescribed penalty on wine-drinking, a habit that was deeply rooted and widely addicted in the Arab society, when the last verse declaring a strict prohibition was revealed: "You who believe, intoxicants and gambling, idolatrous practices, and [divining with] arrows are repugnant acts – Satan's doing – shun them so that you may prosper. With intoxicants and gambling, Satan seeks only to incite enmity and hatred among you, and to stop you remembering God and prayer. Will you not give them up?"[2] It was *taqwā* that stimulated a young girl not to adulterate milk with water. Nevertheless, the mother argued that 'Umar is not aware of it, why should you harbor fear? The girl replied, if 'Umar does not see us, God for sure watches over us and nothing is hidden from Him.[3]

The six meaning of *iḥsān* is mercy, which is a disposition to show compassion, due care and concern, sympathy, and mutual affection for the suffering of others coupled with the wish to relieve their mistress.[4] Mercy is a result of *iḥsān*; when a person practices *iḥsān* and does all good things, he is actually merciful. Mercy is part and parcel of *iḥsān*, so it is not proper to discuss it separately. Only a person who does *iḥsān* has true mercy. Again, mercy appears to be a matter of the heart, which is difficult to define, especially when we attempt to standardize ethical principles that are measurable, verifiable, and standardized. Literally, mercy refers to the

(1) Yūsuf (12: 23).

(2) al-Māʾidah (5:90–91).

(3) See: Abū Nuʿaym al-Iṣfahānī, Ḥilyat al-awliyāʾ & Ibn al-Jawzī, *Ṣifat al-ṣafwah*.

(4) Ibn Abī Uṣaybiʿah, *ʿUyūn al-anbāʾ fī ṭabaqāt al-aṭibbāʾ*, p. 45; Muḥammad ʿAlī al-Bār, "The 4 Principles of Biomedical ethics", a paper presented to CILE, p. 3.

heart's affection, kindness, benignity, and forgiveness.[1] The practical manifestation of mercy is to do what is good and prevent what is harmful and evil, which also belongs to *iḥsān* and then no need to discuss it as an independent principle. For Islam, it is undoubtedly true that mercy has an utmost importance; God describes Himself with two attributes derived from it, namely the All-Merciful and the Ever-Merciful. These two attributes are repeated in the *basmalah* (i.e. *bismillah ar-raḥmān ar-raḥeem*: in the Name of Allah, the All-Merciful, the Ever-Merciful) throughout the Holy Qur'ān and in other occasions. Many *ḥadīths* celebrate the significance of mercy. For God, the Prophet's (PBUH) mission is nothing but a mercy to the whole creation, He (May He be exalted) says: "It was only as a mercy that We sent you [Prophet] to all people."[2] The Qur'ān is also revealed as a mercy for all, God (May He be exalted) says: "We have brought people a Scripture – We have explained it on the basis of true knowledge – as guidance and mercy for those who believe."[3] The Prophet (PBUH) says: "The merciful are shown mercy by the All-Merciful i.e. God. Be merciful on the earth, and you will be shown mercy from Who is above the heavens."[4] He also says, "The similitude of believers in their mutual love, affection, sympathy is that of one body; when one limb suffers, the whole body suffers because of sleeplessness and fever".[5] Books of Sunnah specified independent chapters for the issue of mercy. In his Ṣaḥīḥ, al-Bukhārī entitled: A chapter: "Showing Mercy to

(1) See: *Lisān al-'Arab, al-Qāmūs al-Muḥīṭ* for entry: *raḥim*.

(2) al-Anbiyā' (21: 107).

(3) al-'A'rāf (7: 52).

(4) Reported by Aḥmad, al-Tirmidhī, no. 1924 and Abū Dāwūd no. 4902. al- Zurqānī notes in Mukhtaṣar al-maqāṣid (no. 84) that this is an authentic *ḥadīth*. al-Albānī in commenting on Ṣaḥīḥ al-Tirmidhī declares it as authentic (no. 1924).

(5) Reported by al-Bukhārī in *Ṣaḥīḥ*, no. 6011; Muslim in *Ṣaḥīḥ*, no. 2999.

People and Animals" where he cited several *ḥadīths* on the account of a man (some narrations mention a prostitute), who quenched the thirst of a dog. God then appreciated his/her action and forgave him/her. The Companions asked: "Shall we be rewarded for showing kindness to the animals also?" The Prophet (PBUH) said, "A reward is given in connection with every living creature."(1)

These *ḥadīths* show an inclusive mercy that is equally granted to all, including non-Muslims and even animals. A veterinarian should then show mercy in the treatment of animals. This *Sharī'a* is the law of mercy as Ibn al-Qayyim put it, "[*Sharī'a* is] wholly proved a perfect mercy,"(2) revealed by the All-Merciful and Ever-Merciful God as hundreds of verses confirm, to the Prophet (PBUH) sent to be a mercy for the whole creation. That is why some scholars summarized the objectives of *Sharī'a* in two expressions: Glorifying the Truth (God) and Showing Mercy to the Creation. According to this meaning, mercy, tolerance, benevolence, purity, goodwill, and love of truth, which are – for some scholars – the bedrock of ethical principles,(3) are all inherent in the comprehensive meaning of *iḥsān*.

Comprehensive Scope of *Iḥsān*

Given the linguistic and technical meanings of *iḥsān*, it is crystal clear that this principle is all-inclusive. It encompasses two principles of the four-principle approach advanced by Tom Beauchamp and James Childress since 1976; namely beneficence and non-maleficence. In fact,

(1) al-Bukhārī's *Ṣaḥīḥ*, *al-Adab al-mufrad*, chapter: Showing Mercy to People and Animals. See: *Fatḥ al-bārī* (10/438), no. 6009. It is reported by Muslim, no. 2244.

(2) Ibn al-Qayyim, *I'lām al-muwaqqi'*īn *'an* Rabb al-'Ālamīn (3/3).

(3) See: Walī Allāh al-Dihlawī, *Hujjat Allāh al-Bālighah* (1/191-94); 'Abd al-Raḥmān Ḥabannakah, *al-akhlāq al-Islāmīyah* (1/517).

these two principles stop at the minimum degree of *iḥsān* which necessitates prevention of harm and fulfillment of interests. However, *iḥsān* is more than this. A well-known incident could be cited in this regard. A slave-girl of one Abbasid caliph was pouring water for him as he was preparing for prayer. Accidentally the jug slipped from her hands and fell on his face causing his face to be injured. He raised his sight towards her in anger. She recited "Those who restrain anger".(1) He said to her: "I have restrained my anger". She then recited "...who pardon people".(2) He said: "I have forgiven you". She further recited "...And God loves the doers of good".(3) He said: "Go now you are free".

Iḥsān for Physicians and Institutions

Iḥsān covers a wide scope of manners, including inner and outward moralities. This is applicable to both the physician and the institution in two important aspects: the inner and the outer levels. The inner aspect is reflected in *taqwā*, God-consciousness and God-fearing; consequently, when a physician does something, he feels that God watches over him. This feeling has a profound effect on the physician and his team in their dealings with patients. The same is true for medical institutions and their managers. Being mindful of God, they will not harm others or produce any harmful drugs. On the other hand, the outer aspect is manifested in certain tangible effects where *iḥsān* necessitates non-maleficence and avoidance of any harm. Further, it dictates beneficence, perfectibility, creativity and fulfilling interests on the part of both medical or pharmaceutical institutions in addition to physicians and medical professionals. At the level

(1) Sūrat 'Āl 'Imrān (3: 134).
(2) Ibid.
(3) Ibid.

of institutions, the principle of *iḥsān* requires such medical institutions to have the suitable qualifications and conditions of professionalism. They have to meet all technical and professional requirements, respect specialization, investigate the potential effects of any medicine or intervention in advance and observe all medical, professional and legal regulations and guidelines. This can be summed up using two conditions: sincerity (*ikhlāṣ*) and professionalism (*ikhtiṣāṣ*). The two conditions were emphasized by numerous verses throughout the Qur'ān. For instance, in one verse it is stated, "He (Yusuf) said, 'Set me over the lands treasuries. Surely, I am constantly-persevering, (i.e., guardian) constantly-knowing'."(1) The Arabic word "*Ḥafīẓ*", translated here as constantly-persevering (i.e., guardian), indicates sincerity and ability to fulfil obligations, while the word *'Alīm* (constantly-knowing) refers to knowledge, specialization and expertise. Sincerity is reiterated even in terms of physical labor; however, professionalism here gives priority to physical strength. This meaning can be gleaned from the story of Moses. The Qur'ān reads, "One of the women said, 'Father, hire him: a strong, trustworthy man is the best to hire'."(2) In this context, strength refers to professionalism and experience. In another occasion, eloquence is urgently needed as a manifestation of professionalism. That is why Moses describes his brother Aaron as more fluent and eloquent in calling people to religion, "My brother Aaron is more eloquent than me."(3) Sincerity is an unchangeable condition while professionalism varies based on the kind of work.

(1) Yūsuf (12: 55).

(2) al-Qaṣaṣ (28: 26).

(3) al-Qaṣaṣ (28: 34).

Resolution of IIFA no. 161 (10/17) Concerning *Sharīʿa*-Based Standards of Conducting Biomedical Research on Human Subjects[1]

The IIFA, affiliated with the Organization of Islamic Conference (OIC) holding its 17th session in Amman (Kingdom of Hashemite Jordan) from 28th Jumadah-al-Uwla to 2nd Jumadah-al-Akhirah, 1427 Hijri (24–28 June 2006);

Having reviewed research papers received by the IIFA regarding the *Sharīʿa*-based standards of conducting biomedical research on human subjects as well as the document issued by the Islamic Organization for Medical Sciences in its seminar held in Kuwait from 29th Shawwal to 2nd Dhul-Qiʿdah 1425 Hijri (11–14 December 2004) concerning "International Ethical Guidelines for Biomedical Research Involving Humane Subjects: An Islamic Perspective," and after hearing relevant discussions, the IIFA has resolved the following:

a. First: Endorsing the General Principles of the Document

The Academy ensures approving the general principles and foundations upon which the ethical standards which regulate biomedical research are based, according to the following:

1. Respecting individuals and honoring the human being have strongly rooted, well-established foundations in Islamic *Sharīʿa* as God says, "And

(1) The translation of this resolution is quoted from: Mohammed Ghaly (ed.), Islamic Perspectives on the Principles of Biomedical Ethics (UK: World Scientific Publishing, 2016), p. 287ff.

indeed We have honored the Children of Adam, and We have carried them on land and sea, and have provided them with *al-ṭayyibāt* (lawful good things), and have preferred them above many of those whom We have created with a marked preference" (Qur'ān 17:70). Thus, the autonomy of a person with full competence who volunteers to participate in medical research must be respected. He must be enabled to choose and take proper decisions with full satisfaction and free will without any compulsion, deception, or exploitation in accordance with the *Sharīʿa*-based rule, "No one can interfere with a right assigned to a human being without his/her permission." Likewise, an incapacitated person or one whose capacity is incomplete must be protected from injustice that may come even from his sponsor or guardian. According to a general jurisprudential rule, "The one whose actions are not legally valid (from a *Sharīʿa* perspective) [e.g. a person whose judgment is impaired because of mental illness] has no say." *Sharīʿa* provides for such a person a sponsor or guardian to take care of his affairs in a way that nurtures his personal interests without acting in an any harmful or potentially harmful way.

2. Achieving interest (*maṣlaḥa*) has its origins in Islamic *Sharīʿa* by bringing benefits to and preventing evils from the servants [of God]. In the case of unavoidable evil, it is better to eliminate the bigger evil by committing the lesser one.
3. Justice is the moral commitment to treat everybody in accordance with what is right and good from a moral perspective. It is to give each person his/her

right, whether the person is male or female. Justice is an established principle in Islamic *Sharīʿa*, whose rules have been laid out by Islam and which Islam has made the foundation and basis of success and goodness in life.

4. Excellence (*iḥsān*): It is mentioned in the most comprehensive verse in the Noble Qurʾān to induce all benefits and prohibit all evils: "Verily, God enjoins *al-ʻadl* (justice) and *al- iḥsān* (excellence), and giving (help) to kith and kin and forbids *al-faḥshāʼ* (i.e. all evil deeds), and *al-munkar* (i.e. all that is prohibited by Islamic law: polytheism of every kind, disbelief and every kind of evil deeds, etc.), and *al-baghi* (i.e. all kinds of oppression), He admonishes you, that you may take heed" (Qurʾān 16:90).

b. Second: Standards of Biomedical Research on Human Subjects

The Academy asserts endorsing the standards of biomedical research on human subjects that were included in the document referred to in the introduction of this resolution, recognizing that they organize biomedical research within the framework of Islamic *Sharīʿa* principles and provisions. We call for the Islamic Organization for Medical Sciences to hold a large-scale meeting that includes physicians and jurists to deepen the knowledge of such standards.

Recommendations:

1. The Academy recommends to the officials in Islamic countries that they take concern in supporting research and researchers by allocating

sufficient budgets, providing researchers with suitable conditions, and meeting their scientific and material needs in order to enable them to dedicate themselves to fulfilling their national duties.

2. The Academy recommends to the Islamic countries that they benefit from Muslim scientists abroad "as they are a great asset to the Muslim community (*ummah*)." The Academy recommends that Islamic countries open channels of communication with these scientists and encourage them to collaborate with their peers in Islamic countries to establish solid bases for research in Islamic countries.
3. The Academy recommends to the Islamic Organization for Medical Sciences in Kuwait along with the Ministries of Health in Islamic countries to organize training sessions for those working in medicine and healthcare sectors regarding medical and healthcare jurisprudence (*fiqh*), professional ethics — especially scientific research ethics — and the standards that have been referred to in this resolution. *God, though, knows best!*

The above resolution includes four basic principles that I grouped in three as previously mentioned.

Iḥsān on the part of the Physician

The principle of *iḥsān* implies certain qualifications for physicians and medical professionals.

1. The physician must be knowledgeable, experienced, and proficient in his or her medical profession. S/he has to respect specialization. It was reported that the Prophet (PBUH) asked two physicians who attended a sick person, "which of you is the better

physician?"[1] The Prophet (PBUH) says, "Whoever practices medicine when he is not known for that, he is liable."[2] In our present day, it is also necessary for him or her to obtain a medical degree and an official license from the country in which he or she will be practicing.[3] Moreover, it is necessary to be familiar with the legal rulings pertaining to medical practice to avoid prohibited acts. All this can be summed up by one term; professionalism (*ikhtiṣāṣ*).

2. Respecting fields of specialization. The physician should respect his medical specialization so that he should not treat a disease that is beyond his area of expertise. Rather, he is expected to refer the patient to the appropriate physician or seek advice from the relevantly specialized colleagues. This is dictated by the nature of contemporary medical sciences with their sub-specializations. For example, an ophthalmologist is not expected to know every detail of eye care along with all subdivisions of ophthalmology. Moreover, it is of paramount significance to pay due attention to the patient's psychology. Actually, Muslim jurists highlighted the importance of this issue many centuries ago.[4] To this end, a physician may advise his patient to listen to the Qur'ān and make use of *ruqyya* (healing by listening to certain verses of the

---

(1) Reported by Mālik in al-Muwaṭṭa', vol. 4, p. 328; Ibn 'Abd al-Barr, al-Tamhīd, vol. 5, p. 263.

(2) Reported by Abū Dāwūd, no. 4586, al-Dāraquṭnī, no. 400 and al-Nasā'ī with a good chain of narrators as declared by al-Albānī in Ṣaḥīḥ of al-Nasā›ī, no. 4845. It is also reported by Ibn Mājah. al-Albānī comments in Ṣaḥīḥ of Ibn Mājah (no. 2808) that this tradition is authentic due to external factors. Additionally, al-Suyūṭī declared it authentic in al-Jāmi' al-Ṣaghīr, no. 8596. In commenting on Mishkāt al-maṣābīḥ, al-Albānī considers ḥadīth no. 3434 as ḥasan.

(3) al-Qaradāghī, 'Alī'Alī al-Muḥammadī, *Fiqh al-Qaḍāyā al-Ṭibbīyah al-Mu'āṣirah*, op. cit., p. 110.

(4) Ibn al-Qayyim, *al-ṭibb al-Nabawī*, p. 117.

Qur'ān). This is in agreement with *iḥsān* in the sense of perfectibility and proficiency.

3. The physician must adhere to the laws, systems, regulations, and medical decisions issued by the competent authorities serving to regulate matters of private and public health as long as they do not conflict with the teachings of Islamic *Sharīʿa*. This is congruent with *iḥsān* in the sense of perfectibility and proficiency.
4. The physician needs to have certain personal traits and qualities such as astuteness, acumen, excellence and reliability. Careful and kind treatment with patients brings about trust, which is an indispensable component of a physician-patient relationship. Lack of this trust is the real impetus for many legal suits and claims. Media plays a major role in exaggerating the mistakes and spreading terror among people.(1) In *Principles of Biomedical Ethics*, Tom L. Beauchamp and James F. Childress lay great emphasis on trust as one of the noble ideals at stake within modern medical and health care institutions.(2) On the other hand, physicians may sometimes lack trust in their patients and fear that they may face lawsuits. Thus, they resort to defensive medicine where physicians order tests and avoid treating high-risk patients to reduce their exposure to lawsuits. This had a substantial impact on the behavior of physicians and on medical practice in addition to the high costs incurred by

---

(1) See the paper presented by Muḥammad ʿAlī al-Bār to CILE; "Fatāwá ḥawl al-Ṭibbī al-wa-l-marḍā" in *Fatāwá al-Lajnah al-Dāʾimah lil-Buḥūth al-ʿIlmīyah wa-al-Iftāʾ*, under the supervision of Ṣāliḥ al-Fawzān, no. 119 on 26/5/1404 AH.

(2) Tom L. Beauchamp and James F. Childress *Principles of Biomedical Ethics*, pp. 31, 166.

the patients.[1] In fact, this situation goes in conflict with the sublime values of *iḥsān*.

5. The physician should be characterized by integrity and absolute honesty. These two attributes are necessary for the physician, the medical staff and various medical institutions. Actually, they are necessary characteristics for any person, especially the true believers.
6. The physician must have a live conscience urging him to do good. This conscience manifests the internal morality to be discussed later.
7. The physician is expected to show humility towards God and thank Him for any success and efficacy of medical interventions. He should show humility towards people in general and his patients in particular. It is not proper for a physician to be cruel, haughty or arrogant. Kindness, leniency, smiling, compassion, benevolence, mercy, fulfilling promises are noble manners to be observed by physicians. It is necessary to avoid cruelty, mercilessness, arrogance and other prohibited vices. al-Rāzī states that humility in this medical profession is favorable.[2]

3.1.2 Honoring Human Dignity

Introduction

This principle means respect for the dignity of human subjects. God has honored man and created him in the best fashion. Humankind is distinguished with intellect, free will and choice, and autonomy. The Qur'ān reads, "We have honored the children of Adam and carried them by

---

(1) See the paper presented by Muḥammad ʿAlī al-Bār to CILE, p. 5.

(2) See ʿUyūn *al-akhbār*, p. 151.

land and sea; We have provided good sustenance for them and favored them specially above many of those We have created."[1] This honor is not peculiar to the followers of a certain religion, however, it is exalted in case of believers in return for their righteousness and obedience. God says, "Those who believe and do good deeds will be forgiven and have a generous reward,"[2] "Those are the ones who truly believe. They have high standing with their Lord, forgiveness, and generous provision,"[3] and "They will have known provisions, fruits – and will be honored."[4] This high standing dictates the necessity of respecting man's dignity, autonomy, free will and choice. Man is to be honored, be alive or dead; there must not be any kind of infringement or violation of this dignity.

Respect for Human Rights & Dignity

Islam acknowledges human dignity regardless of one's beliefs. God has chosen man as vicegerent on this earth. The Qur'ān states, "And (remember) as your Lord said to the Angels, 'Surely I am making in the earth a successor'."[5] When the angels wanted to know the wisdom behind this, God told them that man is more knowledgeable than them in terms of construction and population of earth. In addition, God has granted man freedom of belief, "There is no compulsion in religion."[6] Islam is keen to set people free; it prohibits torture, mutilation, and even frightening others. It highly regards human rights, privacy, and possessions. It maintains equality between people with no distinction or

(1) al-Isrā' (17: 70).
(2) al-Ḥajj (22: 50).
(3) al-'Anfāl (8: 4).
(4) al-Ṣāffāt (37: 41-42).
(5) al-Baqarah (2: 30).
(6) al-Baqarah (2: 256).

privilege except on the basis of righteousness. God says, "O you mankind, surely We created you of a male and a female, and We have made you races and tribes that you may get mutually acquainted. Surely the most honorable among you in the Providence of Allah are the most pious; surely Allah is Ever-Knowing, Ever-Cognizant."(1) Liability is also personal as stated by God, "And that man will have nothing except that for which he has endeavored (to achieve),"(2) "No soul will bear the burden of another."(3)

Manifestations of Honoring in Islam

The manifestations of honoring man in Islam can be noticed in the following points:

1. God has created man with His own hands; Adam was the first man to be created. The Qur'ān reads, "God said, 'Iblis, what prevents you from bowing down to the man I have made with My own hands? Are you too high and mighty?'"(4)
2. God created man in the best fashion. The Qur'ān reads, "We create man in the finest state,"... and "He fashioned you (and) so made fair your fashioning; and to Him is the Destiny."(5)
3. God ordered His angels to bow down before Adam, "When We told the angels, 'Bow down before Adam,' they all bowed. But not Iblis."(6)
4. God bestowed man with intellect, reason, the ability of hearing and seeing, and other senses. The Qur'ān enumerates these gifts in the following verse, "It is

(1) al-Ḥujurāt (49: 13).
(2) al-Najm (53: 39).
(3) al-'An'ām (6: 164).
(4) Ṣād (38: 75).
(5) al-Taghābun (64: 3).
(6) al-Baqarah (2: 34).

God who brought you out of your mothers' wombs knowing nothing, and gave you hearing and sight and minds, so that you might be thankful."[1]

5. God breathed His own breath of life into man, giving him spiritual superiority. God says, "When I have fashioned him and breathed My spirit into him, bow down before him."[2] This is the best form of honoring man. That is why every person is obliged to pay respect to others. It is in no way acceptable to assault a person having this Divine breath.
6. God chose man, not Jinn or angels, as a vicegerent on earth. The Qur'ān reads, "And (remember) as your Lord said to the Angels, 'Surely I am making in the earth a successor.' They said, 'Will You make therein one who will corrupt in it and shed blood (Literally: bloods) while we (are the ones who) extol (with) Your praise and call You Holy? Literally: hallow for you)' He said, 'Surely, I know whatever you do not know'."[3] This great honor was not given to the angels who never disobey God, but are rather preoccupied with glorifying and extoling God.
7. God put the whole universe at the service of man as the Qur'ān states, "He [God] has subjected all that is in the heavens and the earth for your benefit, as a gift from Him. There truly are signs in this for those who reflect."[4]
8. God liberated mankind from slavery and submission to any creature regardless of their supreme authority. This is the perfect kind of liberty where man submits only

(1) al-Naḥl (16: 78).
(2) al-Ḥijr (15: 29).
(3) al-Baqarah (2: 30).
(4) al-Jāthiyah (45: 13).

to God, bowing his head to none other. The Messenger (PBUH) was sent at a time when polytheism prevailed among people and different idols and false gods were worshipped. Even some of the followers of heavenly religions believed in trinity of three individuals (Father, Son, Holy Spirit). God saved people from this submission and servitude and called people to monotheism, to believe in His Oneness, to worship none other than Him. Absolute obedience is due to Him alone. There is no god but Him; He has no partner. This is the essence of Islam as explained by Rabaʿī b. ʿĀmir when he told Rustum: "God has sent us to liberate whoever wishes, from the worship of His servants to the worship of God, from the restriction of this world to its vastness and from the tyranny of other religions to the justice of Islam."(1) This is the unique message of Islam which came in an era of polytheism. Such monotheism has profound effects on people's behaviors so that they surrender and bow down only to God.

9. Refusing any intermediaries between God and people. Unfortunately, some followers of heavenly religions believe in some intermediaries. This is evident in the relationship between priests and the lay persons, in the sacrament of confessions with the priest, and notably in the grant of indulgences. The idea of indulgences was occasionally employed as a reward for crusaders who wage holy war against infidels. Such intermediaries are rejected by the Qur'ān as in the following verse, "They take their rabbis and their monks as lords, as well as Christ, the son of Mary. But they were commanded to serve only one God: there is no god but Him; He is far

(1) *al-bidāyah wa-l-nihāyah* (7/39).

above whatever they set up as His partners."(1)

The Frenchman, Etienne Dinet (who took the name "Nasiruddin"), speaks in his book entitled "The life of Muhammad the Prophet of Allah" about the balance, universality and possible future role of the divine message. He says: "A very important thing is the absence of an intermediary between a person and his Lord. This is what practical minded people find in Islam, due to its freedom from mystery and saint worship. It has no need for temples and shrines because all of the earth is a suitable place for the worship of God. Moreover, some of those who believe in God while expressing higher aspirations can find in Islam a pure perspective regarding belief in God. They will find therein the most extraordinary and sublime acts of worship and unimaginable expressions of supplication."(2)

10. Liberating man from undue concern about future, worry, and despair through belief in the Divine decree and predestination without neglecting material causality. This belief provides man with inner peace, a sense of stability and security, self-glory and respect. It prevents people from grieving for what they miss as long as they spared no effort. God says, "No misfortune can happen, either in the earth or in yourselves, that was not set down in writing before We brought it into being – that is easy for God."(3) This belief acts as protection against spiritual instability and imbalance; it provides people with real assurance and tranquility so that they are not obsessed with anxiety and pessimism. Similarly, this belief guards people against being tempted by blessings.

---

(1) al-Tawbah (9: 31).

(2) *The Life of Mohammad the Prophet of Allah*, pp. 362-63.

(3) al-Ḥadīd (57: 22).

11. Respecting human mind and liberating it from superstitions. Islam has a high regard for using mind. It urges people to contemplate and reason. According to Islamic teachings, this act of reasoning and contemplating the universe is an obligation. The Qur᾿ān reads, "Say, 'Look into whatever is in the heavens and the earth.' And in no way do the signs and warnings avail a people who do not believe."(1) There are countless scriptural texts calling people to use their intellectual faculty, urging them to contemplate and ponder the creation of heaven and earth. In fact, mind is the basis of legal responsibility and accountability. It is no surprise that Islam fights superstition, deception, sorcery and seeking help of jinn and demons. It emphatically states that unseen knowledge is only known to God. The Qur᾿ān tells us that, "When We decreed Solomon's death, nothing showed the jinn he was dead, but a creature of the earth eating at his stick: when he fell down they realized – if they had known what was hidden they would not have continued their demeaning labor."(2)

According to the Qur᾿ān, the jinn said, "We tried to reach heaven, but discovered it to be full of stern guards and shooting stars."(3) As for the relationship between mankind and the jinn, God made it clear that the latter do not have any authority over man. God says, "Men have sought refuge with the jinn in the past, but they only misguided them further."(4) Actually, the way to unseen knowledge is revelation; there is no other way. This revelation is represented in the Qur᾿ān

(1) Yūnus (10: 101).
(2) Saba᾿ (34: 14).
(3) al-Jinn (72: 8).
(4) al-Jinn (72: 6).

and authentic Prophetic traditions. It is through revelation only mankind can discover the unseen world. Mind cannot reach this world; consequently, Islam prevents it from attempting to do so and directs it to the seen universe to fulfill the mission of vicegerency and population of earth. Man is created to worship God and fulfill this noble mission. In this way, man becomes prepared and qualified to shoulder the responsibility of righteousness and reform. Thus, the great Greek intellectuals, such as Aristotle and Hippocrates, were preoccupied with metaphysics for hundred years but eventually they did not reach useful conclusions. In contrast, Muslim scholars who followed the Qur'ānic approach and adopted the empirical method did not concern themselves with metaphysics; rather, they directed their attention to humanities, cosmology and natural sciences so that they excelled in various sciences and created a great civilization in less than two centuries. In addition, Islam directs the mind, guides it to discover the secrets of this universe and shows the correct way to fathom many scientific issues. On the creation of the universe, the Qur'ān states that "Are the disbelievers not aware that the heavens and the earth used to be joined together and that We ripped them apart, that We made every living thing from water? Will they not believe?"(1) Some verses provide pretty accurate references to the successive stages of human embryonic development, which are in complete agreement with modern science.

Human Dignity & Bioethics

The International Islamic *Fiqh* Council states in its resolution no. 161 (10/17) that the autonomy of a person with full competence who volunteers to participate in medical research

(1) al-'Anbiyā' (21: 30).

must be respected. He must be enabled to choose and take proper decisions with full satisfaction and free will without any compulsion, deception, or exploitation in accordance with the *Sharīʿa*-based rule, "No one can interfere with a right assigned to a human being without his/her permission." Likewise, an incapacitated person or one whose capacity is incomplete must be protected from injustice that may come even from his sponsor or guardian. According to a general jurisprudential rule, "The one whose actions are not legally valid (from a *Sharīʿa* perspective) [e.g. a person whose judgment is impaired because of mental illness] has no say." *Sharīʿa* provides for such a person a sponsor or guardian to take care of his affairs in a way that nurtures his personal interests without acting in an any harmful or potentially harmful way. Actually, respect for human dignity includes three important principles; namely, respect for autonomy, sanctity of human body, and confidentiality.

3.1.2.1 Respect for Autonomy

Autonomy is self-rule free of controlling interferences by others and freedom from limitations within the individual that prevent choice. The two basic conditions of autonomy therefore are *liberty* (the absence of controlling influences) and *agency* (self-initiated intentional action). Therefore, autonomous informed patients or their families have the right to refuse medical interventions. Ethical dilemmas with the principle of respect for autonomy arise in certain cases when a patient refuses necessary medical interventions. The principlist approach prioritizes the principle of respect for autonomy over other principles and moral demands. Tom Beauchamp explains that many kinds of competing moral considerations can validly override respect for autonomy under conditions of a contingent conflict of norms. For example, if our choices endanger the public health, potentially harm innocent others, or require a scarce and unfunded resource, exercises of autonomy can justifiably be restrained or overridden.[(1)]

Based on the foregoing discussion, it is crystal clear that this principle of respect for autonomy is not universally applicable to all cases and has some exceptions. The IIFA set certain conditions and guidelines for these exceptions in its resolution no. 69/5/7:

Third: The Patient's Permission

1. The patient's permission of the treatment is essential if the patient is in full legal capacity to give it. If he is not, the permission of his (or her) legal guardian shall be sought according to the order of guardianship in *Sharīʿa*, and in conformity with its provisions which limit the scope of the guardian's action to the benefit and interest of the person under guardianship as well as to removing harm from him (or her). If the guardian, however, resolves not to give permission, his decision shall not be taken into consideration if it is clearly detrimental to the person under guardianship. The right of permission shall then be transferred to the next guardian and ultimately to the ruler.
2. The ruler shall order the medical treatment when deemed appropriate as in case of contagious diseases and preventive immunities.
3. In emergency cases, when the life of the victim is in danger, medical treatment shall not depend on permission.

---

(1) Tom Beauchamp, "The Principles of Biomedical Ethics as Universal Principles," op. cit., p. 3.

4. In carrying out medical research, it is imperative to obtain the agreement of the subject if he is totally fit in a way that is devoid of coercion (as in the case of jailed people) and financial enrichment (as in the case of the poor). Moreover, the research to be undertaken must not involve any harm. It is not permissible to carry out medical research on persons that are incapacitated or those of diminished capacity, even with the permission of their guardians.(1)

Dr. Muḥammad ʿAlī al-Bār proved through some studies and statistics that this right of autonomy is not absolute even for the fully competent patient. Moreover, autonomy requires giving the patient the adequate information, but if s/he is not willing to know the results of a medical test, it is better and in their interest to withhold such information in order to give them hope, which will improve their psychological condition and may be helpful for the cure. al-Bār focuses here on the major role of the family especially in Asia, Africa and the Middle East. According to him, the patient, whether he is an elderly or a young person, has to listen to the opinion of his close family regarding the mode of treatment he/she is going to accept. In some places in Africa, the elders of the tribe, decide in serious matters of life and death. The Western attitude of individualism is not accepted in many societies. In most countries of Asia, Africa and the Middle East there is no health insurance for the public at large and the family usually bears the burden of any cost of medical intervention.(2) al-Bār adds

(1) *Journal of Fiqh Academy*, 3 (7) 731-33. This translation is quoted, with slight modification, from Resolutions and Recommendations of the Council of the Islamic Fiqh Academy 1985-2000, p. 139ff.

(2) See the paper presented by Muḥammad ʿAlī al-Bār to CILE, p. 31.

that the patient sometimes delegates the physician to take the suitable decision. The physician should be tactful, try to explain the situation and give information to the patient and/or his family, and reach with them a decision with regard to the course to be taken. As far as he can make it, the physician should explain that the decision should be taken by the patient.(1) If the patient refuses to take a decision or even participate in it, s/he may delegate the decision making to a member of the family, a proxy or even to the physician himself as Beauchamp and Childress mention in their textbook: "Principles of Biomedical Ethics".(2)

al-Bār highlighted the study conducted by some researchers (UCLA) where they examined the different attitudes of 800 elderly subjects (65 years or older) from different backgrounds (Korean, European and African). They found that belief in the ideal of patient autonomy is far from universal. A family centered model places higher value on the harmonious functioning of the family than on the autonomy of its members. Even in cases where family relations are strained, the family becomes furious if one of its members enters a hospital without prior consultation with family elders. The physicians should ask their patients if they wish to receive information and make decisions, or if they prefer that their families handle such matters. The choice is up to the patient.(3) He says: "Many physicians in Arab and Muslim countries try to implement the Western standards of medical ethics; especially in terms of autonomy, however, they face many difficulties with some of their patients particularly the elderly and those suffering from serious

(1) *Ibid*, p. 32.

(2) Tom L. Beauchamp and James F. Childress *Principles of Biomedical Ethics* (New York, Oxford University Press, 5th ed., 2001), pp. 57-104, quoted in al-Bār's paper, p. 32.

(3) For references, see the paper presented by Muḥammad ʿAlī al-Bār to CILE, pp. 32-33.

diseases. They have to adopt a softer attitude and give more hope to patients."[1] This really needs some balance between interests entailed in disclosing all information to the patient and the harms of such disclosure. For example, some patients may refuse medical interventions if they know the correlated effects. If the cancer patient knows that radiotherapy may cause severe burns, he or she may refuse the required treatment. In such a case, it is necessary to strike a balance between interests and harms.

Legal Evidence for Autonomy

Autonomy is supported by many legal proofs and principles that necessitate respect for human dignity and freedom of belief and choice. God says, "There is no compulsion in religion,"[2] "Now the truth has come from your Lord: let those who wish to believe in it do so, and let those who wish to reject it do so."[3] If forcing people to believe is not permissible, then it is in no way acceptable to force someone to accept certain medical intervention unless it may cause harm to others. al-Bukhārī and Muslim reported on the authority of ʿĀʾisha that we poured medicine into the mouth of God's Messenger during his illness, and he pointed out to us intending to say, "Don't pour medicine into my mouth." We thought that his refusal was out of the aversion a patient usually has for medicine. When his condition improved and he felt a bit better, he said (to us) "Didn't I forbid you to pour medicine into my mouth?" We said, "We thought (you did so) because of the aversion, one usually has for medicine." The Messenger said, "There is none of you but will be forced to drink medicine, and I will watch you, except al-ʿAbbās, for he

(1) *Ibid*, p. 34.
(2) al-Baqarah (2: 256).
(3) al-Kahf (18: 29).

did not witness this act of yours."[1] This tradition proves the importance of seeking patient's permission in non-contagious diseases and impermissibility of forcing or coercing a patient into treatment against his will.

3.1.2.2 Sanctity of Human Body

The second principle included under respect for human dignity is the sanctity of human body, whether dead or alive, and prevention of any violation or mutilation. This is the default norm in the Islamic *Sharīʿa*. Accordingly, it is not allowed to use the human body as a subject of medical experimentation except in case of necessity and absence of any other alternatives. In line with this, controversial debate arises among Muslim jurists on the legal ruling of autopsy or post-mortem examination.

Islamic Perspective on Forensic and Academic Autopsy

Autopsy or post-mortem examination is the examination of a body after death. It is carried out for many purposes, including educational and forensic ones. It could be performed for academic purposes as a tool of learning anatomy, or to evaluate any disease or determine the cause of death, is it criminal or not? The early Muslim physicians, particularly, Avicenna, Ibn al-Nafīs, al-Zahrāwī, and Ibn al-Haytham, made influential contributions to anatomy by studying dead animals and corpses of war victims.[2]

Legal Ruling of Autopsy

Muslim jurists unanimously agree on the venerability and sanctity of the human body. Accordingly, violation of

(1) al-Bukhārī, *Ṣaḥīḥ*, no. 6897, 5709, 4458, 6886; Muslim, *Ṣaḥīḥ*, no. 2213.

(2) See: Aḥmad Kanʿān, *al-mawsūʿah al-ṭibbīyah al-Fiqhīyah*, p. 199; Aḥmad Sharaf al-Dīn, *al-Aḥkām al-sharʿīya al-ṭibbīyah* (Kuwait, 1403 AH), pp. 69-70.

the human body, whether during his life or after death, is forbidden in Islam. The Prophet (PBUH) says, "Breaking a deceased body's bones is exactly like breaking them when he is alive."[(1)] Commenting on this *ḥadīth*, Muslim scholars explain that this act is equally sinful based on another narration adding that it "is exactly like in sin". al-Ṭaybī argues that the deceased body should not be disparaged exactly like a living person. Ibn al-Malak understands this tradition as indicating the fact that a deceased person feels pain. Ibn Abī Shaybah quoted Ibn Masʿūd as saying, "Causing harm to a deceased believer is like doing so during his lifetime." [(2)] However, jurists permitted certain autopsies as in the case of a dead pregnant woman to retrieve a living fetus, or to remove money from a dead person's belly.[(3)]

The first contemporary scholar to legitimize postmortems was Aḥmad ibn ʿAbd al-Munʿim al-Damanhūrī (d. 1192 AH/1778 AD), the grand Imam of al-Azhar. Later on, many *fatwās* were issued in this regard. The Islamic *Fiqh* Council of the Muslim World League during its 10th session held between 24-28 Safar 1408H (17-21 October 1987) looked into the post-mortem examination of dead bodies. After a discussion and exchange of views, the Council issued the following resolution:

> Since the necessities which call for the post-mortem examination of dead bodies constitute a good aspect that overcomes the bad aspect of violating the honor of dead bodies, the Council adopted the following resolution:

---

(1) Narrated by Abū Dāwūd, no. 2792, Aḥmad, no. 23173, 23545, 23596, 24188, 24465, 25073, and Ibn Mājah, no. 1605, 1606.

(2) ʿAwn al-maʿbūd, *ḥadīth* no. 2792, Aḥmad in Musnad, no. 24188.

(3) See: Ḥāshiyat ibn ʿĀbidīn (Cairo: 1353 AH), vol. 1, p. 628; Fatḥ al-ʿAlī al-Mālik, p. 135; Ibn Qudāmah, al-Mughnī, vol. 2, p. 551; *al-Mawsūʿah al-fiqhīyah*, Kuwait, vol 16, p. 279ff.

First: It is lawful to do the post-mortem examination of dead bodies for one of the following purposes: a) To investigate a criminal case in order to know the causes of death or crime committed when it is difficult for the judge to know the causes of death, and when it becomes clear that the post-mortem examination is the only way of knowing these causes. b) To confirm a disease that requires post-mortem examination in order to take precautionary measures and appropriate remedies for this disease. c) To impart medical education as is the case in medical colleges.

Second: The post-mortem examination of dead bodies for educational purposes should have the following considerations: a) If the dead body belongs to a known person, it is stipulated that either the person had given permission for his post-mortem examination before his death, or his heirs permitted it after his death. Any post-mortem examination should not be done to the body of an innocent person unless it is necessary. b) The post-mortem examination must be confined to the extent that is necessary so that it should not turn into playing with the dead body. c) The post-mortem examination of female dead bodies must not be undertaken by other than female medical practitioners unless they are not available.

Third: In any case, all parts of the dead body that went through the post-mortem examination must be buried.

The above resolution sets certain conditions for the legitimization of post-mortem examination. Here are other conditions to be met.

1. Autopsy is to take place only after verifying that the person was indeed dead.

2. These examinations are performed only when necessary.
3. It has to be sanctioned, either by the deceased himself/herself or through permission by a member of the deceased's family. However, permission is not necessary in criminal cases on the ground of a preponderant legal interest (Maṣlaḥa). *A fatwā* was issued by Dār al-Iftā' of Egypt to legitimize postmortem examination for scientific purposes when the dead person is unidentified provided that it is limited to the extent necessary.(1)
4. The scope of these examinations must be kept to the minimum, relying on the legal maxim of 'Necessity is measured in accordance with its true proportions.' In principle, human dignity is to be generally respected; it is not permissible to violate the rights of the deceased unless necessary.
5. After the post-mortem examination, the body parts have to be collected and adequately buried.

Forensic Provisions

Procedural laws pay special attention to forensic medicine where relevant provisions are put in force. Egypt's Criminal Procedure Law includes five special articles in this regard (Art: 85-89). Additionally, the Department of Public Prosecutions set 86 articles to regulate forensic medicine.(2) Likewise, The Qatari Law No. 8 of 2003 on Autopsy of Human Corpses states:

Article 2: An autopsy on a human body shall be prohibited, except in legal cases where possible criminal

(1) A fatwā issued by Dār al-Iftā' of Egypt, record 74, no. 454, p. 276; see: Aḥmad Sharaf al-Dīn, *al-Aḥkām al-shar'īya al-ṭibbīyah, op. cit.*, p. 212.

(2) See: Mu'awwaḍ 'Abd al-Tawwāb & Sīnūt Ḥalīm, *al-Ṭibb al-shar'ī*, p. 80ff.

behavior is being investigated, or for medical reasons to help establish the cause of death, which may be otherwise unclear, or for educational purposes, and only after clearly ascertaining and certifying that death has occurred, in accordance with the provisions of this law.

Article 3: The autopsy shall be performed in relation to legal proceedings in the following circumstances:

1. When there is a suspicion that the death was directly caused by a criminal act.
2. When there is a suspicion that the death was somehow associated with or linked to a criminal act.

A forensic physician shall carry out the autopsy in both cases if permission is granted by the competent investigating authority. It is not necessary to obtain the permission of the family of the deceased.

Article 4: An autopsy for pathological purposes shall be performed in cases where the cause of death remains unclear despite clinical evaluation and examination, laboratory and imaging investigations and other medical analyses. The autopsy shall be carried out in a period not exceeding 24 hours since the time of death or the time when the death was certified. In these circumstances, the autopsy shall be carried out only after permission is granted by the minister or another nominated person, and permission must first be sought from the religious court (*Mahkama shar'īyah*). Moreover, the autopsy shall be performed by a physician who is a qualified pathologist. It is not necessary to obtain the consent of the family of the deceased.

Article 5: An autopsy for educational purposes may be carried out to further educational objectives. In these circumstances the autopsy shall be carried out by specialist faculty members in medical colleges, with their students under the supervision and guidance of their professors. It is not permissible to carry out an autopsy for educational purposes without documented permission from the deceased person, composed and witnessed before his death, or the permission of his next of kin with the consent of the religious court. It is also possible to perform an autopsy on deceased persons whose identity, or the identities of their next of kin are not known. In all cases, it is not permissible to carry out an autopsy if the deceased has stated in his will that he did not want his corpse to be subjected to an autopsy.

Article 6: It is prohibited to sell or buy a corpse, or to exchange it for any consideration.

Article 7: It is prohibited to perform an autopsy on the body of a deceased women except by professional women physicians and except when the autopsy is being performed for educational purposes, or in cases of absolute necessity and when women physicians are not available.

Article 8: In all cases, the autopsy shall be carried out in accordance with Islamic *Sharīʿa* rules and provisions defined by the executive resolutions of this law.

Article 9: An Autopsy shall be carried out in the premises specified by the Ministry for this purpose, in accordance with the terms and resolutions issued by the minister.

Article 10: Without prejudice to any more severe penalty stipulated by any other law, any person breaching the provisions of Article 6 of this law shall be punished by imprisonment for a period not exceeding five years and a fine not exceeding 50,000 QR, or either penalty. Furthermore, any person breaching the provisions of Articles 2, 3, 4, 5 and 7 of this law shall be punished by imprisonment for a period not exceeding one year and a fine not exceeding 10,000 QR, or either penalty. In all cases, the court has the right in its ruling, to order the revocation of the doctor's license to practice the profession for a period not exceeding the upper limit of the penalty stipulated for the crime.

Article 11: Only religious courts (*al-Maḥākim al-Shar'īyah*) are competent to investigate and rule on cases related to the implementation of the provisions of this law.

3.1.2.3 Confidentiality

It is also often referred to as medicine-related confidential information or medical profession privacy. This ethical value implies the necessity of maintaining confidentiality regarding all matters seen or heard by the physician from the patient. The physician must not disclose any secret that may harm the patient or any related party. The scope of this concept extends to all the information related to the patient's health, personal history, sexual relations, and so forth. Confidentiality falls under the general scope of higher objectives of Islamic *Sharī'a,* particularly, the principle of preservation of honor. Given the great significance of this objective, God has fixed a prescribed penalty for slander.

Religion has categorically prohibited every type of transgression against a person's honor as it has equally prohibited transgressions against life and wealth. The Prophet (PBUH) says, "Everything belonging to a Muslim is inviolable for a Muslim; his honor, his blood and property."(1) Basically, causing any undue harm to any human being is religiously forbidden. Therefore, disclosing confidential information is prohibited by the *Sharīʿa* and is both professionally and legally liable. Further, this action is considered a betrayal of trust and hence is not a trait of true believers. Rather, God describes true believers as, "And they who are to their trusts and their promises attentive" (al-Qurʾān 23:8). Furthermore, Prophet Muhammad (PBUH) identified betrayal of trust as one of the signs of hypocrisy.(2)

Safeguarding a patient's secrets is an integral part of all human values and is reinforced by all divine religions. Even the ancient oath of Amenhotep, one of the Ancient Egyptian pharaohs, included the statement, "Whatever I hear in my profession or outside of it which should not be disclosed, I will never reveal."(3) Following this came the Hippocratic Oath, taken by medical graduates to this day, which includes, "Whatever, in connection with my professional practice or not, I see or hear, in the life of men, which ought not to be spoken of abroad, I will not divulge, as reckoning that all such should be kept secret."(4)

Early Muslim physicians similarly underscored the importance of confidentiality. In his book *The Best Accounts of the Biographies of Physicians (ʿUyūn al-anbāʾ fī ṭabaqāt*

---

(1) Narrated by Muslim, no. 2564; al-Tirmidhī, no. 1928. Although this Prophetic tradition specifically talks about Muslims, there are many pieces of evidence in support of general applicability to all people.

(2) The Prophet (PBUH) says, "There are three signs of a hypocrite: When he speaks, he lies; when he makes a promise, he breaks it; and when he is trusted, he betrays his trust." It is reported by al-Bukhārī as per *Fatḥ al-bārī* (1/83,84) and Muslim, no 59.

(3) *al-mawsūʿah al-ṭibbīyah al-Fiqhīyah*, p. 556.

(4) Alī Dāwūd, "Akhlāqīyāt al-ṭabīb", a paper published in the *Journal of Islamic Fiqh Academy*, issue 8 (3: 17-18).

al-aṭibbā'), Ibn Abī Uṣaybi'a highlighted some of the oaths taken by the physicians of his era such as, "Those things that I see or hear while treating patients or at other times, which should not be disclosed, I refrain from talking about." He also mentioned some ethics associated with physicians including "perfect morality, sound mind, safeguarding patients' secrets, knowledge of Islamic law, avoiding the practice of abortion, and other similarly admirable behavior."(1)

Islam has prohibited disclosing secrets (except in cases of necessity with specific guidelines) due to the potentially harmful psychological, moral, physical, and financial consequences. In fact, breaching medical confidentiality is harmful to the medical profession itself. If a patient loses confidence in the physician, he may not reveal all the information regarding his condition, which may in turn obscure discovery of the actual disease. Islam places a strong emphasis on the issue of trustworthiness to the extent that a person is obligated to conceal what was said during a gathering if the other party indicates a desire for concealment. In this regard, it has been narrated that the Prophet (PBUH) asserted, "When a man tells someone something and then departs, it becomes a trust (amānah)."(2) This Prophetic narration clearly highlights that gatherings are considered trusts and that the one you consult is considered a trustee. There are many other Prophetic traditions urging Muslims not to disclose secrets and faults. One *ḥadīth* goes as follows, "God would conceal on the Day of Resurrection the faults of the one who conceals the faults of others in this world."(3)

(1) *'Uyūn al-anbā' fī ṭabaqāt al-aṭibbā'* (1/35).

(2) Narrated by al-Tirmidhī, no. 1882. He said, it is a *ḥasan ḥadīth;* Abū Dāwūd, no. 1882; Aḥmad, no. 14531, 14706. al-Ḥāfiẓ al-'Irāqī considered it *ḥasan* in Sharḥ al-Iḥyā' (5/216).

(3) Narrated by Muslim, no. 2580, 2590; al-Bukhārī (51/70, 71).

In its eighth session, the International Islamic *Fiqh* Academy issued resolution No. 79 (10/8) concerning the necessity of maintaining confidentiality in all medical professions except under exceptional cases. It states that:

> **First:** Confidential information is whatever someone tells another with either an anterior or subsequent request to keep it secret. This includes matters which are conventionally known to be of a confidential nature, per se, as well as a person's private matters or defects which he is loath to make public.
>
> **Second:** Confidential information is trust in the hands of the person entrusted with it, in conformity with the Islamic *Sharīʿa* teachings and in consonance with the ethics of magnanimity and proper conduct.
>
> **Third:** The general rule is that divulging confidential information is proscribed and divulging it without a genuine motive is reprehensible from the *Sharīʿa* point of view.
>
> **Fourth:** Secrecy is even more of a duty for individuals working in professions that are adversely affected by indiscretion such as the medical professions. Those in need of advice and assistance usually resort to medical professionals and communicate to them all (intimate) affairs that may help them fulfill their vital tasks properly. This may include information one keeps from all others, including one's own kin.
>
> **Fifth**: On exceptional basis, the duty of secrecy is not binding in cases where keeping the secret may entail

damage for the concerned person greater than the one that ensues from divulging it or when divulging the secret may entail a benefit that exceeds in importance the risks of keeping it. Such cases are of two categories.

a) Cases where the confidential information *must* be revealed on grounds of the rationale of committing the lesser evil in order to avoid the greater one, and the rationale of achieving the public interest which may entail enduring an unavoidable private harm so as to prevent a public one. These cases include two types:
   - Those which involve protecting society against some prejudice;
   - Those which involve protecting an individual against some prejudice.

b) Cases where the confidential information may be broken:
   - To ensure a public interest.
   - To prevent a public damage.

In all such cases the objectives and priorities as set out by *Sharīʿa* in terms of preserving the faith, human life, reason, descendants and wealth.

Sixth: Exceptional cases as to the binding nature of secrecy must be clearly stipulated in the codes of practice for the medical and other professions. Such cases must be clearly defined and enumerated along with all the details as to the manner in which the secret would be divulged, and to whom. The relevant authorities need to familiarize each and every one with these cases.

Then the IIFA issued a recommendation that medical unions and the ministries of health and health care faculties, incorporate this topic in the college curricula, give the subject its due interest and familiarize those working in this field with the whole matter, together with adopting relevant decisions thereon, and benefiting from any research elaborated around the subject.

God though, knows best!

Disclosure of confidential Medical information

According to the Islamic *Sharīʿa*, disclosing any confidential medical information (except for the cases highlighted in the IIFA resolution) is a crime punishable by means of disciplinary punishment. It is a sinful act violating people's rights, which may amount to or even outweigh physical harm. Islam sternly warns against this; the Prophet (PBUH) says, "Do not harm the Muslims, nor revile them, nor spy on them to expose their secrets. For indeed whoever tries to expose his Muslim brother's secrets, God exposes his secrets wide open, even if he were in the depth of his house."(1) This Prophetic tradition is adduced to criminalize disclosure of confidential information. The disciplinary punishment is decided by the judiciary. Article 310 of the Egyptian penal code stipulates that "Whoever among the physicians, surgeons, pharmacists, midwives, or others with whom a secret is deposited by dint of his profession or position, or to whom it is confided, then he discloses it in other than the cases wherein the law obligates him to report it, shall

(1) Narrated by many sources including the compilers of *Sunan* and *Musnad* books on the authority of Abū Barzah and al-Barāʾ. al-Albānī considered it authentic in Ṣaḥīḥ al-jāmiʿ (7984). al-Mundhirī commented in al-Targhīb wa-al-tarhīb that it is of an authentic chain of narrators (3/241). The same view is held by al-Albānī in Ṣaḥīḥ al-Targhīb, *ḥadīth* no. 2339 in addition to al-Ḥāfiẓ al-ʿIrāqī who declared it as having a good chain of narrators in Sharḥ al-Iḥyāʾ (3/175).

be punished with detention for a period not exceeding six months or a fine not exceeding five hundred pounds."

3.1.3 Justice

The third principle among the universal principles and all-inclusive foundations of biomedical ethics is justice. *al-ʿAdl* is the Arabic equivalent of justice; it linguistically means fairness; to claim your rights and fulfill your obligations. It has many connotations and various uses. It could be used as an epithet to mean equal. It is sometimes used as an intensive epithet as though meaning possessing every kind of *ʿadl*. *ʿIdl* means the like of a thing; it signifies the same or the equal. It also signifies the half of a load such as is in either of the two sides of the camel. According to Abū al-Baqāʾ the term "*ʿadālah*" linguistically means straightness, uprightness and justness, while in its technical sense, it denotes upright adherence to the path of truth and purposeful avoidance of religious prohibitions.(1) Some linguists differentiate between *ʿadl* and *ʿIdl*. For them the former is used in relation to what is perceived mentally while the latter is used in relation to what is perceived by the senses, as things weighed, numbered and measured.(2) *ʿAdīl* signifies the equal of a person in weight and measure or size or the like; *ʿAdīlatān* means two sacks because each counterbalances or is equiponderant to the other.(3)

The Qurʾān uses *ʿadl* in contrast to injustice, inequity, transgression, immoderation, and immorality. Accordingly, Muslim jurists use it in the same sense to denote two basic meanings: justice in judgment and relationship with others;

---

(1) Abū al-Baqāʾ, *al-Kulliyāt*, edn. of Muʾassasat alrisāla, 1413 AH., pp. 150, 639.

(2) For a detailed explanation of its linguistic meanings, see: *Lisān al-ʿArab*, *al-Qāmūs al-Muḥīṭ*, *al-Muʿjam al-Wasīṭ* (entry: ʿadl).

(3) al-Rāghib al-Aṣfahānī, *al-mufradāt* (Beirut: Dār al-Maʿrifah), p. 325.

inherent justice through which one attains uprightness. The latter sense is employed by jurists in testimony. On the other hand, the Qur'ān focuses on the first meaning which balances between rights and duties. All heavenly laws and legislations aim to materialize this meaning of justice. In fact, the order of heaven and earth depends on justice.

Justice in the Qur'ān

There is in the glorious Qur'ān unparalleled attention paid to justice. It is a categorical imperative to be observed in all sayings, actions, dispositions, judgements, testimonies, evaluations and relationships. The Qur'ān mentions *'adl* and its derivatives 28 times.(1) Justice is highly acclaimed by all heavenly religions. Messengers and prophets were entrusted with the task of establishing justice. God says, "We sent Our messengers with clear signs, the Scripture and the Balance, so that people could uphold justice,"(2) "I am [Prophet Muḥammad] commanded to bring justice between you,"(3) "God commands you [people] to return things entrusted to you to their rightful owners, and, if you judge between people, to do so with justice: God's instructions to you are excellent, for He hears and sees everything,"(4) "God commands justice, doing good, and generosity towards relatives and He forbids what is shameful [obscenity], blameworthy [maleficence], and oppressive. He teaches you, so that you may take heed."(5)

al-Rāghib al-Aṣfahānī explains that *'adl* (justice) is to

(1) Muḥammad Fu'ād 'Abd al-Bāqī, *Mu'jam alfāẓ al-Qur'ān*, entry: *'adl.*
(2) al-Ḥadīd (57: 25).
(3) al-Shūrá (42: 15).
(4) al-Nisā' (4: 58).
(5) al-Naḥl (16: 90).

equitably act in return for good or evil while *iḥsān* is doing the best in return for the good or the less in return for the evil.[1] The Qur'ān declares, "Good and evil cannot be equal. [Prophet], repel evil with what is better and your enemy will become as close as an old and valued friend."[2] Actually, God considers justice an indication of *taqwā* as in the following verse, "But adhere to justice, for that is closer to awareness of God [*taqwā*]. Be mindful of God: God is well aware of all that you do."[3]

Justice is generally required all the time without limitation, however, it is further accentuated in particular cases, such as:

1. In governance and judgement, God says, "...and, if you judge between people, to do so with justice."[4] As previously explained, God sent down scriptures and messengers to establish justice. God says, "We sent Our messengers with clear signs, the Scripture and the Balance, so that people could uphold justice."[5] Based on this, the majority of jurists, except for some Ḥanafī scholars, hold the view that being just is a prerequisite for nominating a caliph and outright injustice constitutes a sufficient reason to depose a ruler.[6]
2. Maintaining justice among wives. God says, "... then, in case you fear that you will not do justice, then one [wife],"[7] "You will never be able to treat your wives

(1) al-Rāghib al-Aṣfahānī, *al-mufradāt fī gharīb al-Qur'ān*, p. 325.
(2) Fuṣṣilat (41:34).
(3) al-Mā'idah (6: 8).
(4) al-Nisā' (4: 58).
(5) al-Ḥadīd (57: 25).
(6) See: *Ḥāshiyat* ibn ʿĀbidīn (1/638, 4/299); *Jawāhir* al-iklīl (2/221); *Mughnī* al-muḥtāj (3/5, 4/130); *Rawḍat al-ṭālibīn* (6/313); *al-aḥkām al-sulṭānīyah* by al-Māwardī, pp. 6, 22, 66, 35; *al-aḥkām al-sulṭānīyah* by Abū Yaʿlà, pp. 20, 60.
(7) al-Nisā' (4: 3).

with equal fairness, however much you may desire to do so, but do not ignore one wife altogether, leaving her suspended [between marriage and divorce]. If you make amends and remain conscious of God, He is most forgiving and merciful."(1)

3. Maintaining justice in testimony, even when it concerns oneself or relatives, God says, "when you speak, be just, even if it concerns a relative; keep any promises you make in God's name. This is what He commands you to do, so that you may take heed."(2)

In sum, justice is one of the most significant principles of Islam; it is the primary objective for sending messengers and scriptures. As a universal precept, justice is not subject to any exceptions; even in case of necessity, it cannot be compromised. It is to be observed with friends and enemies. The Qur'ān states, "You who believe, be steadfast in your devotion to God and bear witness impartially: do not let hatred of others lead you away from justice, but adhere to justice, for that is closer to awareness of God. Be mindful of God: God is well aware of all that you do."(3)

Justice-Related Terminology

The Qur'ān uses some terms related to ʿ*adl* such as *Qisṭ* meaning equity; *Muqsiṭ* signifying a just person; *Zulm* as injustice; *Jawr* meaning to act wrongfully or deviate from the right course and *baghy* as acting tyrannically.

(1) *Qisṭ*

Linguistically, *qisṭ* is a homonym signifying both equity

(1) (4: 129).

(2) al-'Anʿām (6: 152).

(3) al-Mā'idah (5: 8).

and acting inequitably. The Qurʾān uses the two meanings; God says, "…so that people could uphold justice [*qisṭ*],"[1] "And as for the inequitable [*qasiṭūn*], then they are firewood for Hell,"[2] "And that among us are the Muslims, and among us are the inequitable. So, whoever have surrendered (to Allah), then those are they who earnestly sought rectitude."[3] The verb *aqsaṭ* and its derivatives are used in the Qurʾān in the sense of equity. In Arabic morphology, adding the glottal stop (*hamza*) has a privative effect so that the verb properly signifies to do away with or put away injustice, or the like. God says, "So in case it concedes, then make a reconciliation between them both with justice, and be equitable. Surely Allah loves the equitable (ones)."[4] This verse commands Muslims to justly judge between the two groups and remove or put away any injustice.[5] In this sense, *qisṭ* complements *ʿadl* when they come together. The latter represents the positive aspect in judgement while the former signifies removal of injustice and its root causes. In exposition of this verse, al-Rāzī states that, *iqsāṭ* denotes removal of *qisṭ* (inequity) and *al-qāsiṭ* is the one acting inequitably.[6] The Qurʾānic verses following the above-mentioned one alludes to this subtle difference; they deal with the means to remove grievances and injustice among the believers. God says, "The believers are brothers, so make peace between your two brothers and be mindful of God, so that you may be given mercy."[7] This verse suggests five possible reasons of removing any injustice:

(1) al-Ḥadīd (57: 25).
(2) al-Jinn (72: 15).
(3) al-Jinn (72: 14).
(4) al-Ḥujurāt (49: 9).
(5) al-Rāzī, *al-Tafsīr al-kabīr*, op. cit., vol. 28, p. 129.
(6) Ibid.
(7) al-Ḥujurāt (49: 9).

1. True sense of brotherhood based on belief. This entails maintaining equal rights and effecting such brotherhood so that Muslims feel as if they are one person.
2. Achieving reconciliation between conflicting groups through a just compromise and mutual agreement.
3. Importance of *ḥisba* and reconciliation institutions so that Satan could not sow discord among them.
4. Purity of hearts and being mindful of God.
5. Showing mercy in dealing with others. The Prophet (PBUH) says, "If you show mercy to those who are on the earth, He Who is in the heaven (God) will show mercy to you."(1)

It merits attention that the Qur᾽ān uses *qisṭ* in the sense of equity 25 times,(2) while the imperative *aqsiṭū* is mentioned once (Q 49: 9) and *tuqsiṭū* twice (Q 4: 3, 60: 8). Equity or removing injustice is the intended meaning in all these mentions. The term *alqasiṭūn*, signifying the unjust ones, is mentioned in two verses (Q: 72: 14-15), while the verb *aqsaṭ*, denoting to establish justice, is mentioned twice (Q: 2: 282; 33: 5). Still, *almuqsiṭīn,* i.e. the just people, is mentioned three times (Q: 5: 42; 49: 9; 60: 8). The total mentions of *qisṭ* along with its derivatives are 25 times.

(2) Zulm (Injustice)

Zulm stands for the antonym of *ʿadl* or justice. The Qur᾽ān uses this term along with its derivations 289 times to highlight the danger of injustice and its serious effects on nations and civilizations.

---

(1) Reported by al-Tirmidhī, chapter of al-Birr, *Tuḥfat al-aḥwadhī* (6/51).

(2) (Q: 3: 18, 212; 4: 127, 135; 5: 8, 42; 6: 52; 7: 29; 10: 4, 47, 54; 11: 58; 21: 47; 55: 9; 57: 25).

(3) Baghy

It is to act tyrannically or injuriously. This meaning is employed 10 times in the glorious Qurʾān.[1]

(4) Jā'ir

The Qurʾān uses this word to signify injustice and deviating from the right course in one verse only. God says, "And up to God is adoption of the (moderate) way; (i.e., He has the authority to guide to the moderate way) and (some) of them are trespassing (jā'ir); and if He had (so) decided, He would have guided you all together."[2]

To conclude, the Qurʾān pays utmost attention to justice and removal of inequity and infringement to the extent that it deals with this issue in more than 350 verses. This shows the great significance of justice for individuals, families, groups, nations, and civilizations. Real experiences and Qurʾānic stories prove that injustice in its inclusive sense is a basic reason behind destruction and annihilation of previous nations and civilizations. God says, "Would anyone but the unjust people be destroyed?"[3] In the same vein, God says, "… and in no way would We be causing towns to perish except that their population are unjust."[4] The reality we live in our present-day world testifies to this fact. The biggest problem of our era lies in grievances between peoples and states, or among people with each other or between financial, political and social powers against the vulnerable people. Only justice can save our Islamic world; it can ensure dignity for people beside coherence

(1) However, it is used in the sense of demanding or seeking something in a lot of Qurʾānic verses. See: *al-Muʿjam al-mufahras* (entry: *baghy*).

(2) al-Naḥl (16: 9).

(3) al-ʾAnʿām (6: 47).

(4) al-Qaṣaṣ (28: 59).

and unity for society. The Prophet (PBUH) emphasized this great significance of justice in exposition of this verse, "... and thus We have made you a middle nation (*wasaṭan*) to be witnesses over mankind."[1] He explained that *wasaṭan* means a just nation.[2]

Justice in Medicine

The IIFA resolution no. 161 (10/17) states that justice is the moral commitment to treat everybody in accordance with what is right and good from a moral perspective. It is to give each person his/her right, whether the person is male or female. Undoubtedly, justice is a deeply-entrenched principle in Islamic *Sharīʿa* where its rules have been laid out by Islam. In the realm of medicine, justice is the practical application and underlying foundation of success and goodness in life.

Accordingly, justice is to give everyone his due while requiring them to fulfill their duties. A prime example of the need for general principles of justice is the necessity to distribute health care and its costs fairly in societies. It also entails the principle of fair opportunity and equal treatment, and avoidance of abusing rights and discrimination on the basis of race, color, wealth, or nationality. In this light, justice in Islam is applicable to the state, the physician and medical staff in addition to the medical and pharmaceutical institutions.

Justice in Medicine by the State

Justice in medicine is maintained by a government when it provides health care for all nationals and residents. It is

(1) al-Baqarah (2: 143)

(2) See: Aḥmad in *Musnad* (3/32); al-Tirmidhī comments that this is a *ḥasan ṣaḥīḥ ḥadīth*, *Tuḥfat al-aḥwadhī* (8/298).

fulfilled when health insurance is available for all people, whether it is provided by state-affiliated institutions or any other providers. To establish justice in medicine, the government shall pass the relevant laws and legislations to regulate people's rights and duties and ensure that a decent level of health care be distributed equally to all citizens. Justice in medicine does not necessarily mean that a government is to shoulder all costs of health insurance, health care, and medical research. Tom Beauchamp argues that some governments, especially the United States, tend to pay many useless procedures – a waste of resources that deprives others in society of adequate health care. Other governments have concluded that their resources are so limited that little money can be spent on either public health or health care. The basic ethical problem in every society is how to structure a principled system such that burdens and benefits are fairly and efficiently distributed and a threshold condition of equitable levels of health and access to health care is in place. These ethical objectives are intertwined in the formation of health policy, both internationally and in the policies of individual nations.(1) Justice also includes the ethics pertaining to the distribution of organs for transplantation. Imagine that an institution has used and continues to be attracted to two policies, each of which rests on a basic rule: (1) distribute organs by expected number of years of survival (to maximize the beneficial outcome of the procedure), and (2) distribute organs by using a waiting list (to give every candidate an equal opportunity). These two distributive principles are inconsistent and need to be brought into equilibrium in the institution's policies. Both can be retained in a system of fair distribution if coherent

(1) Tom Beauchamp, "The Principles of Biomedical Ethics as Universal Principles," op. cit., p. 5

limits are placed on the norms. For example, organs could be distributed by expected years of survival to persons 65 years of age and older, and organs could be distributed by a waiting list for 64 years of age and younger. (1)

The principle of justice entails nondiscrimination on the basis of race, color, nationality, etc. People are equal before the law. This equality is cherished as a basic value of Islam since its very beginning. The Prophet (PBUH) declares that "People are all the children of Adam, and Adam was [created] from dust. People should stop boasting about their fathers who have died, while they are but coals of Hell, or they will be more humiliated with God than the dung beetle who rolls dung with his nose."(2) He also affirms that, "There is no superiority for an Arab over a non-Arab, nor for a non-Arab over an Arab. Neither is the white superior over the black, nor is the black superior over the white – except by piety. You are sons of Adam, and Adam came from dust."(3) Despite the recognition of human rights, equality and non-discrimination, these rights can be and are still violated by developing countries or even the most advanced ones such as USA. Tom Beauchamp and James F. Childress argue that more than 40 million U.S. citizens (approximately 18% of the nonelderly population) lack health insurance of any kind. According to them more than 50 million non-elderly adults

(1) Ibid, p. 8.

(2) Reported by al-Tirmidhī, no. 3955 and declared as authentic by al-Albānī in *Ṣaḥīḥ* al-Jāmi', no. 4568. It is also reported by Abū Dāwūd on the authority of Abū Hurayrah, no.5116 and al-Albānī considered it authentic in *Ṣaḥīḥ* of Abū Dāwūd. al-Mundhirī narrated it with an authentic chain of narrators in al-Targhīb wa-al-tarhīb (4/62) and Ibn Taymīyah declared it authentic in *Iqtiḍā' al-ṣirāṭ al-mustaqīm* (1/247). It is reported by Aḥmad (16/300) and declared authentic by Aḥmad Shākir.

(3) Reported by al-Tirmidhī, *Tuḥfat al-aḥwadhī* (4/409) and declared as *ḥasan* by al-Albānī in Ṣaḥīḥ al-Jāmi', no. 3955 but he considered it as authentic in another narration in Sharḥ al-Ṭaḥāwīyah, no. 361. al-Haythamī commented in Majma' al-zawā'id that its narrators are known for reporting authentic traditions. al-Albānī mentions it among the authentic traditions in Silsilat al-Ahādīth al-Ṣaḥīḥah (6/451).

in the U.S., approximately one third of that population, experience a gap in coverage within a two-year period; approximately two-thirds of these same uncovered adults have no insurance for at least one full year.(1)

Structuring, Normativity and Coherence

Actually, measurability and normativity were taken into consideration in the course of articulating the three principles of bioethics; consequently, purely heart-based matters were somewhat excluded. In this sense, these principles are closely linked with the resultant consequences, positive or negative; thus, the regulating frame of reference lies in the legal precept of interests (*maṣāliḥ*) and evils. This precept represents a fundamental premise of *maqāsid* (higher objectives of *Sharīʿa*). However, it should be noted that *maṣāliḥ* are interpreted through the prism of *Sharīʿa* to include benefits and interests both in this world and the life to come. They cannot be in conflict with an established clear-cut text. In the same vein, *mafāsid* (evils and harms) encompass all evils pertinent to this world and the hereafter.

On the other hand, interests and benefits can never be limited to a certain individual or group. They should take into consideration the interests of both individual and community within a balanced approach giving each party its due. This balanced approach prioritizes public interests over private ones, and warding off evils over advancing interests. A corollary concept is the toleration of the lesser of two harms. Interests according to this balanced approach are organized within a hierarchy set by Muslim jurists, particularly scholars of *maqāsid*. Such normativity and structuring fulfill the juristic approach of giving effect to the resultant tangible

(1) Tom L. Beauchamp and James F. Childress *Principles of Biomedical Ethics,* pp. 240, 282.

consequences while taking into consideration the underlying intentions to be determined by concomitant indications. On the other hand, the inner aspect, which does not bring about actual outward actions, constitutes a special affair between the person and his Lord, entirely depending on piety, God-consciousness and *iḥsān* (explained by the Prophet as worshipping God as if one really sees Him).

Based on the foregoing, Muslim scholars classify moralities in relation to their resultant effects on individuals or community into two categories. The first category of moralities results in profound effects and considerable interests. If neglected, such moralities eventually lead to serious evils. This category falls under obligations and compulsory acts. Typical examples include justice as opposed to injustice, beneficence in contrast to maleficence, perfection of work in opposition to negligence, and honesty as contrasted with cheating and deception. Respecting human dignity and autonomy is another prime example of these obligatory moralities. By contrast, any impingement upon these rights, including the basic right of a voluntary, informed consent to medical interventions, is deemed prohibited. These noble values and moralities, with their two aspects of actualization and avoidance, are subject to structuring and normativity. Accordingly, the process of structuring aims at advancing interests and benefits in addition to warding off evils and harms. Besides, it makes use of the positive aspects of utilitarianism. It is established by induction that the *Sharīʿa* rests basically on the idea of promoting people's interests (necessities, needs, and embellishments) and protecting them from all harms. This divine *Sharīʿa* is in full accord with human nature and instinct and stands in stark contrast to monasticism. God says, "But when the righteous are asked, 'What has your Lord sent down?' they will say, 'All that is good'",[1] "Say [Prophet], 'Who has forbidden the adornment and the nourishment God has provided for His servants?' Say, 'They are [allowed] for those who believe during the life of this world: they will be theirs alone on the Day of Resurrection.' This is how We make Our revelation clear for those who understand."[2] This notion is found countless times in the Qur'ān and the Sunnah. On the other hand, the three-principle approach, being based on the concept of promoting people's interests and preventing evils as per the theory of *maṣlaḥa,* distances itself from the negative aspects of utilitarianism. Unfortunately, the utilitarian philosophy is entirely material and so focused on self-interests and personal parochial gains; it totally turns a blind eye to the spiritual dimension and interests of the others.

With regard to the second category of moralities, it does not quite often result in outward effects from the standpoint of interests and evils. Rather, it is all about the general virtues and etiquettes such as cheerfulness and niceness. This kind of virtues is deemed commendable not obligatory. They are interwoven in the three-principle approach through the prism of *iḥsān* and respect for human dignity. In principle, the category of obligations covers necessities and needs; prohibitions cover harms and evils while the remaining categories of commendation, reprehensibility and permissibility could be applied to other cases. Piety and belief belong to the first category of moralities as they bring about tangible effects, whether positive or negative due to their presence or absence. In this light, it can be concluded that *iḥsān* in the sense of piety *(taqwā)* intrinsically covers such virtues.

---

(1) al-Naḥl (16: 30).

(2) al-'A'rāf (7: 32).

Normativity and Internal Morality

Normativity and clear-cut structuring are interwoven in the three principles of bioethics. Their practical outcomes are linked with their concomitant behaviors which could be evaluated and thus subsequent liability could be incurred. Such outcomes are also seen in the light of the consequences and effects of the intervention by the physician or the medical institution. As indicated above, liabilities and duties are determined on the basis of practical effects and external consequences. For instance, beneficence materializes by fulfilling interests, perfecting work, avoiding harm, and warding off evil. These measurable criteria represent the essence of beneficence; however, the perfect form takes shape when mercy and piety are deeply rooted in hearts. The same thing holds true for justice and respect for human dignity.

Given this normativity, these biomedical ethical principles rank as the highest standards of professional medical conduct. Among their unique characteristics is the great emphasis laid on piety, God-consciousness and self-accountability as required by the principle of *iḥsān* in the sense of worshipping God as if one sees Him.[1] Moreover, the principle of respect for human dignity along with its religious dimension ensures this unique feature by means of paying due respect to man, whether alive or dead, and prohibiting any violation of the sanctity of body or soul (even if authorized as in euthanasia). These principles are characterized by certain religious dimension and internal morality reflected in piety and fear of God. By stressing that there is a recompense for good or evil deeds in this world and the life to come, such principles have more far-reaching and lasting impacts on people. If incited to

---

(1) The *ḥadīth* conveying this message is recorded by al-Bukhārī (4777) and Muslim (9).

cause harm or neglect a duty, such innate moral sentiments deter and discourage people even if there are no disciplinary measures to be taken against them. It is to that subject that we now briefly turn.

Impact of Internal Morality

Internal morality, by definition, is the firm belief in God and accountability on the day of Judgement. This belief creates a feeling of God-consciousness and an inclination to obey His commandments. A person who, believes that God sees him in all situations will be wary of disobeying God's commandments or committing any sins. He holds a firm conviction that he will undoubtedly be held accountable for his actions and will suffer due punishment on the Day of Judgment. On the other hand, if he obeys God's orders and maintains positive conduct, he will be rewarded accordingly and will enter Paradise in the Hereafter. Such convictions and religious beliefs serve as an impetus for doing good and avoiding evil or harm. This impetus stands for *taqwā* as put by the glorious Qur'ān. When this *taqwā* is deeply rooted in one's heart, it protects him and prevents him for committing sins. It is a primary objective of worship in Islam and the fruit of sincere belief in God. It is in this sense synonymous with *iḥsān* as an act of worshiping God as if one sees Him. When a person reaches this level of faith, feels God's watchfulness, he will never be able to disobey Him. This internal feeling and firm belief enabled Joseph to resist the temptation by the pretty influential lady. The Qur'ān tells us, "The woman in whose house he was living tried to seduce him: she bolted the doors and said, 'Come to me,' and he replied, 'God forbid! My master has been good to me; wrongdoers never prosper."[1]

---

(1) Yusuf (12: 23).

This internal morality materializes only through virtuous upbringing, persistent purification and self-discipline through acts of worship, constant remembrance of God, regular fasting and self-accountability. It is through this inner morality that faith comes to fruition and people can reap the intended fruits of belief. It is the driving force behind heart purification and righteous deeds. That is why God calls people to seek an effective faith, "You who believe, believe in God and His Messenger and in the Scripture He sent down to His Messenger, as well as what He sent down before. Anyone who does not believe in God, His angels, His Scriptures, His messengers, and the Last Day has gone far, far astray."(1) This is a call for believers to effectuate their belief and act upon it; true belief is to be translated into tangible actions. Indeed, faith dwells in hearts but it has to be manifested in actions.(2) The Prophet (PBUH) tells us that "God does not look at your figures, nor at your attire but He looks at your hearts and accomplishments."(3) Accordingly, the prosperous ones are those who purify their hearts. The Qur'ān reads, "... by the soul and how He formed it and inspired it [to know] its own rebellion and piety, the one who purifies his soul succeeds, and the one who corrupts it fails."(4) Another Qur'ānic passage avers that, "Prosperous are those who purify themselves, remember the name of their Lord, and pray. Yet you [people] prefer the life of this world, even though the Hereafter is better and more lasting. All this is in the earlier scriptures, the scriptures of Abraham and Moses."(5) In these verses God points out that the way

(1) (4: 136).

(2) There is a *ḥadīth* stating this meaning as reported by al-Suyūṭī although its chain of narrators is weak. See: al-Ṣaʿdī, *al-Nawāfiḥ al-*ʿaṭirah, *ḥadīth* no. 287.

(3) Reported by Muslim, in his *Ṣaḥīḥ*, no. 2564.

(4) (91: 7-10).

(5) (87: 14-19).

to success is self-purification so that one becomes inclined to do righteous acts and feels guilty whenever he commits a sin. It is through remembrance of God and preferring the hereafter over this worldly life such purification materializes. The verse ends by stating that all heavenly religions and scriptures lay great emphasis on such moral values that purify souls.

In fact, Islamic history is replete with examples showing the impact of internal moralities. Sometimes, people sacrifice themselves in pursuit of self-purification. This is evident in the case of confessing adultery to receive its prescribed penalty (stoning to death).(1) It is this internal morality that urged the Ansār (people of Medina who supported the Prophet (PBUH)) to benevolently give the *Muhājirīn* (immigrants) preference over themselves. God describes them as the ones who, "... give them preference over themselves, even if they too are poor."(2) Surely, the immigrants have also sacrificed everything for the sake of their faith.

Islam attaches great significance to this moral compass and internal morality. The Prophet (PBUH) says, "If God wants goodness for a servant of His, He will make for him an advisor in his heart."(3) This internal morality includes loving God, doing the best to please Him, and fearing His punishment. These are the driving forces needed for every person. By virtue of these internal moralities Islamic bioethics gain a significant advantage over civil laws and legislations. Ibn al-Qayyim argues that had it not been for the spirit of hope, submission of the heart and bodily organs

(1) See: Muslim, *Ṣaḥīḥ*, chapter of prescribed punishments (3/1323).

(2) (59: 10).

(3) Abū Manṣūr al-Daylamī reported this *ḥadīth* in Musnad al-Firdaws on the authority of Umm Salama. al-Ḥāfiẓ al-ʿIrāqī considered it of a good chain of narrators in commenting on *al-Iḥyā'*.

would not have been possible. It is hope that leads people to obedience; without hope people will not care.[(1)] This moral compass prevents Muslims from resorting to tricks and stratagems to evade religious ordainments. A Muslim firmly believes that God is All-aware; he recalls the ill-fated Jews who tried to evade their religious duties. The Prophet (PBUH) says, "May Allah curse the Jews, for Allah had forbidden them to eat the fat of animals but they melted it and sold it."[(2)] In this regard, Muḥammad ʿAbd Allāh Darāz states that man is inwardly disciplined and groomed. Norms and laws alone cannot establish a utopian ideal city where rights and duties are fully respected. Indeed, the one who fulfills duties out of fear of punishment or prison, is ready to violate them if this goes unpunished.[(3)]

Innate Moral Compass

Internal morality includes something that is found in every person of a sound mind and instinct; it is the innate moral compass that makes people inclined to noble moralities or, at least, to the fundamental ethics generally accepted by all mankind. It is the natural instinct or disposition as the Qurʾān calls it, "So [Prophet] as a man of pure faith, stand firm and true in your devotion to the religion. This is the natural disposition God instilled in mankind – there is no altering God's creation – and this is the right religion, though most people do not realize it."[(4)] These general principles of religion are preached by all prophets from Adam up to Muḥammad (PBUH). The latter states that "There is none born but is created to his true nature (Islam). It is his parents

(1) *Madārij al-sālikīn* (2/42).

(2) Reported by al-Bukhārī (2/774) no. 2110; Muslim, no. 1582.

(3) Darāz, *al-Dīn*, (Egypt: al-Maṭbaʻah al-ʻālamīyah), p. 92.

(4) al-Rūm (30: 30).

who make him a Jew or a Christian or a Magian."[1] These general moralities are part and parcel of faith; they are taken for granted by people. The Prophet (PBUH) indicates that "Imān (faith) has over sixty branches... and the least of which is the removal of harmful object from the road, and modesty is a branch of Imān." In another tradition, he considers modesty as the essential ethic of Islam. The Prophet says, "Every religion has its distinct characteristic, and the distinct characteristic of Islam is modesty."[2]

It is known that modesty is an innate disposition found in all people unless they corrupt it. Ibn al-Qayyim argues that had it not been for modesty, guests would never have been served; trusts would not have been paid back; and help would not have been provided. If it were not for modesty, people would never care for doing good, avoiding evil, fulfilling obligations, or showing kindness towards their relatives and parents. The driving force for such acts is either religious where a person seeks rewards, or a worldly noble incentive out of embarrassment and fear of being exposed or censured by others.[3] In sum, this impetus is intrinsic to mankind. Some may call it an active or live conscience.

In view of the forgoing, it can be concluded that there are four driving forces for morality in Islam.

1. Religious incentive represented in piety and hope.
2. Natural instinct and disposition, or intellect, modesty and live conscience. A Prophetic tradition goes as following, "Righteousness is that which contents the soul and comforts the heart, and sin is that which causes doubts and perturbs the heart, even if people

(1) Reported by al-Bukhārī in his *Ṣaḥīḥ* (1358, 1359, 1385), Muslim (2058) and many others.
(2) Reported by al-Bukhārī in his *Ṣaḥīḥ*, chapter of Imān (1/12) no. 9.
(3) *Miftāḥ dār al-sa'ādah* (1/277-78).

pronounce it lawful and give you verdicts on such matters again and again."[1]

3. Fear of punishment or losing advantages (if law regulates this). Although law is necessary to regulate people's life and their rights and duties, it cannot discipline behaviors and urges people to show *iḥsān*.[2] In its endeavor to reform people and urge them to do good and beneficence and abide by the best practice standards, the Islamic approach pays utmost attention and priority to the religious influence. This religious influence comes to fruition through the following necessary steps:
   a. Implanting the true principles of doctrine and firm belief of God's oneness and omnipotence. It is necessary to have a true love for God, believe that He gives life and death and believe in the day of judgment, hell and paradise. This belief brings about *taqwā* and sensing God's watchfulness in all circumstances.
   b. Abiding by God's commandments and observing the pillars of Islam to strengthen ties with God. Undoubtedly, faithful performance of prayer forbids obscenity and malfeasance; giving *zakāt* purifies souls; fasting disciplines people for a whole month and leads to God-consciousness; pilgrimage represents an extensive moral training to achieve piety and get rid of indecent speech, misbehavior, and quarrelling.
   c. Persistently stressing on the significance of noble character and good morals.

---

(1) Reported by Muslim in his *Ṣaḥīḥ*.

(2) al-Qaraḍāwī, *al-Imān wa-al-ḥayāh*, p. 171.

d. Disciplining, training, striving and purifying souls by means of remembrance of God, supererogatory acts of worship, fasting, and night voluntary prayer. A person should make use of any available means of self-discipline and purification to transform his inner self into one that is self-reproaching, prodded in the direction of righteousness. Such purification has a profound effect on hearts that it purges them from moral flaws such as envy, hypocrisy, malice, etc. By virtue of this purification and discipline, souls change from wicked to virtuous and minds from parochial into receptive and creative. These transformations eventually result in a sea change in morals and attitudes. God says, "God does not change the condition of a people unless they change what is in themselves."(1) Then, law can play an effective role and yield the expected results with the help of this internal morality. Darāz maintains that life is in no way fruitful without cooperation between people of a certain community. This cooperation materializes by virtue of the law which regulates relationships, duties and rights. This law will not serve its function without the help of a specific force to ensure people's respect and law abidance. Religiosity is the mightiest force to serve this purpose. Besides, it ensures social coherence, stability and tranquility.(2)

4. The fourth driving force for morality in Islam is collective ethos. It may be called the collective

(1) al-al-Raʿd (13:11).

(2) Muḥammad ʿAbd Allāh Darāz, *al-al-Dīn*, op. cit., p. 61.

protection force represented in the principle of commanding good and forbidding evil or the institution of *ḥisbah* in the terminology of classical jurists. According to Darāz, it is a collective responsibility of the entire *Ummah* to maintain general order, protect common rights, and prevent outright injustice. Each individual is expected to evaluate his inner state and make sure of its compliance with the spirit of *Sharīʿa*.(1) The Prophet (PBUH) gives an example to explain this collective protection in the following *ḥadīth,* "The likeness of the man who observes the limits prescribed by God and that of the man who transgresses them is like the people who get on board a ship after casting lots. Some of them are in its lower deck and some of them in its upper (deck). Those who are in its lower (deck), when they require water, go to the occupants of the upper deck, and say to them: 'If we make a hole in the bottom of the ship, we shall not harm you.' If they (the occupants of the upper deck) leave them to carry out their design they all will be drowned. But if they do not let them go ahead (with their plan), all of them will remain safe."(2) The entire society is responsible to prevent wrongdoing in order to ensure its own safety. Neglecting this collective duty is a reason for destruction. This is evident in many passages of the Qurʾān. God says, "Those Children of Israel who defied [God] were rejected through the words of David, and Jesus, son of Mary, because they disobeyed, they persistently overstepped the limits; they did not forbid each other to do wrong. How vile

(1) Darāz, *Dustūr al-akhlāq fī al-Qurʾān*, p. 429.

(2) Reported by al-Bukhārī in his *Ṣaḥīḥ* (no. 2493) and al-al-Tirmidhī with an authentic chain of narrators as declared by al-Albānī in commenting on Ṣaḥīḥ al-al-Tirmidhī, *ḥadīth* no. 2173.

their deeds were,"[1] "... how, when some of them asked [their preachers], 'Why do you bother preaching to people God will destroy, or at least punish severely?' [the preachers] answered, 'In order to be free from your Lord's blame, and so that they may perhaps take heed.' When they ignored [the warning] they were given, We saved those who forbade evil, and punished the wrongdoers severely because of their disobedience."[2] This is a function to be practiced by every Muslim. It was institutionalized during the era of rightly-guided caliphs through the mechanism of *ḥisbah.*

Legal Maxims contributing to Normativity

Linking ethics with the principle of *maṣāliḥ* (interests) and *mafāsid* (evils and ḥarms) already ensures normativity and coherent relationship. However, this normativity may be enhanced and a more comprehensive framework can be developed through utilizing a set of legal maxims that serve to outline issues of harm, interest, and the balance between them. Such maxims can help physicians and medical institutions take informed decisions. These rules are as follows:

Governing Legal Maxims for Issues of Harm

1. The rule, "There should be neither harming nor reciprocating harm"[3]

This rule is a Prophetic narration (*ḥadīth*) whose chain

(1) (5: 79-80).

(2) (7: 164-65).

(3) Reported by Mālik in al-Muwaṭṭa' with an authentic chain of narration on the authority of Abū Sa'īd al-Khudrī; al-Ḥākim in al-Mustadrak (2/57-58) commenting that it is an authentic *ḥadīth*; al-Bayhaqī in Sunan (6/96); al-Dāraquṭnī (2/77); Aḥmad in Musnad on the authority of Ibn 'Abbās (1/313); Ibn Mājah in Sunan, no. 2341. It was also reported by Aḥmad on the authority of 'Ubādah b. al-Ṣāmit (5/326), Ibn Mājah, no. 2340, al-Dāraquṭnī on the authority of 'Ā'isha (4/227), al-Ṭabarānī in al-Awsaṭ, no. 270 and al-Dāraquṭnī from Abū Hurayrah (4/228).

of narrators was deemed "acceptable" (*ḥasan*) by many scholars and "authentic" (*ṣaḥīḥ*) by others.(1) This *ḥadīth* indicates that it is prohibited to cause any harm and that harm is not to be removed by way of another harm. A set of rules has been derived from this Prophetic narration such as: harm is to be removed; harm is not to be removed by way of harm; necessity renders the prohibited permissible; need is treated as necessity; necessities and needs must only be assessed and answered proportionately; hardship begets facilitation; and relaxation should be afforded in the case of difficulty.(2)

There are some other maxims related to this *ḥadīth* or general rules, including: "Whatever is permissible because of a certain excuse ceases to be permissible with the disappearance of that excuse"; "When what makes something forbidden no longer exists, what is forbidden shall return [to permissibility]"; "Private harm is tolerated in order to ward off a public one"; "Minor damage will be endured to get rid of major damage"; "In the presence of two evils, the one whose harm is greater is to be avoided by the commission of the lesser"; "The lesser of the two evils is tolerated"; "Warding off harm should always take priority over the accruement of benefit"; "Harm is to be removed as much as possible", "Necessity does not invalidate the right of others"; "Harm is to be warded off whether intended or not"; "Harm is to be warded off as much as possible"; and "Necessity is only considered when it is real and certain, but not when it is conjectured."(3)

---

(1) Jāmi' al-'ulūm wa-al-ḥikam (2/211).

(2) al-al-Suyūṭī, *al-al-Ashbāh wa-al-naẓā'ir* (Cairo: Dār al-Salām), vol. 1, pp. 210-18; Muṣṭafá al-Zarqā, Sharḥ al-qawā'id al-fiqhīyah, pp. 525-830;

(3) al-al-Suyūṭī, *al-al-Ashbāh wa-al-naẓā'ir*, vol. 1, p. 173; Muṣṭafá al-Zarqā, Sharḥ al-qawā'id al-fiqhīyah, pp. 113-64; 'Alī al-Nadawī, Mawsū'at al-qawā'id wa-al-ḍawābiṭ (2/220-223).

2. The rule, "Certainty cannot be overruled by doubt"

In the case of treatment, if there is certainty, positively or negatively, this certainty should not be dispelled by doubt, and it is not allowed to neglect such certainty. For example, if there is definitive evidence that a particular treatment will be of no avail for a particular disease, it is not allowed to neglect this certainty unless we reach a different conclusion based on another certainty, which would in turn be based on proofs that impart certainty. The following rules are related to this maxim: "The basic principle is: what has once existed is [deemed] as continuing," and, "The basic nature of things is permissibility." Imam al-Shāfiʿī once said, "The fundamental principle upon which I base my decisions is that I use certainty, abandon doubt, and do not make use of conjecture."(1) We also have the following rules: "The basic principle is to ascribe the event to the nearest time of occurrence," and "The original rule for all things is permissibility."(2)

How Should a Physician or Patient Decide Regarding Treatment or Research Experiments?

As discussed earlier, medication must be used with the purpose of advancing interests or preventing harms. This raises the question: Is certainty in regards to resulting benefits and/or harms a condition for decision making?

The answer is as follows: The second rule mentioned above ("Certainty cannot be overruled by doubt") refers to situations of absolute certainty, which may only be negated by opposing absolute certainties. However, in cases lacking absolute certainty, the required condition is ensuring the

(1) al-al-Suyūṭī, *al-al-Ashbāh wa-al-naẓāʾir*, vol. 1, p. 156.
(2) Ibid, vol. 1, pp. 151-68; Muṣṭafá al-Zarqā, Sharḥ al-qawāʿid al-fiqhīyah, pp. 35-64.

existence of a predominant hypothesis based on professional principles as to whether treatment should be pursued or not. According to al-'Izz b. 'Abd al-Salām: "Efforts exerted to achieve the interests of this world and the Hereafter and warding off their evils are usually based on a preponderant presumption."[1] He also stated, "Because the preponderant presumption comes true in most cases, the interests of this world and the Hereafter have usually been estimated by this means ...So, it is not allowed to disrupt the interests that will most likely come true for fear of any banes whose occurrence is not guaranteed."[2] He then asserted that it is not permissible to act based on arbitrary assumptions. Rather, assumptions are classified into three categories: low-ranking assumptions, high ranking assumptions, and middle-ranking assumptions.[3] Furthermore, Islamic law established a firm rule that explicitly erroneous assumptions are to be disregarded.[4]

It is not difficult to arrive at an acceptable level of assumption. In fact, it is quite possible to attain this through knowledge, experience, experimentation, and consultation. Imam al-'Izz claims that, "Most of the elements of benefit and harm in this world can be identified by means of human discretion."[5] He continues, "Some beneficial and harmful issues can be recognized by both intelligent and unintelligent individuals, while others are only discernible to intelligent individuals."[6] Hence, the formation of specialized committees that are qualified to make appropriate decisions for complicated situations is imperative.

(1) *al-al-qawā 'id al-kubrá* (Qatar's Ministry of Religious Endowments) (1/6).
(2) Ibid., (2/35).
(3) Ibid.
(4) al- al-Suyūṭī, *al-al-Ashbāh wa-al-naẓā'ir* (1/343).
(5) *al-al-qawā 'id al-kubrá* (1/7, 13).
(6) Ibid., (1/38).

Applying *Fiqh* of Balances in Decision-Making for Contradicting Cases

The *fiqh* of balances (*fiqh al-muwāzanāt*) plays a central role in cases where a conflict arises between benefits and interests, damages and harms, or between benefits/interests, on the one hand, and damages/harms, on the other hand. In these cases, decisions should be made by balancing between the quest to achieve the best, strongest, and most effective benefits and to prevent the most and worst harm and detriment.[1] For situations in which the benefits of a certain action are equal to those of inaction, after consultations and recommendations from relevant committees, the final decision is up to the physician's discretion. If equality, however, is not determined, the issue should be referred to another committee for the decision to be made, while practicing caution and paying due attention to potential harm and detriment as much as possible.

The Muslim Physician's Oath adopted by the Islamic Organization for Medical Science (IOMS) during its first conference held in Kuwait in 1401 AH (1981 C.E.) emphasized the importance of promoting interests and preventing harms as illustrated below.

> In the name of God, The Most Gracious, The Most Merciful,
> I swear by God … The Great
> To regard God in carrying out my profession
> To protect human life in all stages and under all circumstances, doing my utmost to rescue it from death, malady, pain and anxiety
> To keep people's dignity, cover their privacies, and lock up their secrets

(1) Ibid., (1/38).

To be, all the way, an instrument of God's mercy, extending my medical care to near and far, virtuous and sinner and friend and enemy

To strive in the pursuit of knowledge and harness it for the benefit but not the harm of Mankind

To revere my teacher, teach my junior, and be brother to members of the Medical Profession joined in piety and charity

To live my Faith in private and in public, avoiding whatever blemishes me in the eyes of God, His apostle and my fellow Faithful.

And may God be witness to this Oath.(1)

Further Elaboration of Applying *Fiqh* of Balances in Contradicting Cases

There are certain rules derived from the proper application of *fiqh* of balances in case of competing interests or balancing interests and harms. A detailed analysis of such rules is presented here so that physicians, medical institutions, and patients along with their families can make use of them. Much has been written in this respect, but I think, to the best of my knowledge, it is the prominent scholar Yusuf al-Qaraḍāwī who charted this course through his book "*Fiqh al-awlawīyāt: dirāsah jadīdah fī ḍaw' al-Qur'ān wa-al-sunnah*" or (*Fiqh* of Priorities: A Novel Study in Light of the Qur'ān and the Sunnah). Dr. Muḥammad al-Wakīlī contributed to this field in his PhD dissertation on "*fiqh al-awlawīyāt: dirāsah fī al-Ḍawābiṭ*" published in 1997 by the International Institute of Islamic Thought

(1) The English text is taken literally from the official translation. See *Islamic Code of Medical Ethics*. Kuwait: International Organization of Islamic Medicine, 1981: 93.

(IIIT). Similarly, ʿAbd al-Salām al-Karbūlī published his PhD dissertation on *"fiqh al-awlawīyāt fī ẓilāl maqāṣid al-ʿsharīʿah"* in 2008. In addition, a paper co-authored by Dr. Hāyil Dāwūd and *ʿAbd* al-Majīd al-Ṣāliḥīn on the issue of competing interests was published in the journal of The University of Jordan.

In a complementary manner, certain rules can be highlighted to help physicians, medical institutions, and patients and their families to take an informed decision. They include:

First: In case of competing interests and harms

Some scholars maintain the general applicability of the legal maxim stating that, "Warding off harm should always take priority over the accruement of benefit." However, this maxim applies only in cases of equal interests and harms. If they are not equal, the following order shall be observed:

1. A public interest or that affecting the majority of people takes priority over private harm. For instance, if a patient has a contagious disease, his refusal to receive certain medicine shall be not considered. The same holds true when a person is about to marry but he refuses to undergo a necessary medical check. Similarly, the state is authorized to recover organs from deceased persons if they have no relatives. A supporting proof can be gleaned from the story of Moses and al-Khiḍr when the latter intentionally made a hole in the ship. The Qurʾān reads, "The ship belonged to some needy people who made their living from the sea and I damaged it because I knew that coming after them was a king who was seizing

every [serviceable] ship by force."[1] One relevant rule states that private harm is tolerated in order to ward off a public one.[2]

2. A more impactful interest takes priority over the lesser harm. A prime example is the case of a medical intervention with a high probability of success (> 50%).
3. The hierarchy of necessities, needs and embellishments is to be taken into consideration; consequently, a benefit related to necessities takes precedence over any harm related to the category of needs.
4. The ascendant is given priority over the descendant in terms of fulfilling interests and preventing harms. Accordingly, to achieve an interest of the ascendant is a priority over warding off an evil befalling the descendant in case of mutual exclusivity. Based on this, the benefit of saving the life of a mother outweighs the harm of ending the life of her fetus by abortion.
5. A certain benefit is superior to any speculative harm. For instance, preservation of the mother's life is a priority over the life of the fetus given the fact that it is her life that we are certain of saving when aborting the pregnancy, as opposed to the probable life of the fetus.
6. A unanimously agreed on benefit is superior to controversial harm. If the medical staff agrees on the efficiency of a certain intervention but they hold different views concerning the side effects, they shall go on with such an intervention.

---

(1) (18: 79).
(2) Ibn Nujaym, *al-al-Ashbāh wa-al-naẓā'ir* (1/74).

7. A certain benefit should not be missed for fear of any banes whose occurrence is not guaranteed. If a physician knows for sure that a medical treatment is successful but there may be some collateral damages, he should proceed with the treatment. Another relevant rule applies in similar cases where an immediate benefit takes priority over delayed equal harm. However, if such delayed harm is greater, it should be given priority.
8. In case of equal benefits and harms, warding off harm is prioritized over the accruement of benefit. If the medical staff decides that a surgical intervention has a success probability of 50% but the dangerous side effects amount to 50 percent, it is not allowed for them to proceed. However, if there is a 10% chance of success with no complications, they can go on with this procedure after obtaining an informed consent from the patient or his family.
9. Public harm outweighs a private interest; the same thing holds true for such harm affecting a greater number of people as opposed to that affecting only one.
10. Certain harm comes before a speculative interest.
11. Harm befalling the ascendant is given priority over the one affecting the descendant.
12. Any harm affecting others takes precedence over a parochial self-interest.

Second: In case of competing interests

1. A public universal interest comes before a private one. For instance, public vaccination precedes over private interests; mass medication is prioritized over individual treatment; treating the wounded soldiers is given priority over others during war-time, etc.

2. A more impactful interest takes precedence over a lesser one.
3. The ascendant-related interest outweighs the one related to the descendant.
4. A certain interest is superior to a doubtful one.
5. An interest unanimously acknowledged by physicians takes priority over a controversial one.
6. A certain benefit should not be missed for the sake of a less likely one. Likewise, an immediate benefit takes priority over the delayed one.
7. The hierarchy of necessities, needs and embellishments is to be taken into consideration in case of competing interests. This principle is instrumental in construing the legal rulings of cosmetic plastic surgery.
8. Duties and obligations play an important role in settling competing interests. If one of two patients has a medical service contract whereby the medical institution is duty-bound to perform medical treatment, such a person has a priority. However, the other patient should receive medication as much as possible.
9. Strategic interests come before unplanned provisional ones. This particularly applies to medical institutions and laboratories. They have to pay more attention to strategic planning and noble aims rather than to quick profits.
10. A far-reaching permanent effect is decisive in giving priority to one interest over another.

Third: In case of competing harms

1. Warding off public harm or that affecting a lot of people takes precedence over preventing the private one.
2. Doubtful harm is tolerated for the certain one.

3. Agreed upon harm takes priority over a disputed one.
4. A broader harm outweighs another of a limited scope. Prevalence, number of affected persons, and spatiotemporal considerations could be instrumental in setting priorities.
5. Real harm is prioritized over a potential or hypothetical one unless evidence-based research proves more serious complications and consequences in the future. In this case, priority is given to the predicted harm.
6. Harm befalling the ascendant merits more attention than the one related to the descendant in case of contradiction.

The above-mentioned rules serve as a guide for the physician, the medical institution, the patient, and the family in taking an informed decision. Past experiments and meticulous research assessing benefits and evils are also to be taken into account.(1)

The Broad Scope of Medical Ethics that Includes Physicians, Patients, and Others

Medical ethics must primarily stem from the physician himself. These ethics should be inherent qualities in his relationship with the patient since medicine is a means, not an end, for healing a patient. The healing of a patient is the principal end. Therefore, a physician's care for his patients must be unparalleled in its excellence. Likewise, the physician must maintain positive relationships with his colleagues, institution, and society. Given the significant role played by a physician, maintaining the following fundamental ethics and guidelines is crucial:

---

(1) See references of *fiqh* of priorities cited above at the beginning of this section.

The Ethics of a Physician: Guidelines and Behaviors

Islamic *Sharīʿa* has established a set of distinguished ethics (guidelines, rules, and behaviors) for the physician who treats people whether physically, psychologically, or otherwise. Below is a brief outline of these ethics:

First: The physician must be knowledgeable, experienced, and proficient in his or her medical profession. In our present day, it is also necessary for him or her to obtain a medical degree and an official license from the country in which he or she will be practicing (a condition acknowledged by *Sharīʿa*).

Second: The physician's practice must be in alignment with the commonly agreed upon professional regulations.

Third: The physician must be sincerely dedicated to his or her work, trustworthy, protective of the rights of others, and striving towards excellence and innovation.(1)

These are the three fundamental conditions in Islam. They can be summed up using two words: sincerity (*ikhlāṣ*) and professionalism (*ikhtiṣāṣ*). This was reiterated by numerous verses throughout the Qurʾān. For instance, in one verse it is stated, "One of the women said, 'Father, hire him: a strong, trustworthy man is the best to hire.'"(2) In this context, strength refers to professionalism and experience while trustworthiness refers to sincerity and honoring confidentiality.

Fourth: The physician should be knowledgeable of the legal rulings associated with medicine and treating patients.

Fifth: The physician should be characterized by Islam's noble attributes, particularly:

---

(1) For more information, see relevant papers presented by Alī Dāwūd al-Jaffāl", Aḥmad al-Jundī, ʿAbd al-Sattār Abū Ghuddah, Muḥammad ʿAtta, Muḥammad ʿAlī al-Bār, Muṣṭafá ʿAbd al-Rūʾuf, Saʿūd al-Thabītī, published in Group of Scholars (1993). *Islamic Fiqh Academy Journal*, issue 8 (3/10–407).

(2) al-al-Qaṣaṣ (28: 26).

i. God-consciousness, fear of God, and cognizance of God's presence throughout his or her treatment of a patient. The physician should be as the Prophet Muhammad (PBUH) described, "To worship God as if you see Him, and if you do not achieve this state of devotion, then (take it for granted that) God sees you."[1]
ii. Humility towards God, patients, and colleagues and practicing virtue in all interpersonal relationships.
iii. Truthfulness and absolute honesty in regards to sight, behaviors, integrity, and chastity. In addition, it is necessary to refrain from cheating, betrayal, envy, malevolence, and all other diseases of the heart.

Sixth: The physician should respect his medical specialization through enhancing his interest in and study of the field and pursuing creativity and innovation. He should also respect other specializations, so that he should not treat a disease that is beyond his area of expertise but rather refer the patient to the appropriate physician or seek advice from the relevantly specialized physician. Respect for other specializations also entails refraining from practicing any profession that may conflict with the physician's medical profession, such as simultaneously working at a pharmacy.

Seventh: The physician should honor medical confidentiality and abide by the ethical and humanitarian values ratified by Islam. In other words, the temptations of wealth, authority, and desires in this world should never affect his integrity. He should live his life committed to these superior values and not allow his conscience to be compromised with anything this world can offer. This includes even the simplest of transgressions such as granting undue medical leaves or submitting false reports. This is a

(1) Reported by Muslim, no. 8; al-al-Tirmidhī, no. 2613; Abū Dāwūd no. 4695; al-Nasā'ī (8/97).

great responsibility that falls on the shoulders of physicians and all those working within similar professions.

Eighth: The physician should be keen on curing the patient and should not prevent treatment except in cases where there is a legal or scientific justification. In turn, a physician is in no way permitted to participate in ending a patient's life.

Ninth: The physician may not conduct any experimentation on his patients without the patient's consent or without the approval of the specialized authority.

Tenth: The physician must adhere to the laws, systems, regulations, and medical decisions issued by the specialized authorities serving to regulate matters of private and public health. This falls under the Islamic legal obligation of obeying those in authority as long as it does not conflict with any of the *Sharīʿa* texts. This is commanded by God, "You who believe, obey God and the Messenger, and those in authority among you."(1)

These are the ten commandments that physicians must adhere to. They are considered a code of conduct for the medical profession and the solemn covenant. They represent a binding contract and a mandatory commitment that God has commanded us to fulfill in His orders, "O you who have believed, fulfil your contracts" (2) and, "...Honor your pledges: you will be questioned about your pledges."(3)

Physician-Jurists views on Medical Ethics

From the very beginning, Muslim scholars paid due attention to medication and the profession of medicine in line with the Islamic approach in favor of seeking medical treatment. In so

---

(1) (4: 59).

(2) (5: 1).

(3) (17: 34).

doing, they focused on the issue of ethics. Here is an illustrative example to highlight this fact. The physician-jurist al-ʿAbdarī al-Fāsī (d. 737 AH.) wrote his seminal book "*al-Madkhal ilá tanbīh al-ʿummāl bi-Taḥsīn al-nīyyāt wa-altanbīh ʿalá baʿḍ al-bidaʿ wa-al-ʿawāʾid allatī untuḥilat*."(1) He dedicated a chapter to discussing the tools of the physician where a special emphasis is laid on sincerity and devotion. al-ʿAbdarī clarified that a physician must be sincere in practicing his noble profession so that it turns to be one of the best acts of worship through which a physician is not seeking to earn money but to acquire numerous divine rewards. He cited evidence in support of such divine rewards for physicians as they help relieve people's pain and suffering. Moreover, he highlighted the practical ethics and character traits a physician should embody. For example, he argued that a good physician should be compassionate, and sympathetic; he has to retain secrets and avoid disclosing the patient's name in public meetings. If a physician needs to know certain information, he should ask the patient in private (provided that this seclusion is not prohibited). A physician is also required to attentively listen to his patient. al-ʿAbdarī severely blamed those who do not listen attentively and give their patients a chance to express themselves fully. Additionally, he gave some advice to patients and their families.(2) Furthermore, Muslim jurists spoke at great length about monitoring medical practice through the mechanism of *ḥisbah* as will be discussed later.

Physician Liability

The Qurʾān acknowledges the principle of indemnity and compensation which can be applicable to physicians in

---

(1) This book is also known as al-al-Madkhal and was published in four volumes by Dār al-Turāth in Cairo.

(2) Ibid.

certain cases. Similarly, the Sunnah discusses this principle in more detail. A prime example of Prophetic traditions in this respect is a report stating that "There should be neither harming nor reciprocating harm." Here is a brief discussion of the physician's liability.

al-Khaṭṭābī argues that jurists have agreed indisputably that a physician is responsible for any medical error if s/he encroaches or does not act properly. This medical error is compensated for by *al-dīya* (lit. the financial compensation), which is to be borne by the physician's relatives *(ʿĀqilah)*.(1) al-Baghawī states that a physician who errs and causes damage is liable; *al-dīya* is payable but it is shouldered by his relatives.(2) The view of Ḥanafīs merits attention as it allows for the medical institution or the government to assume the role of *ʿĀqilah* and pay the financial compensation on behalf of the physician. Based on this, there is no disagreement among Muslim jurists that an unqualified and unauthorized practitioner who causes injury to a patient will be liable and this liability varies on the basis of actual damage as per the provisions of civil and criminal liability. The same principle is applicable in the positive laws.(3)

There are certain cases in which a physician is immune from liability. To this end, the following requirements must be met:

1. The physician is an authorized and competent practitioner who has the necessary qualification and medical knowledge. In our present day, it is necessary for this practitioner to obtain a medical degree and an official license.

---

(1) Maʿālim al-Sunan, edition of Aleppo (4/39).

(2) Sharḥ al-Sunnah, edition of Damascus (1/341).

(3) ʿAbd al-Qādir ʿAwdah, *al-Tashrīʿ al-jināʾī al-Islāmī*; Shaltūt, *al-Masʾūlīyah al-madanīyah wal-al-jināʾīyah*, p. 8; ʿAlī Badawī, al-qānūn al-jināʾī, p. 400; Kāmil Mūsà and Saʿīd Muṣṭafá, *Sharḥ Qānūn al-ʿUqūbāt*, p. 132.

2. The medical intervention is performed in accordance with the accepted methods of medical practice and profession.
3. The medical intervention is intended for medication purposes, not to escape certain duty such as military service.
4. An informed consent is given by the patient or his family except for certain cases of emergency. Lack of consent is a cause of liability when a medical intervention results in injury.(1) A contract of medical service may regulate such practice and thus it has a binding legal force.

It is mentioned in *Radd al-muḥtār ʿalā al-Durr al-mukhtār* that the barber-surgeon is not held liable as long as he has operated within the required boundaries and was authorized by the patient.(2) In the same respect, Dardīr in *al-Sharḥ al-ṣaghīr* comments that the principle of indemnity applies in the field of medicine in cases of negligence.(3) According to al-Shāfiʿī if someone asks another to let his blood, circumcise his son, or treat his horse, as a result of which loss occurred then the situation is as follows: if the person did what is known for the people of this field in such circumstances which is considered beneficial, he will not be held liable. But if his procedure was at variance with the customary practice, then he is liable.(4) The same rule is acknowledged by the Ḥanbalīs.(5)

---

(1) See: jāmiʿ al-Fuṣūlayn (1/83); badāʾiʿ al-ṣanāʾiʿ (7/305); sharḥ al-Zurqānī (3/283); Ḥāshiyat al-Ṭaḥāwī (4/275); al-Mughnī (6/120); al-al-Suyūṭī, *al-al-Ashbāh wa-al-naẓāʾir*, p. 111; Ibn Ḥazm, al-Muḥalla (10/444). See also: Alī Dāwūd al-Jaffāl, *Islamic Fiqh Academy Journal*, issue 2 (3/95-96); al-Shinqīṭ, Aḥkām al-jirāḥah al-ṭibbīyah (Jiddah: Maktabat al-Ṣaḥābah, 1424 AH), pp. 299-68.

(2) Radd al-muḥtār (5/44).

(3) Dardīr, al-Sharḥ al-ṣaghīr, also known as, Aqrab al-masālik ilā madhhab al-Imām Mālik (4/47).

(4) al-al-Umm (6/166-68).

(5) al-al-Mughnī (6/120-21).

Ibn al-Qayyim listed some cases in which obtaining consent is not necessary. For instance, if a person finds a goat dying, he can slaughter it. However, some literalist jurists argue that a person is not allowed to slaughter it because this act constitutes infringement on the other's right of possession. This argument was refuted on the basis that the right to dispose of other's property is prohibited to prevent any damage or loss. In this particular case of a dying goat, loss is unavoidable unless this immediate action is taken.[1] In the same vein, Ibn Ḥazm discussed a case of a person amputating a cankered hand or extracting a damaged tooth without obtaining the patient's consent. He cited the following Qur'ānic verses: "Help one another to do what is right and good; do not help one another towards sin and hostility"[2] and "So if anyone commits aggression against you, attack him as he attacked you."[3] According to Ibn Ḥazm, the legal ruling should be construed in light of these verses. If this cankered hand proved incurable, the person is not held liable; however, if there is a cure, retaliatory measures are to be taken.[4]

A question may arise here as to the possibility of settling this liability by the medical institution, medical syndicate or hospital on behalf of their physicians. The Ḥanafī jurists were definitely ahead of their time with their discussion of the possibility of paying compensation by the employer. They understood the institution of *'āqilah* to be built on loyalty and patronage. By way of analogy, a medical syndicate to which a physician is affiliated can act as *'āqilah* and settle this liability. The same is true for a medical institution for

(1) Ibn al-Qayyim, *I'lām al-muwaqqi'*īn (2/22).
(2) (5: 2).
(3) (2: 194).
(4) Ibn Ḥazm, al-Muḥalla (10/444).

which a physician works. Moreover, cooperative insurance companies can make an indemnity payment on behalf of an insured physician. Alternatively, the government is the last resort to act as *ʻāqilah* and settle such medical malpractice.

Liability in Islam

According to the Islamic perspective, liability can be seen in various lights. It is not limited to individual liability, conscience-driven responsibility as in solely ethical approaches, or social responsibility. It is not only a kind of moral responsibility that entirely depends on religious morality.[1] Liability in Islam includes four categories: religious responsibility based on the commandments of the religion; moral responsibility (i.e. conscience-driven); social responsibility in which a person has an obligation to act for the benefit of society; and legal liability (based on the law of punishment and compensation). The four kinds can be understood from this Qurʾānic verse, "Believers, do not betray God and the Messenger, or knowingly betray [other people's] trust in you."[2] This verse highlights the bond of belief as a basis of rights and duties. In addition, "do not betray God" indicates accountability before God (i.e. the religious feeling). The word "Messenger" in the verse requires people to obey him in his capacity as a messenger and leader (i.e. the religious and legislative aspect). The legislative aspect can also be assumed by the righteous people of authority. God says, "You who believe, obey God and the Messenger, and those in authority among you."[3] The Prophet (PBUH) says, "Whosoever obeys my commander obeys me, and whosoever disobeys my commander disobeys

(1) Muḥammad ʿAbd Allāh Darāz, Zād al-Muslim, compiled by Aḥmad Faḍīlah, p. 181.

(2) (8:27).

(3) (4: 59).

me."[1] Likewise, the phrase "or knowingly betray [other people's] trust in you" refers to moral responsibility that includes all covenants, contracts and pacts; consequently, it encompasses in this sense many religious and moral values in addition to social responsibility.[2]

Mechanisms of Monitoring & Evaluation

There are various tools of monitoring and evaluation from an Islamic perspective. They include:

1. God's watchfulness. The Qur᾽ān highlights the advice given by Luqmān to his son, "'My son, if even the weight of a mustard seed were hidden in a rock or anywhere in the heavens or earth, God would bring it [to light], for He is all subtle and all aware."[3] Every person will be held accountable on the Day of Judgment and will be questioned about life, knowledge, acts, etc. This may be dubbed as "the Divine court of justice". God says, "And all of them will be coming up to Him upon the Day of the Resurrection, every one singly."[4] If not telling the truth, people's limbs and organs will testify against them. God says, "on the Day when their own tongues, hands, and feet will testify against them about what they have done."[5] Taking this watchfulness seriously results in *taqwā* that guards people against vice. A prime example is found in the story of Joseph who resisted seduction saying, "God forbid!" [6]
2. Live Conscience or the constantly self-blaming

(1) Reported by al-Bukhārī, chapters on Government, *ḥadīth* no. 6725.

(2) Muḥammad ʿAbd Allāh Darāz, *Ḥaṣād Qalam*, compiled by Aḥmad Faḍīlah (Cairo: Dār al-Qalam), pp. 204, 279.

(3) (31:16).

(4) (19:95).

(5) (24: 24).

(6) Yusuf (12: 23).

soul. The Qur'ān praises this soul as God swears, "by the self-reproaching soul".[1] It is a live soul that constantly blames the one who commits vice such as wrongdoing, transgression, maleficence, etc. It serves as a conscience-led court. God says, "On the Day of Resurrection, We shall bring out a record for each of them, which they will find spread wide open."[2]

3. Executive authority reflected in the various punishments and penalties. This authority is assumed by the state-affiliated administrative, judicial and regulatory bodies. We may call this an Authority-led Court.
4. Monitoring by Family and society. This kind of monitoring decides one's good or bad reputation. Society can play a key role in this respect through the mechanism of *ḥisbah*.

The above mechanisms of monitoring and evaluation are employed in Islamic upbringing. These four methods can be gleaned from the glorious Qur'ān; God says, "Say [Prophet], 'Take action! God will see your actions – as will His Messenger and the believers – and then you will be returned to Him who knows what is seen and unseen, and He will tell you what you have been doing."[3]

Public Order (*ḥisbah*) and Medicine

The early Muslim society has witnessed the development of traditional regulative and monitoring institutions such as *ḥisbah*. Its main function was to maintain public order and decorum. This institution was termed as *ḥisbah* because the person assumes this role for the sake of God. In principle, it

(1) (75:2).
(2) (17:13).
(3) (9:104).

is a practical application and development of the injunction of enjoining good and forbidding evil. Through *ḥisbah* this injunction has taken an institutional shape giving the official person certain disciplinary and moral authority while the right to enforce penalties is exclusively reserved to the judiciary.

As far as medicine is concerned, *ḥisbah* treatises discuss in detail some regulative functions in terms of treatment procedure, medical instruments and ethical and professional requirements. The following points can be highlighted in this regard:

1. *Ḥisbah* treatises set well-defined entry requirements and qualifications for physicians.
2. Physicians of every hospital have to choose a chief physician known for his knowledge and practical expertise. This chief physician must take an oath that he will maintain public order and morals and ensure the strict application of professional medical standards.
3. It is necessary to appoint an entity to test and examine physicians in their respective fields of specialization.
4. Clear identification of physician duties and responsibilities.
5. Resorting to the chief physician to decide in case of doubt or controversy.
6. *Ḥisbah* treatises speak at length about the physician's liability and the cases when he is held accountable for the medical intervention. Many other issues were tackled in such treatises.(1)

---

(1) See *ḥisbah* treatises including: Ibn Taymīyah, *al-Ḥisbah*; Muḥammad al-Tamīm, *Nihāyat al-rutbah fī ṭalab al-ḥisbah;* Ibn al-Rifʿah, *al-rutbah fī ṭalab al-ḥisbah*; Ibn Iyās al-Ḥanafī, *badāʾiʿ al-zuhūr fī waqāʾiʿ al-duhūr,* ed. Muḥammad Muṣṭafá, edition of Būlāq; al-al-Qifṭī, tārīkh al-ḥukamāʾ.

Nature of Penalties

Every person is responsible for his own acts; consequently, penalties are to be imposed on an individual basis. No one is held accountable for acts committed by any other party. This principle is emphasized in many passages of the Qur'ān. For instance, God says, "You are accountable only for yourself,"[1] "Say, 'Should I seek a Lord other than God, when He is the Lord of all things?' Each soul is responsible for its own actions; no soul will bear the burden of another. You will all return to your Lord in the end, and He will tell you the truth about your differences,"[2] "Whoever accepts guidance does so for his own good; whoever strays does so at his own peril. No soul will bear another's burden, nor do We punish until We have sent a messenger,"[3] "No burdened soul will bear the burden of another: even if a heavily laden soul should cry for help, none of its load will be carried, not even by a close relative. But you [Prophet] can only warn those who fear their Lord, though they cannot see Him, and keep up the prayer – whoever purifies himself does so for his own benefit – everything returns to God,"[4] "If you are ungrateful, remember God has no need of you, yet He is not pleased by ingratitude in His servants; if you are grateful, He is pleased [to see] it in you. No soul will bear another's burden. You will return to your Lord in the end and He will inform you of what you have done: He knows well what is in the depths of [your] hearts,"[5] "Has he not been told what was written in the Scriptures of Moses and of Abraham, who fulfilled his duty: that no soul shall bear the burden

---

(1) (4:84).
(2) (6:164).
(3) (17:15).
(4) (35:18).
(5) (39:7).

of another; that man will only have what he has worked towards; that his labor will be seen, and that in the end he will be repaid in full for it,"[1] "God does not burden any soul with more than it can bear: each gains whatever good it has done, and suffers its bad,"[2] "You are not responsible for my actions nor am I responsible for yours,"[3] "Say, 'You will not be questioned about our sins, nor will we be questioned about what you do,"[4] and "He is responsible for the duty placed upon him, and you are responsible for the duty placed upon you."[5]

These Qur'ānic verses categorically state that every person is accountable for their own deeds. None is questioned for others' crimes unless a person is convicted as an accomplice, or a guardian. The latter maybe questioned for negligence in his guardianship duties. The following Qur'ānic verses can be seen in this light. God says, "Those who disbelieve say to the believers, 'Follow our path and we shall bear [the consequences for] your sins,' yet they will not do so – they are liars. They will bear their own burdens and others besides: they will be questioned about their false assertions on the Day of Resurrection."[6] This Qur'ānic passage makes it plain that they incited others to disbelieve and deviate from the true path; thus, they are accomplice in this crime and will be liable. Two important things were declared in this respect. First: the subordinate people who followed others will shoulder their full responsibility; they were supposed to make up their minds instead of blindly imitating others. The Qur'ān rebukes such people for not using their minds,

(1) (53: 36-41).
(2) (2:286).
(3) (10:41).
(4) (34:25).
(5) (24:54).
(6) (29: 12-13).

"They will say, 'If only we had listened, or reasoned, we would not be with the inhabitants of the blazing fire,' and they will confess their sins. Away with the inhabitants of the blazing fire!"(1) Accordingly, they will not be pardoned and their punishment will not be mitigated. Secondly, the instigators are evidently accountable for their active role in encouraging others to disbelieve and willingness to take on responsibility instead of them. God warns those people, "[It will be said to them], 'You have done wrong. Having partners in punishment will not console you today."(2) Even Satan will disavow the actions of his followers on Judgment Day. The Qur'ān reads, "When everything has been decided, Satan will say, 'God gave you a true promise. I too made promises but they were false ones: I had no power over you except to call you, and you responded to my call, so do not blame me; blame yourselves."(3) Their responsibility is also established in another verse stating that, "On the Day of Resurrection they will bear the full weight of their own burden, as well as some of the burden of those they misled with no true knowledge. How terrible their burden will be!"(4) Both parties will have their share of responsibility. The only exception is the case of duress. God says, "With the exception of those who are forced to say they do not believe, although their hearts remain firm in faith,"(5) "He has expounded whatever He has prohibited to you – except whatever you are constrained to."(6)

The responsibility of the principal party varies on the basis of its influence over others. If a person exercises

(1) (67: 10-11).
(2) (43:39).
(3) (14:22).
(4) (16:25).
(5) (16:106).
(6) (6:119).

greater influence or power over a subordinate, his sin and punishment will be proportional to that influence.[1] A person is to be held accountable for his own acts and other acts he has incited or caused. God says, "We keep an account of everything in a clear Record."[2] The Prophet (PBUH) says, "Whoever introduces a good practice that is followed, he will receive its reward and a reward equivalent to that of those who follow it, without that detracting from their reward in the slightest. And whoever introduces a bad practice that is followed, he will receive its sin and a burden of sin equivalent to that of those who follow it, without that detracting from their burden in the slightest."[3] This meaning is further accentuated by the Prophet's saying, "The first son of Adam takes a share of the guilt of every one who murders another wrongfully because he was the initiator of committing murder."[4] In commenting on this first murder the Qur'ān states, "On account of [his deed], We decreed to the Children of Israel that if anyone kills a person – unless in retribution for murder or spreading corruption in the land – it is as if he kills all mankind, while if any saves a life it is as if he saves the lives of all mankind. Our messengers came to them with clear signs, but many of them continued to commit excesses in the land."[5]

Positive Upbringing as Means of Inculcating Noble Morals

Legislations and positive laws are not enough on their own to ensure morality; this is a fact that had proven remarkably true throughout years. Rather, it is the positive upbringing,

(1) Muḥammad ʿAbd Allāh Darāz, *Zād al-Muslim*, compiled by Aḥmad Faḍīlah, p. 181
(2) (36:12).
(3) Reported by Muslim, no. 1017. al-al-Nasā'ī reported this *ḥadīth* in his collection and al-Albānī declared it as authentic, no. 2553.
(4) Reported by al-Bukhārī, no. 7321; Aḥmad in Musnad, no. 8316.
(5) (5:32).

sound disposition and virtuous milieu that have far-reaching influence over people. Penal laws only have a limited effect on preventing crimes. Taken this into consideration, it may be appropriate here to briefly shed some light on the upbringing approach to be adopted in order to inculcate general and medical morals. Indeed, man is the cornerstone in all human activities, especially in relationships with others. Accordingly, raising a righteous reformer is a sublime aim. All possible efforts have to be exerted to fulfill this aim and nurture a heart of mercy, compassion and sympathy; it is a heart full of faith, piety, beneficence and love for others; it is free from vestiges of envy, hypocrisy, hatred, etc.

To this end, it is necessary to purify and refine one's soul to become a constantly self-reproaching and experience inner peace. Such soul is highly responsible and feels deep sorrow for wrongdoing and negligence. This self-refinement and sincere endeavor to purge the heart from any spiritual diseases including overanxiety, malice, wicked lusts, excessive anger, greed, recklessness, cowardice, etc.(1) Developing a mindset that gives priority to public interests over parochial gains is of primary concern for this approach. Such a mindset considers these social and public interests in close relation with their general objectives and universals. The glorious Qur'ān and the noble Sunnah pay utmost attention to inner upbringing. They provide some auxiliary means to raise this upright man and ensure ethical conduct and noble character. To begin with, the Islamic doctrine is instrumental in this kind of nurturing. It establishes a close link between man and his God; it constantly reminds him of Judgment Day, the reward and punishment in the grave, and the final abode of Paradise or Hell. Consequently,

---

(1) For more details, see: al-Ghazālī, Iḥyā' 'ulūm al-dīn.

this doctrine helps restrain man from evil practices and maleficence and prompts him to do good and beneficence. It ingrains some deep-rooted belief in God's watchfulness and reward. This belief serves as a restraint and deterrent. In addition, acts of worship and the five pillars of Islam are inseparably linked to morality. In terms of ritual prayers, God says, "keep up the prayer: prayer restrains outrageous and unacceptable behavior. Remembering God is greater: God knows everything you are doing."(1) As for *zakāt* (alms giving), God says, "Take of their riches a donation to purify them and to cleanse them thereby; and pray for them; surely your prayer is sereneness (i.e., tranquility) for them; and God is Ever-Hearing, Ever-Knowing."(2) The same holds true for fasting; the Qur᾽ān states, "You who believe, fasting is prescribed for you, as it was prescribed for those before you, so that you may be mindful of God."(3) As regards pilgrimage, God says, "The pilgrimage takes place during the prescribed months. There should be no indecent speech, misbehavior, or quarrelling for anyone undertaking the pilgrimage."(4) All beliefs and acts of worship are intended to nurture the Muslim's inner self in order to be ready to demonstrate this in practice. God says, "The servants of the Lord of Mercy are those who walk humbly on the earth, and who, when the foolish address them, reply, 'Peace'."(5)

The Qur᾽ān directs people towards righteousness, beneficence, reform and public welfare. The reflective reading of the Qur᾽ān proves this fact. It sometimes addresses the natural disposition of people or touches their

(1) (29:45).
(2) (9: 103).
(3) (2: 183).
(4) (2: 197).
(5) (25: 63).

feelings to prod them into doing good. On other occasions, it uses reason, cogent arguments, marvelous signs and other methods appealing to minds and souls.

By diversifying its discourse and style, the Qurʾān touches both the inner and the external aspects of man. It directs man towards the good in all walks of life. In so doing, it addresses both the spiritual and material sides in an amazingly balanced fashion away from total separation and detachment. Consider for example the following verses in which God says, "Believers! When the call to prayer is made on the day of congregation, hurry towards the reminder of God and leave off your trading – that is better for you, if only you knew – then when the prayer has ended, disperse in the land and seek out God's bounty. Remember God often so that you may prosper."[1] These verses touch on one's deep faith to promptly answer the call to prayer and leave behind any other business. After performing this prayer, man is advised to seek his maintenance while sticking to God's remembrance in both cases. Remembrance of God is ideally observed by heart and tongue; however, it could sometimes be practiced by the heart if one is preoccupied with his own business. Remembrance of God using the heart has an enlivening effect that ennobles one's soul and helps it remain attached to God. This attachment naturally brings about uprightness and self-reform. In this way, a person feels the presence of God and His watchful eye; God sees and hears everything; knows our inner thoughts and whispers; He is closer to us than our jugular vein.[2]

The great emphasis laid by the Qurʾān on God's watchful eye is not intended to frighten or threaten people; rather, it

(1) (62:9-10).

(2) Muḥammad ʿAbd Allāh Darāz, Zād al-Muslim, p. 305.

seeks to reform people and ensure their happiness, well-being, and prosperity. This materializes through purification and discipline as a natural corollary of this belief and God-consciousness. The Qurʾān states, "The one who purifies his soul succeeds and the one who corrupts it fails."(1)

Morality and Live Conscience

All methods of upbringing in Islam primarily aim at raising a righteous benevolent compassionate Muslim who loves others and has a soul intrinsically inclined to doing good and preventing evil. Such a Muslim is characterized with internal morality serving as a self-restraint. Whenever lust arises in his heart or temptation comes, this internal morality restrains him. God describes such persons as "Those who are aware of God think of Him when Satan prompts them to do something and immediately they can see [*Mubṣṣirūn*]."(2)

Islam seeks to instill this feeling of God-consciousness (*taqwā*) in the hearts, souls and minds of Muslims so that it controls one's thoughts and actions. This *taqwā* as illustrated elsewhere in this book makes a Muslim always aware of God and feel His watchful eye. It is synonymous with *iḥsān* as worshipping, fearing or working for God as if you see Him, and if you do not achieve this state of devotion, then (take it for granted that) God sees you. The Arabic word "*Mubṣṣirūn*" used in the above verse refers to the perceptive faculty of the mind. It signifies knowledge, intelligence, understanding and skill. A person with this trait (*Baṣīrah*) possesses true intuitive perception and intelligence.(3) This trait is highly acclaimed in many passages of the Qurʾān. For instance, God says, "Say, 'This is my way: based on

(1) (91: 9-10).

(2) (7:201).

(3) see: *Lisān al-ʿArab, al-Qāmūs al-Muḥīṭ, al-Muʿjam al-Wasīṭ.*

clear evidence [*baṣīrah*], I, and all who follow me, call [people] to God – glory be to God! – I do not join others with Him.'"[1] If sight is the faculty of seeing by one's eyes, this trait is the faculty of perception by heart and mind. It enables man to unveil truth and anticipate consequences. Put differently, it is foresight and correct intuition through which one can expect the outcomes of his actions in this world and the one to come. It is the ability to distinguish right from wrong as a result of piety and God-consciousness. God says, "Believers, if you remain mindful of God, He will give you a criterion [to tell right from wrong] and wipe out your bad deeds, and forgive you: God's favor is great indeed."[2]

A question may arise here as to how such *taqwā* can be achieved. The Qur'ān tells us that it comes as a result of deep belief in God and His attributes, the Day of Resurrection, and other articles of faith. Sincerity, devotion, love for the sake of God, and avoiding sins, lusts and evils ingrain this watchfulness and piety. It can also be reached through much prayer, obligatory and supererogatory ones, in addition to fasting and other obligations. In terms of the objectives of fasting, the Qur'ān states, "You who believe, fasting is prescribed for you, as it was prescribed for those before you, so that you may be mindful of God."[3] As for pilgrimage, God says, "It is neither their meat nor their blood that reaches God but your piety. He has subjected them to you in this way so that you may glorify God for having guided you. Give good news to those who do good."[4]

Whenever a person establishes a closer relationship with

(1) (12:108).
(2) (8:29).
(3) Sūrat al-al-Baqarah (2: 183).
(4) (22:37).

God through obligatory and voluntary acts of worship, his soul becomes stronger and piety increases in his heart. Conversely, if he indulges himself in sins and evils, this takes his heart away from piety. God says, "No indeed! Their hearts are encrusted with what they have done."(1) This idea is oft-repeated in many verses where a close link is drawn between obedience and guidance to the good deeds. For instance, the Qur᾿ān clarifies that, "But We shall be sure to guide to Our ways those who strive hard for Our cause: God is with those who do good."(2) Other verses confirm this principle; God says, "There is the one who gives, who is mindful of God, who testifies to goodness – We shall smooth his way towards ease. There is the one who is miserly, who is self-satisfied, who denies goodness – We shall smooth his way towards hardship and his wealth will not help him as he falls,"(3) and "God has endeared faith to you and made it beautiful to your hearts; He has made disbelief, mischief, and disobedience hateful to you. It is people like this who are rightly guided."(4)

Therefore, whenever faithfulness and sincerity are deeply rooted in one's heart, Satan cannot mislead him. This is evident in the story of Joseph as the Qur᾿ān narrates, "We did this in order to keep evil and indecency away from him, for he was truly one of Our chosen servants."(5) Satan has already admitted this fact; "Iblis then said to God, 'Because You have put me in the wrong, I will lure mankind on earth and put them in the wrong, except, among them, Your chosen servants"(6) and "Iblis said, 'I swear by Your might!

---

(1) (83:14).
(2) (29:69).
(3) (92:6-11).
(4) (49:7).
(5) (12:24).
(6) (15:39-40).

I will tempt all but Your true servants."[1] The Qur'ān again confirms this fact in the most definitive terms, "You [Satan] will have no power over My servants, only over the ones who go astray and follow you,"[2] and "He has no power over those who believe and trust in their Lord; his power is only over those who ally themselves with him and those who, because of him, join partners with God."[3] Actually, persistent self-refinement and purification transform the soul into a constantly self-blaming one. It turns a spiritually defective heart into a healthy and peaceful one. God says, "Truly it is in the remembrance of God that hearts find peace."[4] When a person is truly mindful of God, he experiences God's protection and preservation. God told Moses and Aaron that, "Do not be afraid, I am with you both, hearing and seeing everything."[5] That is why the Prophet (PBUH) assured Abū Bakr saying, "What do you think of two, the third of whom is God?"[6] The Qur'ān narrates it as, "When the two of them were in the cave, he [Muhammad] said to his companion, 'Do not worry, God is with us,' and God sent His calm down to him, aided him with forces invisible to you, and brought down the disbelievers' plan. God's plan is higher: God is almighty and wise."[7] God also says, "Wait patiently [Prophet] for your Lord's judgement: you are under Our watchful eye. Celebrate the praise of your Lord when you rise. Glorify Him at night and at the fading of the stars."[8] The Qur'ān

(1) (38:82-83).
(2) (15:42).
(3) (16:99-100).
(4) (13:28).
(5) (20:46).
(6) Reported by al-Bukhārī, no. 4663, 3653 and Muslim, no. 2381.
(7) (9:40).
(8) (52:48-49).

and the Sunnah provide a raft of examples in support of this notion.

Undoubtedly, unwavering faithful belief and worship have profound positive influence over people; they yield tremendous results in this world and the hereafter. By the same token, disbelief and disobedience has serious effects in this worldly life and the one to come. In view of the above, a true believer has a pure righteous heart that loves beneficence; he is characterized with modesty that guards against vice, and live conscience that motivates him to do good and avoid evil. This perfection is nothing without true belief in God and the Day of Judgment. However, God has created in every person a natural disposition inherently inclined to beneficence; a mind guiding them to the best; modesty preventing them from acts in stark contrast with this disposition; and mercy to sympathize with the weak ones. Such natural disposition, modesty, good reputation, collective ethos, righteous companionship and laws of punishment and compensation can keep one's conscience alive. This is commonly shared by all people to help illuminate the world when the influence of religion dwindles; however, they cannot eventually survive without the illumination of religion and Divine revelation. God declares that "… light upon light – God guides whoever He wills to his Light; God draws such comparisons for people; God has full knowledge of everything."[1]

Linking Ethics to *Maqāṣid* Ecosystem

By *maqāṣid* ecosystem I mean the various sets of general objectives in terms of creation and creation of human, in addition to the general objectives of *Sharīʿa* and the particular

(1) (24:35).

objectives of medicine. It also includes objectives pertaining to the legally competent persons, *fiqh* of consequences and blocking means to evil.[1] The following section provides a brief discussion of this ecosystem of *maqāṣid*.

First: Linking Ethical Principles to Objectives of Creation

The universe is mentioned in many Qurʾānic verses which outnumber the passages of legal rulings. The following general objectives of creation can be deduced from such verses:

1. Creation is a proof of God's existence, omnipotence, all-inclusive knowledge, beside the other Divine attributes as indicated by the Qurʾān and the Sunnah.
2. To prove God's Divinity, as creation entails a creator; thus, this creator deserves to be worshipped. Most of Qurʾānic proofs take this as a point of departure.
3. God's worthiness of worship is established through the blessing of creation.
4. It is through creation, man can ensure happiness, well-being, and sustenance; consequently, man ought to be thankful to God. (See: Qurʾān; 2:22, 29, 168, 169, 172, 173).
5. To test man so that people are rewarded by Paradise in return for good deeds, or punished by Hellfire for evils and sins. God says, "… who created death and life to test you [people] and reveal which of you does best."[2]
6. To positively construct this universe; God created the universe in order for man to worship Him and contribute to the development of this world.

---

(1) For further details on this subject, see: al-al-Qaradāghī, *al-ḥaqībah al-Iqtiṣādīyah*, (Beirut: Dār al-Bashāʾir al-Islāmīyah). vol.1

(2) (67:2).

Actually, there are various objectives for the different kinds of creation. For instance, the creation of this worldly life has particular objectives different from those of the hereafter. It is beyond the scope of this book to dwell on the different particular objectives. Undoubtedly, everything is created for a purpose; we may realize some of these purposes to the exclusion of others. God says, "Our Lord! You have not created all this without purpose – You are far above that! – so protect us from the torment of the Fire."[1] Based on this, establishing a link between ethical principles and these objectives becomes obvious; abiding by such principles brings about mercy for the entire universe. Taking into consideration the fact that this universe is subjected to man, a physician has to do the best to make use of it, harness its resources and discover its secrets to find the suitable medication. These principles urge man to constantly aspire for creativity and sustainable innovation. The Qur'ān states, "Above everyone who has knowledge there is the One who is all knowing."[2] In addition, such ethical principles lead man to show mercy and beneficence towards this universe and our environment. They help establish harmony and balance in all human acts through a holistic perspective including mankind, religion and the entire universe.

With regard to the objectives of human creation, they are countless; here are the most significant ones.

1. Realizing that worship is holistic; it encompasses life and death.
2. Trial is intended to test people and distinguish the righteous from the wicked. God says, "Exalted is He who holds all control in His hands; who has power

(1) (3:191).
(2) (12:76).

over all things, ho created death and life to test you [people] and reveal which of you does best – He is the Mighty, the Forgiving."[1]

3. Fulfilling the mission of vicegerency and positive construction of the earth and the entire universe in accordance with the Divine approach of righteousness and reform.
4. To compensate people for their deeds either by Paradise or Hell.

In view of the above, it can be concluded that ethics guard people against greed and indifference and motivate them to serve humanity as much as possible.

Second: *Maqāṣid* of Legally Competent People

The general objectives pertaining to the legally competent people (*Mukallafūn*) refer to the good intents of physicians, patients, and human subjects. When these intents are good, they yield positive results and produce tremendous effects on the heart, soul, health and conduct. The source of good deeds is one's heart; the Qurʾān reads, "...the Day when neither wealth nor children can help; when the only one who will be saved is the one who comes before God with a heart devoted to Him."[2] These positive results include:

1. Acceptance by God. The Prophet (PBUH) says, "(The value of) an action depends on the intention behind it. A man will be rewarded only for what he intended."[3] This tradition indicates that the validity or acceptance of acts depends on their underlying intents and objectives.
2. Changing habits into worship. al-Shāṭibī argues that

(1) (67:1-2).
(2) (26:88-89).
(3) Reported by al-Bukhārī, no. 5589 and Muslim, no. 1907.

a single act may have as its purpose a certain thing and it will amount to worship, but a different thing may be intended by the same act so it will no longer be worship; in fact, one thing may be intended and it will amount to faith, but another thing may be intended and the same act will turn into disbelief, like prostrations before God and before idols.[1] The above *ḥadīth* is the basis of the legal maxim stating that "Acts are judged according to their intentions".

3. Preventing deception and cheating. Whenever, a good intention exists, there will be no room for deception, cheating, betrayal, etc. This has special significance in the field of medicine.

On the other hand, ill intentions have their destructive effects on work, perfectibility and creativity. Cheating and deception come among their most dangerous effects. Taking this into consideration, it is necessary for physicians among others to have good intentions. Evidently, the spirit of any work lies in the intention behind it; it serves as the impetus and motive. Sometimes, one's intention could be better than his action.

Third: Linking Ethical Principles to The Eight Higher Objectives of *Sharīʿa*

Medical ethics are not mere virtues or embellishments; rather, they are primary intents for all heavenly religions. They are perfected by the Qurʾān. The different issues of medical ethics can fall under the five categories of legal rulings. Some of them are obligations while some malpractices amount to grave sins and prohibitions. Still, other practices with no concomitant negative effects on

---

(1) *al-Muwāfaqāt* (2/255); see also: ʿUmar al-Ashqar, Maqāṣid al-Mukallafīn, edition of Kuwait.

people can be either recommended or reprehensible. For instance, the recommended practices include altruism and showing too much generosity or courage without being reckless, while reluctance to help without causing harm could be reprehensible.

In line with this holistic approach to ethics in Islam, it is more appropriate to frame medical ethics in light of the higher objectives, intents, wisdom and philosophy of *Sharīʿa*. A thorough induction reveals that the *Sharīʿa* seeks to fulfil the three levels of necessities, needs and embellishments for five or six things. This is confirmed by many classical scholars including al-Juwainī, al-Ghazālī, al-'Izz b. ʿAbd al-Salām, Ibn Taymīyah, Ibn al-Qayyim, al-Shāṭibī in addition to the majority of contemporary scholars beginning with Ibn ʿʿĀshūr.(1) The six objectives are: preservation of religions, life or soul, intellect, progeny, honor, and wealth. Elsewhere I added the security of the legitimate state and the security of society among the general objectives. Collectively, these eight objectives take into consideration the objectives of individuals in addition to those of society and the state. Each objective has three levels: necessities, needs and embellishments, and requires two aspects: actualization and avoidance (to advance interests and ward off evils). By applying this approach to the field of medicine, these objectives are chiefly concerned with the physician, the patient (or his guardian) and the medical institution as follows.

1. The Preservation of the Higher Objective of "Religion"

The preservation of religion in this context refers to two

(1) For further details, see: *al-Muwāfaqāt*, ed. ʿAbd Allāh Darāz (Beirut: Dār al-Maʿrifah, 1415 AH); Ibn ʿĀshūr, *Maqāṣid al-sharīʿah al-Islāmīyah*, ed. Muḥammad al-Ḥabīb ibn al-Khūjah, edition of IIFA; Aḥmad al-Raysūnī, *Naẓarīyat al-maqāṣid ʿinda al-Imām al-Shāṭibī*, the International Institute of Islamic Thought; al-Qaradāwī, *Dirāsah fī fiqh maqāṣid al-sharīʿah*, Dār al-Shurūq.

issues. The first issue is concerned with the preservation of Islam's principles and rulings, as Islam is the last of all divine religions. Since our discussion is focused on medical ethics, all divinely established ethics, values, ideals, and virtues are verily categorized under medical preservation and care according to their respective levels of strength, obligation, and so forth. Medical preservation likewise includes all common ethical principles and virtues such as abstaining from murder and theft; preventing evil and harm; honoring promises and contracts; saving those at risk; exonerating the innocent; and practicing honesty, integrity, sincerity, altruism, truthfulness, kindness, generosity, and empathy, in addition to all other morals as identified in the Qur᾿ān and Prophetic traditions. The general principles of Islam are similarly included, such as justice, equality, seeking counsel, and respecting human rights. It is imperative that the concept of preservation and care in medicine incorporates both elements of positive and negative obligations, whereby people's interests and benefits are promoted, and any harm or corruption is prevented from reaching them. The Prophet (PBUH) expounded the meaning of *al-birr* as noble character; he says, "Virtue is noble behavior, while sin is that which creates doubt and you do not like people to know about it."[1]

The second issue is the preservation of the patient's religion and avoiding any practices that may undermine it. Therefore, the physician should not attempt any experiment or prescribe a cure that conflicts with the patient's religious beliefs except in cases of extreme necessity or unequivocal need. In such cases, a physician may only use a proscribed treatment in the absence of alternative permissible treatments. This is in accordance with the following Islamic

(1) Recorded by Muslim, no. 2553 and al-al-Tirmidhī, no. 2390.

principles: "Necessity overrides religious prohibitions," and, "Dire need for medical treatment can acquire the status of necessity."(1) A physician's ethical conduct entails that he respects the patient's beliefs and does not exploit a patient's vulnerability to impose other beliefs. For example, this is often practiced by Christian missionaries who exploit the dangerous triad of disease, ignorance, and poverty to proselytize religion. On the other hand, the patient is also responsible for maintaining his or her religion. The patient must adhere to the legal rulings of *Sharīʿa* when seeking treatment, especially given that undergoing treatment may often be obligatory if rejecting it would lead to definite harm. Similarly, treatment may be prohibited if it utilizes forbidden means, except in cases of necessity.

It is important to note that preserving this higher objective also entails abstinence from everything that is deemed religiously forbidden and prohibited by *Sharīʿa* in regards to a person's life or physical body (both externally and internally). This includes allowing a fetus to be killed, donating vital organs, altering natural appearance, human cloning, abortion, and all similar practices that God has forbidden. Likewise, these are all considered unethical actions if practiced by a physician and are simultaneously categorized under the preservation of life as is explained below.

2. *The Preservation of the Higher Objective of "Life"*(2)

This higher objective refers to a person's physical

---

(1) al-al-Qaradāghī, ʿAlīʿAlī al-Muḥammadī, *Fiqh al-Qaḍāyā al-Ṭibbīyah al-Muʿāṣirah,* op. cit., p. 225.

(2) For more details, see entry on nafs in: al-al-Rāghib al-Aṣfahānī, *al-mufradāt fī gharīb al-Qurʾān*. The intended meaning here is life; it denotes man with all his bodily organs in addition to his internal parts. It also includes the psyche or soul, which could either be at peace (content, self-assured, and unwavering) or unsettled due to psychological diseases.

body, including all internal and external organs. Ethical principles in this regard entail that the physician and the patient prevent any malevolence and harm from coming to a person's life and that they promote a person's welfare and interests. Consequently, the use of any medication, treatment, or experiment that harms one's body, organs, or internal systems or does not result in benefits is considered unethical, and both the physician and the patient are forbidden from utilizing it. This is because, in Islam, a person does not own his or her life, organs, internal systems, or any other part of the body; instead they all belong to God the Almighty. The issue of organ donation during one's life is tied with this Islamic principle. The primary ruling for this issue is prohibition, unless it has been categorically proven that donating the organ will not result in any harm to the donor and that it is in the best interest of the patient. It is similarly for this reason that the donation of unpaired vital organs like the heart or liver is absolutely forbidden. Likewise, killing a patient for the sake of relieving him from an incurable disease (euthanasia) is considered unethical in Islam and in all divine religions, even if permitted by the patient, as it is not a right he has. In fact, it is considered a transgression against one of the rights of God the Almighty. Plastic surgeries that alter a person's original attributes also fall into this category, as do issues of cloning, abortion, and genetic manipulation. In the case where a patient has passed away, organ donation is considered lawful given that consent has been provided through the patient's will or by his or her heirs and that it is in the best interest of the recipient. Resolutions in regards to these rulings have been issued by different *fiqh* academies as following.

IFC Resolution:

The Islamic *Fiqh* Council during its eighth session held at the headquarters of the Muslim World League in Makkah Mukarramah between 28 Rabī al-āk̲h̲ir, 1405 AH. – 7 Jamādá al-Ūlá 1405 AH. (19-28 January 1985) and on the request made by the Muslim World League Office in the United States to the Council, looked into the issue of transplanting the organ of one human being into another, who is in need of that organ to make up his idle organ in the wake of great strides made by modern medical science with the use of latest technology.

The Council reviewed the study prepared by Sheikh ʿAbdullah Ibn ʿAbd al-Raḥmān al-Bassām in this regard, and its contents that included the disagreement of opinion among contemporary *fiqh* scholars on permissibility of transplanting the human organs and arguments of every group of scholars in favor of its views in the light of the relevant *Sharīʿa* evidences. After thorough discussions among its members, the Council was of the view that the arguments of those who permit transplant are stronger, therefore it adopted the following resolution:

First: The transplant of an organ from the body of a living human being into the body of another human being who is in need of this organ in order to save his life or to restore the function of that organ is a lawful act and it is not against human honor with regard to the person whose organ has been taken. In the transplant, there is also a great benefit and good support to the person who needs the organ transplant and this is a legitimate and praiseworthy work, if the following conditions are met:

1. That donation of an organ by the donor does not harm him in a way disturbing normal life, because the *Sharīʿa* rule states that any harm must not be removed by another similar or more serious harm; in such a case, the donation of organ would be a suicidal act, which is not permissible in the Islamic *Sharīʿa*.
2. That donation of organ by the donor is voluntary without any compulsion.
3. That the organ transplant is the only possible medical option for the treatment of the needy patient.
4. That success of the transplant operation is almost certain.

Second: The following cases would be permissible in the light of Islamic *Sharīʿa* on priority basis:

1. That the organ is taken from a dead human being in order to save another human being who is in need of it, provided that the person whose organ is taken, had given his permission for it in his lifetime.
2. That the organ is taken from an animal whose meat is lawful for eating and it is legally slaughtered or any other animal in case of necessity for its transplant into a human being who is in need of it.
3. That a part of the human body is taken for its transplant or patching on his own body such as taking a part of skin or bone from a human being for its transplant or patching on some other part of his body, which needs such operation.
4. That an artificial piece of metal or another material is placed in the body of a human being in order to treat a case of sickness such as joints, the heart tube, etc.

The Council is of the view that all these four cases are permissible in the Islamic *Sharīʿa* under the above-mentioned conditions.(1)

IIFA Resolution No. 54/5/6 on Transplantation of Brain Tissues and Nervous System

The Council of the Islamic *Fiqh* Academy, in its sixth session held in Jeddah, Kingdom of Saudi Arabia, from 17 - 23 Sha'baan, 1410 AH. (corresponding to 14 - 20 March, 1990),

Having studied the papers and recommendations on this subject which was one of the subjects discussed in the sixth medical and *Fiqh* Seminar held in Kuwait, from Rabīʿ al-Awwal 23 to 26, 1410 AH. (October 23 - 26, 1989), held in cooperation between the Academy and the Islamic Organization for Medical Sciences of Kuwait,

Taking into consideration the conclusions of the aforesaid seminar that transplant here is not intended to mean transfer of a human brain from one person to another; rather it is to treat the failure of certain tissues in the brain in properly discharging chemical and hormonal material and to replace these tissues with similar tissues obtained from another source, or to treat a gap of nervous system which has resulted from some injury.

RESOLVES

First: If the source of the tissues is the suprarenal gland of the same patient and are accepted by the

(1) This translation is quoted with slight modification from: Muslim World League Islamic Fiqh Council, Resolutions of Islamic Fiqh Council: From 1st to 18th Sessions During 1398-1427H (1977-2006).

patient's body, because they are from the same body, the transplant is permissible in accordance with *Sharīʿa*.

Second: If the source of the tissues to be transplanted is an animal fetus, there is no objection to this method if its success is possible, and there is no contravention of any rule laid down by *Sharīʿa*. Physicians have mentioned that this method has been successful in different species of animals and it is hoped that it will prove successful if adopted with necessary medical precautions to avoid the body's rejection of the transplanted organ.

Third: If the source of the tissues to be transplanted is live tissues from the brain of a premature human fetus (in the tenth or eleventh week of pregnancy), the *Sharīʿa* ruling may differ in the following way:

A. The First Method:

Taking it directly from the human fetus in his mother's womb by surgically opening the womb. The removal of the brain tissues of the fetus leads to its death. This is prohibited under *Sharīʿa*, except if it follows an unintentional natural abortion or a lawful abortion to save the mother's life, and the death of the fetus becomes obvious. In such a case, the conditions pertaining to the use of fetus as stated in Resolution No. 59/8/6 of this session must be observed.

B. The Second Method

This method may be adopted in the near future and it means the culture of brain tissues in special laboratory to benefit from them. There is no objection from *Sharīʿa* point of view to this method if the source of cultured tissues is lawful and they are obtained by lawful means.

Fourth: Child born without a brain

As long as the child is born alive, no part of his body may be taken away, unless it is proven that he is dead by the death of his brain stem. He is not different from other sound infants in this respect. If he dies, taking parts of his body must be in accordance with the terms and conditions applicable to the transplant of organs of the dead, such as obtaining the required permission, unavailability of a substitute, evident need and such other conditions indicated in Resolution No. 26/1-4 of the Fourth session of this Academy. There is no objection under *Sharīʿa* to keep this brainless child on the artificial instruments up to the death of his brain stem in order to preserve the life of transferable organs and to facilitate benefiting from them by their transplant according to the aforementioned conditions. Verily, Allah is All-Knowing![(1)]

IIFA Resolution No. (57/8/6): "TRANSPLANT OF GENITAL ORGANS"

The Council of the Islamic *Fiqh* Academy, in its sixth session held in Jeddah, Kingdom of Saudi Arabia, from 17 - 23 Sha'baan, 1410 AH. (corresponding to 14 - 20 March, 1990),

Having studied the papers and recommendations on this subject which was one of the subjects discussed in the sixth medical and *Fiqh* seminar held in Kuwait, from Rabīʿ al-Awwal 23 to 26, 1410 AH. (October

(1) This translation is quoted, with slight modification, from Resolutions and Recommendations of the Council of the Islamic Fiqh Academy 1985-2000.

23 - 26, 1989), in cooperation between the Academy and the Islamic Organization for Medical Sciences of Kuwait.

RESOLVES

First: Transplant of sexual glands

Since the testicles and ovaries continue to bear and discharge hereditary attributes to the transferee, even after they are transplanted in a new grantee, their transplant is prohibited by *Sharīʿa.*

Second: Transplant of genital organs

Transplant of some genital organs which do not transfer hereditary attributes, except the genitals organs, is permissible for a legitimate necessity, in accordance with *Sharīʿa* standards and regulations indicated in Resolution No. 26/1/4 of the Fourth session of this Academy. Verily, Allah is All-Knowing![1]

IIFA Resolution No. (58/9/6): Restoration of an Organ Amputated in *Qiṣāṣ* (retaliation) or *Ḥadd* (prescribed punishment)

The Council of the Islamic *Fiqh* Academy, in its sixth session held in Jeddah, Kingdom of Saudi Arabia, from 17 - 23 Sha'baan, 1410 AH (corresponding to 14 - 20 March, 1990,

Having studied the papers forwarded to the Academy on the subject of "Restoration of an organ amputated in *Qiṣāṣ* or *Ḥadd*" and having listened to the discussions on the subject;

Keeping in view that the objective of *Sharīʿa* in

(1) Ibid.

enforcing "*Ḥadd*" punishment is deterrence, and this can only be achieved by maintaining the effect of the punishment, so that it may be a permanent lesson for the offenders and may eradicate the opportunities of further crimes;

And keeping in view that the restoration of an amputated organ requires an instant operation according to modern medical science; therefore, it cannot be carried out unless there is a previous arrangement and medical preparation, which may result in diminishing the seriousness of the enforcement of "*Ḥadd*" and its required effect,

RESOLVES

First: It is not permissible, in *Sharīʿa*, to restore an organ amputated in "*Ḥadd*" because the object of the punishment can be achieved only if its effects persist after punishment, and this is the only way to prevent any neglect in the enforcement of the punishment, and any possible conflict with the rules of *Sharīʿa*.

Second: Since the "*Qiṣāṣ*" (retaliation) has been ordained in order to establish equity and to give justice to the aggrieved person, and to secure the right of living in society and to provide peace and stability, therefore, it is not permissible in *Sharīʿa* to restore an organ amputated "in *Qiṣāṣ*" except in the following situations:

1. The aggrieved person gives permission to the offender after the enforcement of "*Qiṣāṣ*" to restore the amputated organ.
2. The aggrieved person has been able to restore his own organ.

Third: If an organ has been amputated by mistake in the judgment or in the execution, it is permissible to restore the same. Verily, Allah is All-Knowing!

IIFA Resolution No. (56/7/6) On Use of Fetus as a Source of Transplant

The Council of the Islamic *Fiqh* Academy, in its sixth session held in Jeddah, Kingdom of Saudi Arabia, from 17 - 23 Sha'baan, 1410 AH. (corresponding to 14 - 20 March, 1990),

Having studied the papers and recommendations on this subject which was one of the subjects discussed in the Sixth Medical and *Fiqh* Seminar held in Kuwait, from Rabīʿ al-Awwal 23 to 26, 1410 AH. (October 23 - 26, 1989), in cooperation between the Academy and the Islamic Organization for Medical Sciences of Kuwait,

RESOLVES

First: Fetus cannot be used as a source of obtaining organs to be transplanted in another person, except in certain cases and under certain conditions which must be fulfilled:

A) No abortion can be provoked in order to use the fetus for transplant of its organs in the body of another person. The operation should be restricted to a case of natural abortion or an abortion for a lawful purpose, and no surgical operation should be resorted to in order to remove the fetus unless it is essential to save the mother's life.

B) If the fetus has a chance of remaining alive, medical treatment must be directed to keep it alive, and not for using it in organ transplant. If it cannot survive, it must not be used except after its death and under the conditions stipulated in Res. No. 26/1/4 adopted by this Academy at its Fourth session.

Second: Organ transplant operation must not, at all, be used for commercial purpose.
Third: Supervision of organ transplant operation must be entrusted to a specialized and reliable body. Verily, Allah is All-Knowing!

IIFA Resolution No 100/2/10: HUMAN CLONING

The Council of the Islamic *Fiqh* Academy, holding its Tenth session in Jeddah (Kingdom of Saudi Arabia), from 23 to 25 Ṣafar 1418H (28 June to 3 July 1997);
Having taken cognizance of the research papers prepared and relating to "Human Cloning" and of recommendations issued by the 9th *Fiqh* and Medical seminar organized by the Islamic Organization for Medical Sciences of Kuwait, in cooperation with the Islamic *Fiqh* Academy and other institutions, and held in Casablanca (Morocco), from 9 to 12 Ṣafar 1418 AH. (14 to 17 June 1997);
Having listened to discussions held around this topic, with the participation of *fiqh* scholars and physicians;

CONCLUDES THE FOLLOWING:

PREAMBLE:

God Almighty has created human being in the best of its form and has surrounded it with His Solicitude. God says:

> *"We have honored the sons of Adam, provided them with transport on land and sea, given them for sustenance the best and purest and conferred on them special favors above a great part of our Creation" (Q17:70).*

God Almighty has endowed man with a spirit, honored

him by legal competence, appointed him as His regent on earth, allowed him to colonize this planet and has honored him by a mission compatible with his nature – this indeed is perhaps man's very nature. God says:

> *"So set thou thy face steadily and truly to the Faith; (Establish) God's handiwork according to the pattern on which He has made mankind: no change (let there be) in the work (wrought) by God: that is the standard Religion, but most among mankind understand not" (Q30:30*).

Islam insists on the necessity of preserving man's innate nature, by maintaining the five universal principles: religion, life, reason, offspring and wealth; and by protecting man from any corruptive modification both at the level of causes and consequences, as witnessed by the following *qudsī ḥadīth* quoted by al-Qurṭubī from the narration of al-Qāḍī Ismāʿīl: "I have created my servants all pure, but Satan has come to deviate them from their religion... and ordered them to change my creature".

God Almighty has taught man what he was ignorant of and has ordered him to research, observe, think and meditate. In many verses of the Holy Qurʾān, God Almighty calls out man: "Don't they see?", "Don't they look out?", "Doesn't man see that We created him from a drop of sperm?", "These are signs for those who understand", "This is a reminder for the conscious minded", "Read! In the Name of Your Lord Who has created".

Islam does not set up any obstacle or any obstruction to the freedom of scientific research that constitutes a means to discover the order established by God Almighty in His creation. Nevertheless, Islam stresses that the door cannot be left wide open, without restriction, to the generalized implementation, without limit, of the results of scientific research, without examining them closely in the light of *Sharīʿa, so* as to authorize what is lawful and prohibit what is not. It is not allowed to apply a discovery just because such an application is technically possible. It has to be a useful science serving public interest and protecting people from harm. Science must respect human dignity, his place in the world and the purpose for which the Almighty God has created him. Man should never be a field for experimentation. In no way, should his identity, his specificity and his particularity be violated. Science should neither shake the stability of social structure, nor destroy the foundation of parenthood, marriage links and family structures as they have been known through the history of mankind and preserved by the Divine Law on sound and strong bases set up by God. One innovation of our time concerns a topic that has attracted public attention, through the mass media; it is "Cloning". It was therefore necessary to let people know the position of *Sharīʿa* on this issue, after having it studied, in all its details, by an elite group of experts and scholars specialized in this field.

DEFINITION OF CLONING

It is generally known that the order set up by God stipulates that any human being created by God is the result of the encounter between a spermatozoid and an ovule, the nucleus of each contains a number of chromosomes equal to half the number of chromosomes contained in the cells of the human body. When the spermatozoid of the father (the husband) unites with the ovule of the mother (wife), the result transforms into an embryo containing a complete genetic map and capable of reproducing itself. Once it fixes itself in the womb of the mother, this embryo gradually develops to become a complete being that will be born by the will of God. Thus, the initial cell divides itself into two identical cells, then four, eight, and so on, until reaching the stage of determining the differentiation of the embryonic being. If one of the cells of the embryo divides itself into two identical parts, we obtain identical twins. Such an experience has been possible with some animals and has resulted in giving birth to identical twins. This operation has been considered as a form of cloning or procreation, inasmuch as it yields identical copies or species.

This technique has been called "cloning by division". There is another method of cloning a fully-grown being. It consists in taking the nucleus of a cell containing the complete DNA of a subject and injecting it into an enucleated avocet. A new embryo containing a complete DNA and capable of reproducing itself is therefore created. Implanted into the uterus, the embryo develops, reaches its full shape and becomes a living being. This type of cloning is known as "nuclear transfer" or "Nucleus replacement". This is what is called "cloning" and this operation has led to the birth of Dolly the sheep. But this new creature is not an identical copy of the original, because the enucleated ovule of the mother still contains remains of the nucleus in the area surrounding the removed nucleus. These remains have a noticeable effect on the transformation of the characteristics inherited from the cell. To the best of our knowledge, such an experience has not yet, been applied to human being.

Cloning is therefore giving birth to one or several living beings, either by transplanting the nucleus of a cell into an enucleated ovule, or by dividing a fertilized egg before the tissues and limbs differentiation stage. No one ignores that such operations do neither constitute a total creation, nor a partial one. God Almighty says: "... Or do they assign to God partners who have created (anything) as He has created, so that the creation seemed to them similar? Say: "God is the Creator of all things: He is the One, the Supreme and Irresistible" (Q13: 16). God Almighty says: "Do ye then see? The (human seed) that ye throw out, is it ye who create it, or are We the Creator? We have decreed death to be your common lot and We are not to be frustrated from changing your forms and creating you again in (forms) that ye know not. And ye certainly know already the first form of creation: why then do ye not celebrate His praise?" (Q56:58-62). God also says: "Do not man see that it is We who created him from sperm? Yet behold! he (stands forth) as an open adversary! And he makes comparisons for Us and forgets his own (origin and) creation, saying: "Who can give life to (dry) bones and decomposed ones (at that)? Say: "He will give them life Who created them for the first time! For He is well versed in every kind of creation. The Same Who produces for you fire out of the green tree, when behold! Ye kindle therewith (Your own fires)! Is not He Who created the heavens and the earth able to create the like thereof?" Yeah, indeed! For He is the Creator Supreme, of skill and knowledge, (Infinite)!" Verily, when He intends a thing, His Command is "Be" and it is!" (Q36:77-82).

The Almighty God says: "Man We did create from a

quintessence (of clay); then We placed him as (a drop of) sperm in a place of rest, firmly fixed! Then We made the sperm into a clot of congealed blood; then of that clot (We made) a (fetus) lump; then We made out of that lump bones and clothed the bones with flesh; then We developed out of it another creature. So, blessed be God, the Best to create!" (Q23:12-14).

On the basis of the studies previously presented to the Academy, the discussions held thereon, and the principles of *Sharī'a,*

It is decided that:

1. It is prohibited to clone human being, such as in the above-mentioned two cases or by any other method that results in the multiplication of human species.
2. In case of violation of *Sharī'a* prescriptions underlined in the first paragraph, consequences of such acts should be brought to the notice of the Academy so as to clarify *Sharī'a* rules thereon.
3. All cases implying the intervention of a third party in the procreation process, whether a uterus, an ovule, a spermatozoid or a body cell for cloning, are prohibited.
4. It is permitted by Sharī'a to use cloning techniques and genetic engineering in the fields of microbiology, botanic and zoology, and thus within the limits prescribed by *Sharī'a,* in order to serve general interest and prevent inconvenience.
5. The academy invites Islamic countries to adopt laws and rules in order to close all direct and indirect avenues for local or foreign institutions, research institutes and foreign experts so as to

prevent them from using Islamic countries as experimentation fields for the propagation of cloning.

6. The Council of the Academy and the Islamic Organization for medical Sciences shall jointly ensure the follow-up of the issue of cloning and of any new discovery in this field. They shall establish the terminology of cloning and organize seminars and meetings in view to popularize *Sharīʿa* rules on the subject.
7. The Council calls for the establishment of specialized committees comprising experts and *fiqh* scholars, in order to set up the rules of ethics to be observed in the field of biomedical research in Islamic countries.
8. The Council calls for the creation and strengthening of scientific establishment and institutes conducting research in biology and genetics, but in field other than human cloning, in compliance with *Sharīʿa* rules, so that the Islamic world would not be left in a state of complete dependency in this field.
9. The Council calls for approaching scientific discoveries from an Islamic standpoint. It invites all mass media to adopt a suitable attitude congruent with the religious prescriptions in covering such issues; to avoid using these discoveries in a way incompatible with the spirit of Islam; and raise public awareness so that people can take an informed stance, as required by Almighty God who says: "When comes to them some matter touching (public) safety or fear, they divulge it. If they had only referred it to the Apostle or to those

charged with authority among them, the proper investigators would have tested it from them (direct)" (Q4: 83). Verily Allah is All Knowing!

Paying Due Attention to Psyche

It is worth mentioning that the term life in this context may also refer to a person's soul, which could either be at peace (content, self-assured, and unwavering) or unsettled due to psychological diseases. Once again, the preservation of this higher objective may require a balancing of both positive and negative obligations and refraining from the use of any treatment or medication that may have negative psychological or emotional effects. In these cases, the physician must attempt to balance between informing the patient of all necessary details regarding the disease and treatment and withholding any information that may lead to the patient losing hope or rejecting treatment.

3. Ethical Principles Associated with Preserving the Higher Objective of "the Intellect"

Linguistically, the word *'aql* is defined as the cognition and realization of matters as they are in reality and the ability to distinguish between them.(1) The technical definition, however, has stimulated extensive philosophical debates. According to Muslim scholars, it is defined as the instinct through which God has distinguished man from the rest of creatures. In its absence, there can be no accountability (*taklīf*) placed on a person.(2) It also refers to the process of grasping theoretical knowledge. In his definition, al-Ghazālī explained that, "*'Aql* can encompass a number of meanings...

(1) See: *Lisān al-ʿArab, al-Qāmūs al-Muḥīṭ, al-Muʿjam al-Wasīṭ.*

(2) Iḥyāʾ ʿulūm al-dīn, op. cit., (3/4); Ibn al-Qayyim, Miftāḥ dār al-saʿādah (1/117).

amongst them are two meanings that are relevant to our discussion: the first refers to the awareness and recognition of reality…and the second refers to the grasp of knowledge… in other words, comprehension."[1] Intellect in Islam holds a high status. It is an indispensable condition for affirming belief and mandating accountability, the comprehension of knowledge, juridical reasoning (to deduce legal rulings), and the development and progress of civilizations.

The ethical principles associated with intellect, in terms of positive and negative obligations, require that the physicians exert utmost efforts to preserve and advance intellect, while also preventing any harm from coming to it. Consequently, it is unethical to use any medication that may potentially damage a person's intellectual abilities. The patient must likewise avoid anything that harms his or her intellectual capacity and must exert effort towards intellectual development and prosperity. Freedom and independence are central to the intellect. The patient should not be denied the right to freely decide whether to undergo treatment or participate in research experiments, provided that his or her decision does not conflict with an explicit legal text or public interest. Such cases include when a patient suffers from a serious contagious disease or when another person may be directly harmed, such as the enforcement of pre-marital medical check-ups that takes place in certain countries.

4. Principles of Medical Ethics Associated with the Higher Objective of "Wealth"

These principles are evident in the physician's or the medical institution's requirement to charge patients

(1) Iḥyāʾ ʿulūm al-dīn (3/4).

reasonable fees. Needless to say, exploiting a patient in order to gain extra money is unethical behavior. Similarly, the patient should not squander his or her money on extravagant, superfluous medication. It is also considered unethical for a terminal patient to offer the physician or other persons money with the purpose of depriving his or her heirs from their rightful inheritance. The principles of justice and beneficence apply to this objective.

5. Principles of Medical Ethics Associated with the Higher Objective of "Offspring"

The purpose here entails protecting the patient from harm, realizing the patient's welfare and interests, and doing our best to avoid any possible distortion of lineage. Arising from this, abortion is considered an unethical act with the exception of some cases in which the mother's life is in danger. In addition, it is the physician's ethical duty to preserve lineage during artificial insemination and any other similar procedures. The three principles, namely, justice, beneficence, and respect for human dignity apply to this specific objective of offspring.

6. Principles of Medical Ethics Associated with the Higher Objective of "Honor"

It is not permitted for a physician or a medical institution to act in any manner or disclose any secrets in regards to the patient that may potentially be disparaging of his or her honor, dignity, or character. On the contrary, the physician must protect and preserve the patient's honor and dignity (this objective is also related to preserving the patient's psychological and emotional well-being). This principle specifically relates to people's dignity and their moral rights.

7. *Principles of Medical Ethics Associated with the Preservation of Communities and Societies*

This refers to the protection and preservation of public welfare and interests along with individual interests. It requires the protection of a society's political, social, economic, and environmental security from any potential harm or malfeasance. It also requires that medical insurance be distributed equally and justly among members of socicty without any form of discrimination.

This has been firmly established as a basic legal right for all individuals. Based on this, any practices performed by the physician (or the medical institution), whether for treatment or research, must be intended to increase benefit, not harm. Therefore, any action that results in the overall corruption of the society and the environment or leads to injustice and inequality is considered an unethical act. For this reason, the resolutions issued by the *fiqh* academies stipulated that DNA fingerprinting, gene therapy, or the like is permissible only if it does not cause any harm to humans, animals, or the environment.(1) In fact, the preservation of public interests is prioritized over individual interests. Hence, a patient's independent will in rejecting treatment is discounted if he or she suffers a contagious disease that poses a danger to society. The three principles apply to this objective.

8. *Principles of Medical Ethics Associated with the State*

This involves the obligation of adherence to the laws and regulations that have to be transparently issued by the state. It includes preserving the state's medical and rehabilitation institutions, maintaining its security, advancing its interests,

(1) al-al-Qaradāghī, *al-ḥaqībah al-Iqtiṣādīyah* (1/190ff).

and protecting it from harm or corruption. Consequently, any action practiced by the physician that contradicts the state's established laws and regulations or that places its security at risk is considered unethical. The principles of beneficence and justice apply to this higher objective.

Fourth: Linking Ethics to the Universal Six Objectives

In this case, we exclude the last two objectives while extending the scope of the six objectives to include society and the state.

In sum, it is evident that the theory of drafting principles of biomedical ethics based on the higher objectives of *Sharīʿa* is a comprehensive theory and successfully integrates the four principles of biomedical ethics. As explained, maintaining any of the eight higher objectives requires two elements: preventing harm and malfeasance and preserving interests and benefits. These represent two of the four principles in the principle-based approach. They fall under the principle of *iḥsān* (beneficence). I also found that the principle of respect for autonomy falls under two of the higher objectives of *Sharīʿa*, preserving religion and preserving life. We further found that the principle of justice falls under the higher objectives of preserving communities and societies as well as preserving religion.

This theory also encompasses the principle of equality through the two higher objectives of preserving communities and societies and preserving religion. Likewise, it ensures the protection of a person's psychological and emotional well-being through the higher objective of preserving honor. Finally, it includes the principle of freedom and similar rights through the higher objective of preserving the intellect. It also covers the internal attributes of both the physician and the patient such as sincerity, altruism, and parental compassion, all of which fall under the higher objective of preserving religion. The institution as a corporate body is also considered in this theory so the aforementioned three principles apply to it or its representatives.

Fifth: Linking the three Principles to *Fiqh* of Consequences

1. Ascertaining Effective Cause (taḥqīq al-manāṭ)(1) in Medicine

Taḥqīq al-manāṭ is an *uṣūlī* terminology denoting the process of ascertaining effective cause of legal rulings. By applying it to the field of medicine, it means exerting the utmost effort on the part of the physician or the medical institution to ensure three things:

1. The physician diagnoses an illness alone, or with the help of a colleague, a number of consultant physicians, or another medical institution. In other words, attempting all technical means and advanced techniques including x-ray examinations and medical tests to find out the nature of an illness.
2. To accurately determine the suitable medical prescriptions or any possible interventions.
3. To apply the best possible means in administering medicines. The Prophet (PBUH) says, "Make use of medical treatment, for Allah has not made a disease without appointing a remedy for it, with the exception of one disease, namely old age."[2] Another version

---

(1) For more information on *taḥqīq al-manāṭ*, see: Abd Allāh ibn Bīyah, Itharāt tajdīdiyyah fī ḥuqūl al-uṣūl; Bashīr ibn Mawlūd Juḥaysh, Fī al-ijtihād al-tanzīlī, p. 43ff; al-al-Qaradāghī, "Taḥqīq al-manāṭ Fī al-Taḍakhkhum" a paper submitted to *the seminar on Fiqh al-wāqi'* held in Kuwait, 2013.

(2) Reported by Abū Dāwūd in al-Sunan, along with *'Awn al-ma'būd (10/334);* al-Tirmidhī considers this tradition as *ḥasan ṣaḥiḥ*, *Tuḥfat al-aḥwadhī* (5/201, 6/190, 6/12, 6/121). It is also reported by Ibn Mājah, al-Nasā'ī and al-Ḥākim.

states that "God has not sent down a disease but also sent down a cure for it. Those who know it are aware of it, and those who do not know it are ignorant of it."(1) This tradition clearly shows that God has created a cure for every illness but the problem lies in ignorance, misdiagnosis, improper administering of medication, etc.

2. Fiqh of Consequences & Blocking Means to Evil

Fiqh of consequences is concerned with identification of potential consequences and future implications of any medical intervention. It is a kind of anticipation and having a future outlook by making use of modern scholarship and techniques. al-Shāṭibī avers that heeding the outcomes of actions is consistent with the higher objectives of the law, whether the actions concerned are in accordance with the law or in violation thereof. Therefore, the *mujtahid* is not to judge a human action, be it one of commission or omission, until after he has given careful thought to the consequences to which the social action will lead. A given action may be intended to acquire certain benefit or prevent some sort of evil, however, it may result in an opposite outcome. If generally permitted, the action intended to secure a benefit may lead to an equal or greater evil. In this specific case, this permissibility cannot be accepted. The same is true for the action intended to ward off an evil as it may lead to even a greater one.(2)

If paying heed to consequences is instrumental in exercising *ijtihād* and giving *fatwā* to such an extent that

---

(1) Recorded by Aḥmad in *Musnad (6/159)*. Aḥmad Shākir comments that its chain of transmission is sound. It is also reported by Ibn ʿAbd al-Barr in al-Tamhīd where he considers it authentic and so does al-Suyūṭī in al-Jāmiʿ al-Ṣaghīr, no. 1783.

(2) al- Shāṭibī, *al-Muwāfaqāt*, vol. 4, pp. 552-53

a permissible thing can be rendered prohibited or vice versa, its importance is further accentuated in the field of medicine. It is obligatory for the physician or the medical institution to carefully consider repercussions and potential consequences of every treatment. The expected effects on the health, psyche, mind, and bodily systems are to be taken into consideration and the final decision is to be premised on the rules of interests and evils as stated above.

As far as blocking the means to evil is concerned, it is equally important and legally required. It aims at preventing all practices leading to evils. That is why God urges people not to insult the disbelievers' idols and deities. God says, "[Believers], do not revile those they call on beside God in case they, in their hostility and ignorance, revile God."(1) All jurists consider blocking the means to evil and *fiqh* of consequences in construing the legal rulings although some of them debate their authority as legal indicants. It is beyond the scope of this book to dwell on this issue. Evidently, some scholars of *uṣūl*, including Ibn Taymīyah, Ibn al-Qayyim, and al-Shāṭibī, pay special attention to these principles.(2)

The physician and the medical institution have to take these principles into consideration. They entail a careful examination and deliberation of the tools and methods on the one hand and the outcomes and repercussions on the other hand. Failure to do so could have serious negative impacts. As regards medicine, the principle of blocking the means to evil could be put in effect by virtue of analytical and experimental studies, or a forward-looking approach. Indeed, medicine primarily deals with the most noble and precious creature, i.e., human beings. God declares, "If

(1) (6:108).

(2) al-Shāṭibī, *al-al-Muwāfaqāt* (4/552-53).

anyone kills a person – unless in retribution for murder or spreading corruption in the land – it is as if he kills all mankind, while if any saves a life it is as if he saves the lives of all mankind. Our messengers came to them with clear signs, but many of them continued to commit excesses in the land."[1]

Given this great significance, the IIFA issued an important resolution (92/9/9) that is quoted verbatim below.

Resolution no. 92/9/9: Sadd al-dharāʾiʿ (Blocking the Means to Evil)

The Council of the Islamic *Fiqh* Academy, holding its Ninth Session in Abu Dhabi, State of the United Arab Emirates, from 1 to 6 Dhū al-Qaʿdah, 1415 AH. (1-6 April, 1995)

Having considered the research papers forwarded to the Academy on the subject of Sadd al-dharāʾiʿ,

Having listened to the debate around the subject,

RESOLVES

1. Blocking the means to evil is one of the Islamic *Sharīʿa* principal rules. It is defined as the prohibition of an otherwise permissible matter but which may be used as a proper or stepping stone to achieve evil or transgression.
2. Blocking the means to evil is not confined to matters that call for questioning or caution, rather it may extend to all that could be used as bridge way to anything illicit.
3. Blocking the means to evil calls for barring the way against any subterfuge leading to the commitment

(1) (5:32).

of prohibited acts or to nullify any of the Sharīʿ requirements, though a subterfuge differs from "*al-Dharīʿah*" (an evasive legal device) in that the former is dependent on the existence of deliberate intent whereas the latter is not.

4. Blocking the means to evil is of several categories:
   - There is unanimous agreement of opinions as to the prohibition of the first category. It includes devices that are stipulated in the Holy Qurʾān and the Sunnah of the Prophet (PBUH), and those which are definitely or most probably conducive to evil action, whether the medium used is itself permissible, delegated or obligatory. Such is the case of contracts which are concluded for the purpose of committing a prohibited action by providing for it in the contract.
   - The second category is subject of a consensus as to its optimal character. This category includes cases where the social benefit exceeds the harm that may be caused.
   - The third category is subject of disagreement: it includes cases where the intention is apparently a healthy one but still shrouded in the suspicion that it is intended only as a passageway to something prohibited, in view of its frequent use to such intent.
5. The criteria for allowing an evasive legal device is that it scarcely leads to evil doing or that its social benefits are more likely than any resulting evil assaulted with it.
6. The criteria for prohibiting an evasive legal device lies in the fact that it is definitely or in most cases

conducive to evil, or that the evil likely to arise from it is more important than any benefits associated with it. Verily Allah is All-Knowledge![1]

Source of Morality

Islamically speaking, the source of moralities is the Divine revelation, represented by the Qur'ān and the Sunnah. However, the sound intellect can realize them. Actually, universal moralities represent the natural disposition as emphasized by the Islamic *Sharī'a*. This *Sharī'a* stipulates the legal rulings of obligation and approbation for abidance by such moralities, or prohibition and reprehension for violating them. From a positivist standpoint, the intellect is the source of morality. However, this standpoint is based on a utilitarian philosophy giving priority to the individualistic interests and hedonism. It is a philosophy completely detached from spiritual and doctrinal values. Consequently, countless violations took place, even in the field of medicine. A lot of economic and social crises arose as a corollary to the moral crisis. History shows that only belief in God and the Day of Resurrection and piety can save humanity from serious repercussions and deviation. This belief preserves the firmly entrenched traditions of the nation and remains a defense against absorption by others.

Morality: Source of Obligation & Authority

These medical ethics deduce their obligation and authority from the Islamic *Sharī'a* which makes mandatory the adherence to beneficial medical ethics and prohibits immoral conduct, as ordained throughout numerous Qur'ānic

---

(1) *Journal of Fiqh Academy*, 3 (9) 5. This translation is quoted, with slight modification, from Resolutions and Recommendations of the Council of the Islamic Fiqh Academy 1985-2000.

verses and Prophetic traditions. In turn, it becomes the responsibility of the individual to abide by these ethics even if the state did not decree binding legislations for regulating them. This fact gives ethics in Islam a distinctive character. Combined with the force of law, such religion-driven ethics become more impactful.

To sum up, ethics acquire their legal binding force from:

1. The Qurʾānic verses and Prophetic traditions requiring adoption of such ethics. The three principles of bioethics are not mere embellishments; rather, they are obligations. Abiding by them pleases God and brings about prosperity and salvation. Conversely, failing to stick to them is a cause of God's wrath and punishment. A lot of Qurʾānic and Prophetic dicta establish this fact.
2. Any contractual agreement providing for the adherence to these moral principles.
3. Any applicable laws and legislations enforcing these moral principles.
4. Institutional by-laws stipulating them.

Morality: The Driving Force

The real incentive or driving force behind morality lies in the firm belief in God and the Day of Judgement. By adhering to morality, a person aims at pleasing God, seeking His reward of paradise and avoiding His punishment of hell. This is a unique feature of Islamic ethics; it combines such effective incentives along with the primary objective of advancing people's interests and avoiding evils. These interests are not limited to the worldly ones, rather, they include those pertaining to the hereafter as well. If adequately materialized, this driving force leads people to avoid maleficence and selfishness. As a result, a person desires for others what he desires for himself. When this driving force becomes more impactful, a person puts the interests of others before his own. The Qur'ān reads, "They give them preference over themselves, even if they too are poor."[1]

A Sea Change within Souls and Minds

By means of its beliefs, rituals, pillars, branches of faith, and continuous purification Islam seeks to make quite a profound change to people's souls. It looks for cultivating a constantly self-blaming soul that is satisfied with God's decree instead of such a self that is attached to worldly lusts and persistently incites people to evil. Moreover, Islam wants to transform hearts through the sound doctrine, belief in God and the Day of Judgment, acts of worship, rituals, and branches of faith. It seeks to change the spiritually defected hearts and free them from vestiges of disbelief, whims, superstitions, envy, hatred, arrogance, haughtiness, hypocrisy, etc. In so doing, Islam transforms those hearts into righteous ones full of faith, beneficence, humbleness, etc. God says, "...the Day when neither wealth nor children can help, when the only one who will be saved is the one who comes before God with a heart devoted to Him."[2]

Likewise, Islam wants to transform minds from being in a state of laziness and inertia into one of creativity, innovation and initiative so that people aspire for excellence in every aspect to have a promising future and make life always better. To conclude, Islam lays down a basic principle that "change begins within souls, minds and hearts." The Qur'ān says, "God does not change the condition of a people unless they change what is in themselves."[3]

---

(1) (59:9).
(2) (26: 88-89).
(3) (13:11).

Clear-cut Yardstick

The Prophet (PBUH) set a clear-cut criterion to measure morality within souls, minds, and hearts. This criterion requires a person to put himself in another person's situation or predicament and treat them the way he would want to be treated. The Prophet says, "No one of you shall become a true believer until he desires for his brother what he desires for himself "[1] If we apply this clear-cut criterion in dealings with others, it will be adequately sufficient. True belief can be measured against this yardstick. It is a holistic one that can be employed for medical and non-medical practices.

Unique Features of Islamic Bioethical Theory

The theory of three principles of medical ethics is characterized with some unique features:

1. It is a holistic theory composed of three universal principles covering all medical ethics and applying to the physician, the medical staff, the pharmaceutical institution, and different hospitals. It also applies to the state as it is legally responsible for providing health care, whether directly or indirectly.
2. It clarifies the general principles of practical professional ethics and code of conduct. It is not a mere theoretical framework that has nothing to do with practical reality. It is not a set of spiritual values and internal moralities with no real effect in practice.
3. It is based on transparency, clarity, and applicability. The three-principle approach is clear-cut, comprehendible, and applicable. Every person, even a non-Muslim, could put it into effect as this approach depends on the practical conduct in general and its actual effects.

(1) Reported by al-Bukhārī, book of belief, *ḥadīth* no. 13 and Muslim, no. 45.

4. It is characterized by cohesion. The three principles are interrelated; beneficence, justice, and respect for human dignity are complementary.
5. Although these principles are practical, they emanate from deep belief and piety in line with the meaning of *iḥsān* as an act of worshiping God as if one sees Him. There is no contradiction between this fact and the practical nature of this theory because this belief and piety serve as a driving force. Whenever *iḥsān* materializes, it provides a strong impetus to live by these ethical principles. In such a case, laws and legislations become only auxiliary means (as in the story of Joseph and the milk-seller family).
6. It highlights some lucid Islamic terminology in addition to establishing a solid link with the higher objectives of *Sharīʿa*. In so doing, it reinstates the medical ethical principles back to the *Sharīʿa* and its objectives and terminology.
7. The theory delineates its source, structure, normativity and measurability. In addition, it highlights its impetus, driving force and governing legal rules and lays the foundation of applicable *fiqh* of priorities and balances.

Final Thoughts on Liability

Islam does not confine itself in the delineation of medical ethics to religious and moral aspects only. Rather, it sets some practical measures to be taken as necessary. These measures include:

1. Putting under interdiction the ignorant physician by suspending or revoking his license.(1)
2. Applying the principle of indemnity to the incompetent and unlicensed physician. Such a

(1) This view is hold by Abū Ḥanīfah as indicated in *badāʾiʿ al-ṣanāʾiʿ* (5/200).

physician is liable to pay compensation in cases of damages.[1] In certain circumstances, this incompetent physician can carry criminal liability. The Prophet (PBUH) says, "Whoever practices medicine when he is not known for that, he is liable."[2]

3. In case of transgression or negligence on the part of the physician, he commits an unethical act and thus will be held accountable. This physician shall carry civil and even criminal liability when the relevant conditions are met. The punishment is to be determined by the state. In our present-day world, I think there is dire need to enact a particular law to regulate the punishments and compensations in case of medical errors. This law is expected to set guidelines and regulations of medical research and experiments involving human subjects in consonance with the principles of Islamic *Sharīʿa.* The relevant procedures, conditions and guidelines shall be clearly set out by this law after thorough meticulous studies in order to establish justice without negligence or excess. This specific issue needs further elaboration but the scope of the present study does not permit a detailed treatment of this aspect.

---

(1) See: Ḥāshiyat ibn ʿĀbidīn (3/184); Ibn Taymīyah, al-siyāsah al-sharʿīyah, pp. 120-33; ʿAbd al-Sattār Abū Ghuddah, Fiqh al-ṭabīb; ʿAbd al-Qādir ʿAwdah, al-Tashrīʿ al-jināʾī al-Islāmī (1/63, 704).

(2) Reported by Abū Dāwūd, no. 4586, al-Dāraquṭnī (3/117). Ibn Ḥajar in commenting on the traditions of al-Mishkāh considers it as *ḥasan* (3/392); al-Suyūṭī declares it as authentic in al-Jāmiʿ al-Ṣaghīr, no. 8596; Ibn Daqīq al-ʿĪd points out that this tradition is authentic according to the methodology of some traditionists. Similarly, Ibn Mufliḥ al-Maqdisī considers it *ḥasan* in *al-Ādāb al-sharʿīyah* (2/438); Ibn Kathīr notes in Irshād al-faqīh that this tradition has a good strong chain of transmission (2/266). To conclude, this tradition could be cited as a proof.

Representing the Three Principles in Medical Ethical Codes

A lot of medical codes of conduct have been published. One of the most comprehensive code is the Islamic Code for Medical and Health Ethics which consists of 108 articles. Here we highlight the place of the three principles (beneficence, respect for human dignity and justice) in these articles.

Article No.	The Principle
1	*Iḥsān* or beneficence
2	beneficence
3	Dignity
4	The part dealing with piety comes under the category of beneficence while the remaining part dealing with the belief and custom of the patient belongs to the principle of respect for human dignity.
5	Beneficence as this article tackles the necessity of performing medical tests.
6	Dignity
7	Dignity and the necessity to refer the patient to a specialized physician.
8	This article comes under beneficence. The last part applies to the principle of respect for human dignity.

9	Its first part comes under the principle of beneficence while the last part of the article relates to human dignity.
10	Beneficence
11	Beneficence. The last part dealing with the necessity of giving proper care relates to the principle of human dignity.
12	Beneficence & Dignity
13	Dignity
14	Dignity
15	Dignity
16	Beneficence
17	Beneficence
18	Dignity
19	Dignity
20	Justice
21	Dignity
22	Dignity
23	Dignity & Beneficence
24	Beneficence
25	Beneficence & Dignity

26	Beneficence & Dignity
27	Dignity
28	Dignity & Beneficence
29	Beneficence
30	Dignity
31	Dignity
32	Dignity & Beneficence
33	Dignity
34	Dignity
35	Dignity
36	Dignity
37	Beneficence
38	Dignity
39	Dignity
40	Dignity
41	Beneficence
42	Beneficence
43	Beneficence
44	Beneficence
45	Beneficence

46	Beneficence
47	Beneficence
48	Beneficence
49	Beneficence & Dignity
50	Beneficence
51	Beneficence
52	Beneficence
53	Dignity
54	Beneficence
55	Beneficence
56	Justice
57	Dignity & Beneficence
58	Dignity & Beneficence
59	Dignity & Beneficence
60	Dignity & Beneficence
61	Dignity & Beneficence
62	Dignity
63	Beneficence
64	Dignity
65	Beneficence

66	Beneficence & Dignity
67	Dignity
68	Dignity
69	Dignity
70	Dignity
71	Beneficence
72	Dignity
73	Beneficence
74-83	The three principles apply to these articles.
84-93	The two principles of beneficence and respect for human dignity apply.
94-101	The three principles apply in a very clear way.
102-108	The three principles apply in a very clear way.

At last, all praise is due to God; may the peace and blessings of Allah be upon our master Muḥammad (PBUH) and upon his family and Companions!

APPENDIX

THE ISLAMIC CODE FOR MEDICAL AND HEALTH ETHICS

CHAPTER ONE: PHYSICIAN ETHICS

Article 1:

A physician should be sincere in performing his work, enjoy high moral values, be grateful towards his teachers and trainers, and acknowledge the efforts of others. He should serve as an example in taking care of his own health and giving due attention to the requirements of his body and to his general appearance, and he should refrain from anything that may influence the esteem accorded to his profession inside and outside his place of work.

CHAPTER TWO: THE PHYSICIAN'S DUTIES TOWARDS THE PATIENT

Article 2:

A physician should listen carefully to the patient's complaint, sympathizing with him in his suffering, treat him well, and be gentle while examining him. He should avoid any condescending attitude in dealing with the patient, and avoid any ridicule or derision of the patient, regardless of the patient's educational or social level, or religious or racial background. A physician should respect his patient's opinion, particularly in matters that concern the latter personally, but that should not keep the physician from giving the appropriate instructions.

Article 3:

A physician should treat all his patients equally, without any discrimination based on their prestige, their social or moral status, the physician's own feelings towards them, their religious or racial background, their political orientation, or their gender, nationality, or color.

Article 4:

A physician should fear God when dealing with his patients; show respect for their beliefs, religions, and traditions when engaging in the process of examination, diagnosis, and treatment. He should avoid any violations of Islamic law, such as being alone with a member of the opposite sex or looking at the private parts (*'awra*) of a patient except in as much as the process of examination, diagnosis, and treatment requires; in the presence of a third party; and after obtaining permission from the patient.

Article 5:

A physician should ask only for the tests needed for the patient, without adding any tests not justified by the patient's case. He should base his whole diagnosis and treatment on the best available evidence and data, and refrain from using any unauthorized, unaccepted, or scientifically unrecognized methods of diagnosis or treatment. Moreover, he should ask only for the medications or surgical operations that are called for in the patient's case.

Article 6:

A physician should honestly explain to the patient or anyone representing him the type, causes, and complications of the illness, and of the usefulness of diagnostic and therapeutic procedures. The physician should also explain clearly the proper options of diagnosis and treatment in as much as the patient's physical and psychological condition allows.

Article 7:

A physician should not hesitate to refer the patient to a doctor specialized in the type of disease the patient has or to a doctor who has more effective equipment whenever the patient's case calls for such a referral, nor to refer him to a doctor whom the patient wishes to consult. It is unacceptable for a physician to delay the referral when it is in the patient's interest. The physician should make the patient's medical record accessible when referring him to another doctor, and to give the patient, without delay, an adequate medical report of his case.

Article 8:

A patient or a member of his family has the right to invite another efficient doctor for consultation, after the original physician's consent has been obtained. The latter, however, has the right to discontinue his services, without having to give any reason, if the patient or a member of his family insist on consulting another doctor unacceptable to him.

Article 9:

A physician should never decline or discontinue to treat an emergency patient under any circumstances, unless the patient refuses to follow his instructions or seeks, without the consent of the physician attending him, the services of another doctor. Nor should a physician decline or discontinue to treat a patient, unless the case is not within his field of specialization.

Article 10:

A physician should continue to give an emergency patient the proper treatment until it is no longer needed or until care for the patient is taken over by another doctor.

Article 11:

A physician should continue to extend proper care to patients with incurable, terminal, or fatal diseases, and to console them and give them hope to the last minutes of their lives.

Article 12:

To the best of his ability and with all the preventive and therapeutic means available to him, whether material or psychological, a physician should relieve the patient's pain and give him the feeling that the physician is eager to give him proper care and attention.

Article 13:

A physician should see to it that the patient is enlightened as regards his illness and his health in general, as well as to the way to maintain his health and follow proper and effective methods of disease prevention. This should be through face-to-face enlightenment or through the employment of other effective methods when available.

Article 14:

A patient should not be examined or treated without his consent, except in cases when emergency medical intervention is required and informed consent cannot be obtained for any particular reason, or when the disease is communicable or poses a threat to public health or to others, and in accordance with the laws in force. In the case of a patient with full legal competence, his consent can be expressed orally or implicitly. When the patient is a minor, an unconscious adult, or a person who fails to meet one or more of the competence conditions, consent should be given by someone who legally represents him. For surgical operations and for treatment and examinations that have potential side effects, consent should be informed and given in writing.

Article 15:

A physician is entrusted to investigate the health care programs suitable for the patient's case. He should ascertain the usefulness of a course of treatment before choosing it and applying it to the patient. He should follow the patient's case until he fully recovers, if the disease is curable. When a patient asks for an ineffectual course of treatment, the physician should convince him that it is useless.

Article 16:

Taking into consideration the stipulation of Article 4, a physician should make sure to observe the following while examining a patient:

1. He should make a record of the patient's condition and of personal and family medical history before beginning to diagnose and treat the case.
2. He should be careful and efficient in, and give sufficient time to, the examination and diagnosis process.
3. Prescriptions should be made in writing and should be clear, with dosages and method of administration specified. The patient or his family members, as the case requires, should be made aware of the importance of following the method of treatment prescribed by the physician and of the serious potential side effects of the medical or surgical treatment.

4. Side effects resulting from medical or surgical treatment should be monitored and treated promptly when possible.

Article 17:

A physician should make sure that surgical operations are performed under the following conditions:

1. The physician who performs an operation should have the specialization and medical experience that qualify him to do the required type of surgery.
2. The surgical operation should be performed at a therapeutic institution or health establishment which is sufficiently equipped for the performance of such a surgery.
3. Proper laboratory and radiology tests should be made to confirm that surgical intervention is necessary and appropriate as a treatment for the patient and to make certain that the patient's health condition allows the surgery to be performed.
4. The surgeon attending the patient has the obligation of performing the surgery himself. He may be helped by a resident at the hospital or some other surgeon, with no need for the patient's consent. The surgeon may also authorize an assistant of his to perform certain procedures of the surgery, provided that they are done under the surgeon's supervision and with his help, and that he bears the legal responsibility for them.

Article 18:

A patient should be made aware of his health condition and of available treatment alternatives, if he can grasp this information. A physician should not force a treatment on a patient without his consent, nor force him to sign, unwillingly, data in his medical file.

Article 19:

A physician should gently, honestly, and wisely and without undue exaggeration explain to the patient the consequences of declining to follow a treatment and the resulting complications. The physician should also take the patient's admission if the latter declines to follow the treatment, and when he refuses to give it, a statement signed by the physician and a member of the nursing staff should be added to the patient's medical file, in order to clear the physician from any responsibility.

Article 20:

When a patient is referred to one of the institutions in which the physician holds shares, the following should be observed:

1. The establishment should offer outstanding services that are not inferior to others in type or quality.
2. Referral to the establishment should be warranted by the incapability to deal with the patient's condition. The patient should not stay in the establishment he is referred to longer than necessary.
3. The physician should inform the patient that he, the physician, has a financial interest in the establishment to which he is referring the patient. In all cases the patient should be given the freedom of choice.

Article 21:

A patient should be checked out of the health establishment where he is receiving treatment only if his health condition allows it, or if he expresses his desire to leave despite being made aware of the consequences of his departure. In the latter case, a written statement should be obtained from the patient or, when he is not fully competent, from a family member of the first, second, third, or fourth degree of kinship and should be included in the patient's medical file.

Article 22:

A physician should not take an active part in terminating the life of a patient, even if it is at his or his guardian's request, and even if the reason is severe deformity; a hopeless, incurable disease; or severe, unbearable pain that cannot be alleviated by the usual pain killers. The physician should urge his patient to endure and remind him of the reward of those who tolerate their suffering.

Article 23:

A physician should cooperate with the other members of the medical team involved in providing care to the patient, and he should make available to them, whenever he is asked to do so, what information he has of the patient's condition and of the method of treatment he, the physician, has been using.

Article 24:

A physician should give to his patient an advance notice of any travel or absence plans he has and should tell him how to act when the physicians is absent. Under all circumstances, a suitable physician should be available in the absence of the doctor in charge of the patient to guarantee that the latter continues to receive treatment.

Article 25:

If invited to examine a patient being treated by a colleague, a physician should observe the following rules:

1. Even if there are no clear justifications, he should answer the invitation for consultation if it comes from the attending doctor. The consulted physician should disclose his findings to his colleague, rather than to the patient himself.
2. The consulted physician should reassure the patient, reduce his anxiety, and use his own discretion in determining what the patient should know and what should be reserved to the attending physician.
3. He should guard against any word or suggestion that implies any discredit or disparagement of the attending doctor or any underestimation of the latter's efforts in treating the patient. This should be particularly observed when the consulted physician's point of view differs from that of the attending doctor.
4. If the patient desires to terminate the service of the original physician, the latter has to be informed of that decision.
5. The attending doctor has the right to consult another colleague in the same field of specialization after the first consulted doctor has given his opinion and made his recommendations.

Article 26:

When a physician is commissioned to extend health care to individuals with limited freedom, he should abide by the following:

1. He should provide them with the same type and level of health care available to persons with no freedom restrictions.
2. He should not, actively or indirectly, perform anything that amounts to collaboration in torture procedures or other forms of cruel or inhuman treatment, or to

complicity in, enticement of, or keeping silent about such acts.

3. He should never use his professional knowledge or skills to help in the interrogation of people with restricted freedom in a way that is hazardous to their physical or psychological condition. Nor should he participate in any restricting procedure against them.
4. If he notices that a restricted person has been or is being subjected to torture or abuse, he should report it to the proper authorities.

Article 27:

Physicians who attend minors, should explain to these patients, each to the extent of his comprehension skill, the nature of the medical procedures or interventions applied.

Article 28:

When treating a child patient, a physician should defend his patient's interest if the family or relatives of the child fail to appreciate the case fully or if they fail to carry out their duty towards the child.

Article 29:

A physician attending a patient who takes any addictive material should deal with his patient seriously, carefully, and confidentially. He should endeavor to apply the best treatment procedures to his patient, whether in special institutions or at his own office if treatment equipment is available. In doing so, the physicians should observe the laws in force.

CHAPTER THREE: MEDICAL CONFIDENTIALITY

Article 30:

A physician may not disclose a personal secret that has come to his knowledge through the performance of his profession, whether the patient confides the secret to him, or the physician comes to know it in the course of his work, except in the following situations and similar cases that are stipulated in national laws:

1. if disclosure of a person's secret is done at his own request, which should be in writing or if disclosure of a secret is in the interest of the patient or of society;
2. if the laws in operation require disclosure of the secret, or an order to disclose it is made by a judicial authority;
3. if the purpose of disclosing the secret is to prevent a crime, in which case the disclosure should be strictly to the official authority concerned and to no other party;
4. if disclosure of a person's secret is in the interest of the patient's spouse, provided that it is made to the couple, and not to one without the other;
5. if the physician makes the disclosure in defending himself before a judiciary authority at its request and in as much as the defense requires; and
6. if the purpose of disclosing the secret is to prevent the spread of an infectious disease that would be harmful to social members, provided that the disclosure is made only to the concerned health authority.

Article 31:

When minor patients ask to be treated in secret, without their guardians knowing about it, the physician in charge should attempt to find out the reason behind the desire to keep the condition secret from the minor's family, should encourage the patients to get their family involved, and should correct any misconceptions the minor may have.

Article 32:

A physician may treat underage patients and may refrain from revealing any information that may cause harm to the minors in question, unless the existing laws stipulate otherwise.

Article 33:

Before releasing any information about a patient to third parties – such as researchers, pharmaceutical companies, and data collecting institutions – a physician should obtain the patient's informed consent in writing.

Article 34:

A patient has the right to obtain, upon request, a detailed report of his medical condition from his attending physician, based on the latter's own examination. The physician, however, should not write a medical report or give testimony on a subject not within his field of specialization, and his report or testimony should be true to the facts that he has learned through his own examination of the patient.

Article 35:

A physician may discuss a patient's case, diagnosis, and treatment, as well as the expected development of the case, with the patient's lawyer, provided that the patient or his guardian consent to that.

Article 36:

A physician may release information about a patient to

an insurance agent, provided that the patient or a legal representative of his should consent in writing. The information released should be only what relates to the insurance item involved. Before disclosing the information, the physician should make the patient aware of the consequences of such disclosure.

Article 37:

Physicians and all health staff members should do their utmost to guard the confidentiality of medical reports, including those stored in computer memory. Data should be entered into computers only by authorized people. The date and timing of adding any new data entries should be scheduled, and the person adding or modifying an entry should sign his name.

Article 38:

A patient or a representative of his should be informed when the health institution has a computer data base before the physician sends any data related to that patient to the computer department for storage. All parties who can access the data should be specified in advance. Revealing such information to the patient is an important element in getting his informed consent. Security measures, in proportion with the extent of sensitivity of the patient's data, should be taken to prevent any information leakage or any access to the database by unauthorized persons.

Article 39:

A patient or someone acting on his behalf should be informed before any report containing data that concerns the patient is distributed. Moreover, the attending doctor should be informed before any data or information relating to the patient is released to parties outside health care establishments, so that no disclosure of such data is made before the patient's consent is obtained.

Article 40:

Confidential information may be disclosed only to parties that keep it highly secret, in accordance with existing laws and regulations, and should be restricted to the data that meets the purpose specified when such disclosure is requested and to the time period specified. All such parties should be told that releasing the data to them does not mean they can pass these data to other parties, apply them for purposes other than what is specified when the data are requested, or use them against the patient's interest.

Article 41:

Computers should be equipped with backup and retrieval functions to avoid the loss of any data when some failure occurs in the programs or server used. Before a file is deleted, a printout should be submitted to the attending physician.

Article 42:

As soon as the attending physician receives a copy (a printout or a copy saved on a hard, compact, or floppy disk) of stored data, they should be deleted from the data base. The computer department should inform the attending doctor in writing that the deletion is done. A patient has the right to request the deletion of some of the data that concern him, subject to the laws in operation.

Article 43:

Very strict measures should be taken to prevent free access to the database, including the introduction of systems to discover any attempts to break into it by any unauthorized party.

CHAPTER FOUR: PHYSICIAN DUTIES TOWARDS SOCIETY

Article 44:

A physician should be an active member of society, interacting with it, influencing it, and taking interest in its affairs. His actions should also aim at satisfying God, and he should never get involved in any practices or behaviors that are unethical or harmful to society.

Article 45:

A physician should help society in dealing with elements of health enhancement, disease prevention, and protection of the natural and social environment. He should live up to his responsibility of promoting health awareness and education. He should take advantage of patient visits to offer advice on the proper styles of healthy life and to discourage all health-damaging life styles.

Article 46:

A physician should use his skill, knowledge, and experience to improve the quality of health services offered to the community.

Article 47:

A physician should endeavor to conserve health resources and use them in the best possible way and make optimal utilization of these resources, setting an example by his own behavior.

Article 48:

A physician, particularly when holding an official position, should take an active part in setting regulations, drawing health policies, and solving health problems, thus serving the interests of the community.

Article 49:
In the case of communicable diseases, a physician should follow relevant regulations, report cases of the disease to the proper authorities, and take all necessary measures.

CHAPTER FIVE: SOCIAL ISSUES

Utilization of Health Resources

Article 50:
Physicians bear the moral responsibility of employing all the professional experience they have to contribute to the decision-making process relevant to the distribution or rational utilization of limited medical resources in a way that protects patient interests and observes the principle of equity and equality.

Article 51:
The decision-making process concerning the distribution of limited medical resources should be based on the medical, scientific, and moral criteria applicable to the patient's health condition. These criteria include the extent of the patient's need for these limited resources, the duration of treatment, the likelihood of the patient's death, and, in certain cases, the amount of materials needed for the treatment to succeed.

Article 52:
A physician should not abandon his role as a patron of the patient entrusted with the task of guarding the patient's interest, particularly what concerns his treatment needs.

Article 53:

Patients who are denied certain medical resources have the right to know the reason for that. The policies practiced by some institutions of controlling scarce medical resources should be made known to the public. Moreover, these policies should be subject to the occasional revision of supervisory medical authorities.

Article 54:

A physician should not make a decision to admit a patient into a hospital, to discharge him, or to engage in any diagnosis or treatment procedure for the purpose of financial gain and without considering the actual need of the patient.

Article 55:

Physicians should prescribe medicines and medical aids, equipment, or other approved therapeutic methods only on the basis of medical considerations and patient needs and not under any type of pressure. A physician should not accept offers from other parties.

Article 56:

Every physician should endeavor to suggest policies aimed at equity in providing a decent standard of health care to all social members.

Article 57:

When selecting the preventive and therapeutic procedures and approaches which guarantee a decent standard of health care, physicians should observe the following ethical considerations:

1. the extent to which a patient benefits from the course of treatment,

2. the likelihood of benefit to the patient from the treatment,
3. the duration of that benefit,
4. the cost of the treatment, and
5. the number of patients benefiting from the treatment.

Patients With AIDS or Any Other Communicable Disease

Article 58:

It is the right of a patient infected with AIDS or with another communicable disease to receive the treatment and health care that his condition warrants, regardless of the cause of his infection. The physician is obliged to treat such a patient, taking the necessary precautions to protect himself and others.

Article 59:

A patient with AIDS or another communicable infection should be told how to prevent further deterioration of his condition and to avoid transmitting the disease to other people.

Article 60:

A physician who knows that he himself is HIV-positive or a carrier of some other communicable disease must not engage in any activity that involves a clear risk of transmitting the disease to his patients, his colleagues, or others. In such a case, the physician should consult the proper authority at the health establishment where he works to determine the tasks he may perform.

Article 61:

Taking the stipulation of Article 28 (d) into consideration, a physician should inform the spouse of a patient with AIDS or another communicable disease of his or her spouse's infection in accordance with existing regulations and in the presence of the patient.

Euthanasia and Physician-Assisted Death

Article 62:

Human life is sacred, and it should never be wasted except in the cases specified by *Sharīʿa* and the law. This is a question that lies completely outside the scope of the medical profession. This particularly applies to the following cases of what is known as mercy killing:

1. the deliberate killing of a person who voluntarily asks for his life to be ended,
2. physician-assisted suicide, and
3. the deliberate killing of newly born infants with deformities that may or may not threaten their lives.

Article 63:

The following cases are examples of what is not covered by the term "mercy killing":

1. the termination of a treatment when its continuation is confirmed, by the medical committee concerned, to be useless, and this includes artificial respirators, in as much as allowed by existing laws and regulations;
2. declining to begin a treatment that is confirmed to be useless; and
3. The intensified administration of a strong medication to stop a severe pain, although it is known that this medication might ultimately end the patient's life.

Abortion

Article 64:

A physician should not cause a pregnant woman to abort,

unless when medical considerations call for it, such as when the mother's health and life is being threatened. Abortion, however, is permissible before the end of the fourth month of pregnancy when it is definitely established that continued pregnancy involves a risk of a serious injury to the mother. This, however, should be confirmed by a medical committee of specialists of no less than three members, one of whom familiar with the disease for which the termination of pregnancy is recommended. The committee members should prepare a report in which they specify the definite risk that threatens the mother's health if the pregnancy continues. When abortion is recommended, the mother and her husband or guardian should be advised of the fact and their written consent obtained. All other exceptional cases, including pregnancy resulting from rape, should be referred to the authorities of Islamic *fatwa* and legislation, and to the laws and regulations in force.

Organ Transplants

Article 65:

The procedure of transplanting organs from a living donor or a dead body is one of the most important methods of life saving, a method in which the mutual love, sympathy, and compassion of social members is clearly manifested, provided that Islamic ethical and legal controls are exercised.

Article 66:

When physicians declare the death of a certain patient who may have donated some of his organs, they should not get directly involved in removing these organs from his body or in the consequent implanting procedures, and should not be the physicians attending the potential recipients of these organs.

Article 67:

Before initiating the procedures of organ transplantation in accordance with the applicable legal regulations, a physician should explain to the donor the medical consequences and hazards he may be exposed to as a result of the procedure. He should also obtain, before the operation, the necessary statements from the donor that indicate his awareness of all such consequences.

Article 68:

It is not permissible to transplant an organ from the body of a living minor to another individual. An exception may be made in the case of regenerative tissues if the law of the nation allows it.

Article 69:

It is not permissible to subject the human body and its components to commercial transactions, and any commerce in organs, tissues, cells, or human genes is prohibited. It is forbidden to advertise the need or the availability of organs in return for a price to be paid or received. A physician should under no circumstances take part in such commercial traffic. Physicians, as well as all other health professionals, should not undertake organ transplant procedures if there is anything that suggests to them that the organs to be transplanted were subject to commercial transactions.

Article 70:

A physician who undertakes an organ transplant procedure should guarantee that full medical care is provided to the donor, ensuring that he would not suffer in any way as a result of that procedure.

Article 71:
Physicians are forbidden to transplant testicles or ovaries.

Cases of Violence

Article 72:
A physician has the right to report to the proper authorities the cases of violence he learns of in the course of his work, particularly when the victim is a juvenile, a woman, or a helpless person who cannot defend himself either because of old age or due to physical or mental illness, if the physician believes that such an action on his part protects the victim from further physical, mental or psychological violence.

CHAPTER SIX: ADVERTISEMENT AND THE MEDIA

Article 73:
What is meant by advertisement and the media is for the doctor to resort, directly or through an intermediary, to conventional visual, auditory, or printed advertisement media – such as newspapers, magazines, visual or auditory broadcasting, and ordinary or electronic mail, as well as other media – to transmit information that introduces the physician, his field of specialization, and his experience.

Article 74:
An advertisement may list the physician's degrees, fields of specialization, professional history, experience, and other objective data, as long as none of them is misleading.

Article 75:
An advertisement should not include information with the purpose of misleading the receiver, giving a false image, or hiding the side effects of an advertised treatment. Likewise, the advertisement should not be

indecent, jeopardize the dignity of the profession, or offend professional colleagues.

Article 76:
A physician should not claim for himself or his establishment to have diagnostic or therapeutic skills or services for which he is not qualified or which he is not licensed to perform.

Article 77:
A physician should not exploit a patient's ignorance in the field of medicine to mislead him by claiming that the physician is capable of performing certain diagnostic or therapeutic procedures that have no scientific basis, or by offering a guarantee to cure certain diseases. The content of an advertisement should include only true information, with no exaggeration, and should not include statements in any form that imply superiority to others or discredit them.

Article 78:
A physician should have his name, qualifications, address, and contact data in any local or national directory or in other, similar highly regarded publications. Physicians and specialists who work in the private sector may notify their colleagues and other health establishments of the services and practices they perform.

Article 79:
Although it is necessary to use printed, auditory, and visual media extensively for the purpose of health education and health awareness, it is also necessary to take all precautions to avoid abusing these media for the promotion of a physician in a manner contradictory to the advertisement controls listed above.

Article 80:
Physicians who work in private-sector health establishments or specialized clinics should avoid advertising the services offered by these establishments in statements in the mass media, papers or articles they write, and the like.

CHAPTER SEVEN: PHYSICIAN DUTIES TOWARDS THE ESTABLISHMENT HE WORKS AT

Article 81:
A physician should protect the reputation and dignity of the establishment at which he works, and should actively contribute to the organization, development, and improvement of the establishment and its performance.

Article 82:
He should abide by the laws, bylaws, and regulations applied in that establishment.

Article 83:
He should safeguard its property and use it most rationally.

CHAPTER EIGHT: RELATIONS WITH COLLEAGUES

Article 84:
A physician should behave politely and decently towards his colleagues, and base his relations with them on reciprocal trust, constructive cooperation, and mutual respect. He should refrain from direct criticism of a colleague in front of patients. He should endeavor to teach physicians in his medical team and trainees working with him, and should be precise and honest in evaluating them, giving every member his due, without exaggerated praise and without giving the same evaluation to diligent and negligent staff members.

Article 85:
If a physician finds that the intervention of one of his colleagues or superiors may undermine his proper medical performance, or if he fears that such an intervention may be hazardous to the patient, he should have an oral discussion of the matter with the colleague or superior concerned. When they fail to reach an agreement, the matter should be referred in writing to the proper authority for consideration and for making the proper decision.

Article 86:
A physician should not charge any fees for examining or treating a colleague, or a member of the immediate family of a colleague (a spouse, a parent, or a child), unless it is a reimbursement for additional expenses paid by the examining or attending physician.

Article 87:
A physician should never try to compete with a colleague in a dishonest manner in any professional undertaking.

Article 88:
A physician should settle amicably any differences he may have with a colleague. If no settlement is reached, the matter should be referred to the proper authority for a final decision.

Article 89:
When a physician substitutes for a colleague at the latter's office, he should never take advantage of the situation to serve his own interests. He should inform every patient, before examining him, that he is substituting temporarily for the office owner.

Article 90:

When a physician is asked to visit a patient being treated by another doctor who could not be contacted, the new physician should allow his colleague, as soon as he is back, to carry on with the treatment and inform him of the measures taken, unless the patient or his family want the new doctor to continue.

Article 91:

A physician should never demand any share of the fees from one of his colleagues or assistants, unless he has actually taken part in the examination or treatment.

Article 92:

A physician should respect his non-physician professional colleagues, appreciate their role in the treatment extended to the patient, and refrain from criticizing them in front of patients. He should base his relations with them on reciprocal trust and constructive cooperation to serve the patients' interest. He should endeavor to teach and train them, and make sure they abide by the principles of professional ethics.

Article 93:

In dealing with members of the supporting medical staff, a physician should observe the following:

1. He should respect and honor them and make any professional observations to them in a friendly and proper manner;
2. give any instructions to them in writing and with no ambiguity, and make sure, as much as possible, that these instructions are carried out;
3. listen objectively and without any condescension

to their observations, criticism, and reservations concerning his treatment instructions; and

4. help in and contribute to their scientific and career advancement and in the updating of their knowledge and skills.

CHAPTER NINE: PHYSICIAN RIGHTS

Article 94:

A physician has the right to be provided by society with the means of training, acquiring scientific qualification, and drawing regulations that guarantee the high quality of health establishments and their performance, in accordance with internationally recognized standards.

Article 95:

A physician has the right to have the opportunity of continuing education through conferences, seminars, scientific gatherings, libraries, scholarships, courses for the refinement of information and skills, and other means. He should not fail to keep up and interact with the latest professional developments in his field of specialization.

Article 96:

A physician has the right to be treated by society with due respect and appreciation and be accorded all the human and civil rights enjoyed by others, normal people. He should not to be suspended or prevented from practicing unless this is done within the limits of the law. During any investigation or judicial procedure, his dignity must be respected, he should have legal protection, and he should enjoy the right to defend himself when he commits any violation of the law.

Article 97:
A physician has the responsibility to extend the needed care to a patient of his but not to cure him.

Article 98:
When a physician is treating a patient for a fee, it is permissible for them to reach an agreement that payment is contingent on recovery.

Article 99:
A physician should not be influenced physically or morally or forced to perform or refrain from performing a task related to his professional practice, unless this is done within the limits of the law. He should not be forced to testify against his conscience and should enjoy the full immunity due to him when invited to give an opinion or a technical testimony before a court of law or an investigation authority.

Article 100:
A physician may refer a patient to another doctor or health establishment for diagnosis or treatment, in accordance with the regulations that cover such cases, taking into consideration the following:

1. The doctor to whom the patient is referred should have specialized experience that can benefit the patient.
2. The first physician should communicate, verbally or in writing, to the doctor to whom he is referring the patient, the information he believes to be necessary for continuing the treatment.
3. The referral should not be prompted by a belief that the patient's case is incurable or by financial motivation.

Article 101:

A physician has a claim on the health authority members to assist him in carrying out his instructions, to discuss things with him in order to get an explanation whenever possible, and to observe and never go beyond the limits of their profession in their fields of specialization.

CHAPTER TEN: PHYSICIAN DUTIES TOWARDS HIS PROFESSION

Article 102:

A physician should maintain the dignity and reputation of the medical profession, observe the standards of medical practice, and strive to upgrade the cognitive and scientific aspects of his profession through research, studies, articles, and continuing education and training.

Article 103:

In dealing with a patient, a physician should avoid everything that might undermine his integrity and honesty, or discredit the medical profession. He should strive not to lose the patient's confidence through resorting to deception or fraud, having an inappropriate affair with the patient or one of his/her family members, or making material gain through irregular methods. He should also refrain from seeking fame at the expense of professional ethics and principles.

Article 104:

A physician should give testimony to concerned authorities whenever he is required to do so. Moreover, he should not fail to write honest and precise medical reports according to existing regulation.

Article 105:

A physician infected with some communicable disease must not engage in any activity that involves a clear risk of transmitting the disease to his patients, his colleagues, or others. In such a case, the physician should consult the competent authority at the health establishment where he works to determine the tasks he may perform.[1]

Article 106:

A physician should refer a patient to a practitioner of complementary (folk, traditional, alternative) medicine only when the latter is licensed to practice such medicine by the proper health authority.

Article 107:

A physician should serve as an example in maintaining his health and in all his actions. He should take all necessary precautions to protect himself from all potential hazards while practicing his profession.

Article 108:

A physician should never

1. use intermediaries or illegitimate means, whether paid for or not, to attract patients;
2. allow his name to be used for the promotion of medicines, drugs, or any other type of treatment, or for commercial purposes in any form;
3. demand any kind of fee or compensation in return for undertaking to prescribe particular medicines or equipment to patients or for referring them to a health establishment, therapy clinic, nursing home,

---

(1) Translator's note: This article is a duplicate copy of Article 60.

pharmacy, or any specific place of medical tests and examination or of trading in medical aids and equipment, or act in any way as an agent for another physician or health institution;

4. offer medical consultations for companies that offer such consultation through communication media;
5. engage or participate in telemedicine consultations for telecommunication companies providing this service;[1] and
6. sell any medications, prescriptions, or medical equipment or aids in his clinic, while practicing his job, for commercial purposes.

(1) Translator's note: This item is not included in the formal English copy published on the website of the Islamic organization for Medical Sciences. Moreover, the IOMS online version of this code contains 107 articles.

BIBLIOGRAPHY

Sciences of the Qur᾽ān

al-Qurṭubī, *al-Jāmiʿ li-aḥkām al-Qur'ān* Cairo: Matḅaʿat Dār al-Kutub al-Misṛīyah, 1387 AH.

al-Rāzī, *al-Tafsīr al-kabīr*, Dār Iḥyā' al-turāth al-ʿʿArabī; Beirut: Dār al-Kutub al-ʿʿIlmīyah, 1421 AH

al-Ṭabarī, *Jāmiʿ al-bayān*, ed., Maḥmūd Shākir, Cairo: Dār al-Maʿārif; ʿMaṭbaʿat Būlāq, 1328 AH.

Collections of the Sunnah

ʿAbd al-Razzāq, *al-Muṣannaf,* Beirut: al-Maktab al-Islāmī.

Abū Bakr ʿAbd al-Razzāq, al-Muṣannaf, ed. Ḥabīburraḥmān Aʿẓamī, Beirut: al-Maktab al-Islāmī.

Abū Dāwūd, al-Sunan, along with *ʿAwn al-maʿbūd* (al-Medinah: al-Maktabah al-Salafīyah).

Aḥmad, *Musnad* (Beirut: al-Maktab al-Islāmī, 1391 AH).

al-Bayhaqī, *al-Sunan al-Kubrā* (Ḥaidarābād: Dār al-Maʿārif).

al-Bukhārī, *Ṣaḥīḥ along with Fatḥ al-bārī*, (Cairo: al-Maktabah al-Salafīyah, 1380 AH).

al-Dārimī, Sunan (Egypt, 1st ed., 1386 AH).

al-Dāraquṭnī, Sunan, ed. al-Sayyid ʿAbd Allāh al-Yamānī (Cairo: Dār al-maḥāsin, 1386).

al-Ḥākim, al-Mustadrak (Ḥaidarābād, 1340 AH).

al-Nasā'ī, al-Sunan, along with Zahr al-rubá (Cairo: ʿMaṭbaʿat ʿĪsá al-Bābī al-Ḥalabī, 1383 AH).

al-Shāfiʿī, Musnad (Qatar: Wizārat al-Awqāf wa-al-Shu'ūn al-Islāmīyah, 1428/1999).

al-Suyūṭī, al-Jāmiʿ al-ṣaghīr (Cairo: al-Maṭbaʿah al-Khayrīyah, 1321 AH).

al-Tirmidhī, al-Sunan, along with *Tuḥfat al-aḥwadhī* (Cairo: al-Fajjālah, 2nd ed., 1385 AH).
Ibn Abī Shaybah, *al-Muṣannaf* (Beirut: Dār Qurṭubah, 1427 AH).
Ibn Mājah, al-Sunan, ed. Muḥammad Fu'ād ʿAbd al-Bāqī (Cairo: ʿMaṭbaʿat ʿĪsá al-Bābī al-Ḥalabī, 1972).
Mālik, al-Muwaṭṭa' (Beirut: Dār al-Maʿrifah, 1420 AH).
Muslim, *Ṣaḥīḥ,* ed. Muḥammad Fu'ād ʿAbd al-Bāqī (Cairo: ʿMaṭbaʿat ʿĪsá al-Bābī al-Ḥalabī, 1374 AH).

Other Sources

ʿAbd-al-Karīm b. Muḥammad al- Rāfiʿī, Fatḥ al-ʿAzīz sharḥ al-Wajīz, printed along with al-Majmūʿ (Cairo: Sharikat al-ʿUlamā').
ʿAbd Allāh ibn ʿUmar al-Bayḍāwī, al-Ghāyah al-qaṣwá fī dirāyat al-Fatwā, ed. ʿAlī Muḥyī al-Dīn al-Qaradāghī (Dār al-Iṣlāḥ, 1982).
ʿAbd al-Raḥmān ibn Muḥammad al- ʿĀṣimī, ḥāshiyat al-Rawḍ al-murbiʿ (Riyadh: al-Maṭābiʿ al-Ahlīyah lil-Ūfsit, 1392 AH).
Abū ʿAbd Allāh Muḥammad ibn ʿAbd al-Raḥmān al-Dimashqī, Raḥmat al-ummah fī ikhtilāf al-a'immah (Cairo: ʿMaṭbaʿat ʿĪsá al-Bābī al-Ḥalabī,2nd ed., 1386 AH).
Abū ʿAbd Allāh al-Shaykh Muḥammad Aḥmad ʿIllaysh, Fatḥ al-ʿAlī al-Mālik fī al-fatwá ʿalá madhhab al-Imām Mālik (Cairo: ʿMaṭbaʿat ʿĪsá al-Bābī al-Ḥalabī, 1378 AH).
Abū al-baqā' al-Ḥusaynī, al-Kulliyāt (Beirut: Mu'assasat al-Risālah, 1413 AH).
Abū Bakr al-Rāzī al-Jaṣṣāṣ, Aḥkām al-Qur'ān (Beirut: Dār al-Fikr).
Abū Yūsuf al-qāḍī, al-Kharāj, ed. Dr. Muḥammad Ibrāhīm al-Bannā.
Abū Zakarīyā Yaḥyá ibn Sharaf al-Nawawī, Rawḍat al-ṭālibīn (Damascus: al-Maktab al-Islāmī).
Aḥmad al-Dardīr, al-Sharḥ al-ṣaghīr ʿalá Aqrab al-masālik ilá madhhab al-Imām Mālik (UAE: Ministry of Endowment, 1989).

Aḥmad al-Raysūnī, Naẓarīyat al-maqāṣid, International Institute of Islamic Thought.
Aḥmad b. Muḥammad al-Ṣāwī, Bulghat al-Sālik li-Aqrab al-masālik ilā madhhab al-Imām Mālik (Cairo: ʿMaṭbaʿat ʿĪsá al-Bābī al-Ḥalabī).
Aḥmad b. Yaḥyá al-Murtaḍá, al-Baḥr al-zakhkhār (Beirut: Muʾassasat al-Risālah, 2nd, 1366 AH).
Aḥmad ʿUmīrah, ḥāshiyat ʿUmīrah (Cairo: ʿĪsá al-Bābī al-Ḥalabī).
ʿAláʾ al-Dīn Abī al-Ḥasan ʿAlī ibn Sulaymān, al-Mardāwī, al-Inṣāf fī maʿrifat al-rājiḥ mina al-khilāf, ed. Muḥammah Ḥāmid al-Fiqī, edition of al-sunnah al-Muḥammadīyah, 1375 AH.
al-Albānī, Irwā› al-ghalīl (Beirut: Dār al-Fikr al-Islamī).
al-Āmidī, *al-Iḥkām Fī Uṣūl al-Aḥkām* (Cairo: Maṭbaʿat Muḥammad ʿAlī Ṣubayḥ, 1968).
al-Bazdawī, Kashf al-asrār (KSA, 1430 AH).
al- Fayyūmī, al-Miṣbāḥ al-munīr (Cairo: ʿMaṭbaʿat ʿĪsá al-Bābī al-Ḥalabī).
al-Ghazālī, *al-Mustaṣfá* (Cairo: al-Maktabah al-Tijārīyah, 1356 AH).
______, *al-Wasīṭ fī al-madhhab,* ed. ʿAlī Muḥyī al-Dīn al-Qaradāghī (Dār al-Iʿtiṣām; Qatar's Ministry of Endowments*),* manuscript of Dār al-Kutub, no. 212, 206.
______, *Iḥyāʾ ʿulūm al-dīn* (Cairo: ʿĪsá al-Bābī al-Ḥalabī).
al-Ḥākim, Muḥammad ibn ʿAbd Allāh al-Nīsābūrī, al-Mustadrak (Ḥaidarābād, 1340 AH).
al-Ḥaṣkafī, al-Durr al-mukhtār sharḥ Tanwīr al-abṣār (Cairo: ʿMaṭbaʿat ʿĪsá al-Bābī al-Ḥalabī).
ʿAlī al-Nadawī, *al-qawāʿid al-fiqhīyah* (Damascus: Dār al-Qalam).
ʿAlī Ḥaidar, Durar al-ḥukkām fī sharḥ Majallat al-aḥkām (Riyadh: Dār ʿĀlam al-Kutub, 2003).
al-Ḥamawī, al-aḥkām al-nabawīyah fī al-ṣināʿah al-ṭibbīyah, ed. Aḥmed al-Jamal (Beirut: Dār Ibn Ḥazm).
al-Ḥaṭṭāb, Mawāhib al-Jalīl fī sharḥ Mukhtaṣar al-Shaykh Khalīl (Beirut: Dār al-Kutub al-ʿIlmīyah, 1st ed., 1995)

al-Isnawī, al-Tamhīd fī takhrīj al-furū' 'alá al-uṣūl, ed. Dr. Hītū (Beirut: Mu'assasat al-Risālah).

al-Juwaynī, al-Furūq, Manuscript of al-Sulayminyyah, no. 146 Uṣūl Fiqh.

______, al-kāfiyah Fī al-jadal, ed. Dr. Fawqīyah.

al-Jurjānī, *al-ta'rīfāt* (Beirut: Maktabat Libnān, 1985).

al-Kasānī, badā'i' al-ṣanā'i' (Cairo: al-Imām).

al-Khaṭīb al-Baghdādī al-Faqīh wa-al-mutafaqqih (Dammam, Dār Ibn al-Jawzī, 1996).

al-Khatīb al-Shirbīnī, Mughnī al-muḥtāj (Cairo: 'Maṭba'at 'Īsá al-Bābī al-Ḥalabī, 1377 AH)

al-Mawardī, al-nukat wa-al-'uyūn, Kuwaiti Ministry of Endowment.

al-Mawwāq, al-Tāj wa al-Iklīl, with Mawāhib al-Jalīl (Egypt: dār al-sa'ādah, 1329 AH)

al-Nawawī, *ādāb* al-*'ālim* wa-al-muta'allim (Tehran: Dār Iḥsān).

______, *al-Majmū'* (Cairo: Sharikat al-'ulamā').

______, Sharḥ Ṣaḥīḥ Muslim (Cairo: al-Maṭba'ah al-Miṣrīyah).

al-Qaradāghī, 'Alī al-Muḥammadī, *Fiqh al-Qaḍāyā al-Ṭibbīyah al-Mu'āṣirah* (Beirut: Dār al-Bashā'ir al-Islāmīyah, 2nd ed., 2008).

al-Qaraḍāwī, *al-ḥalāl wa-al-ḥarām* (Beirut: al-Maktab al-Islāmī).

______, *Dawr al-qiyam wa-al-akhlāq fī al-iqtiṣād al-Islāmī* (Cairo: Maktabat Wahbah, 1415 AH)

al-Qarāfī, al-Furūq (Beirut: Dār al-Ma'rifah).

Āl Taymīyah, al-Musawwadah fī uṣūl al-fiqh, Dār al-Kitāb al-'Arabī.

______, *al-Iḥkām fī tamyīz al-fatāwā* 'an *al-aḥkām wa taṣarrufāt al-qāḍī wa al-imā*, ed. *'Abd* al-Fattāḥ Abū Ghaddah.

______, al-Dhakhīrah (Beirut: Dār al-Gharb al-Islāmī).

al-Rāghib al-Aṣfahānī, *al-mufradāt fī gharīb al-Qur'ān* (Beirut: Dār al-Ma'rifah).

al-Rāzī, al-maḥṣūl (Beirut: Mu'assasat al-Risālah, 1997).

al-Sarakhsī, al-Mabsūṭ (Cairo: Maṭba'at al-Sa'āda, 1331 AH).

al-Shāfi'ī, Aḥkām al-Qur'ān (Beirut: Dār al-Kutub al-'Ilmīyah, 1395 AH).

______, *al-Umm* (Beirut: Dār al-Ma'rifah) & (Cairo: Dār al-Sha'b).

al-Shāṭib, al-Muwāfaqāt, ed. 'Abd Allāh Darāz (Beirut: Dār al-Ma'rifah, 1415 AH)

al-Shawkānī, Fatḥ al-Qadīr (Beirut: 'Ālam al-Kutub).

______, Irshād al-fuḥūl ilá taḥqīq al-ḥaqq min 'ilm al-uṣūl (Cairo: Dār al-Kutabī, 1413 AH).

______, Nayl al-awṭār (Cairo: Maktabat al-kullīyāt al-Azharīyah, 1398 AH).

al-Shīrāzī, al-Muhadhdhab (Cairo: Maṭba'at 'Īsá al-Bābī al-Ḥalabī)

al-Suyūṭī, *ād*ab al-futyā, ed. Muḥyī Hilāl (Baghdad: al-Irshād).

______, *al-Ashbāh wa-al-naẓā'ir* (Beirut: Dār al-Kitāb al-'Arabī, 1407 AH)

______, *al-Ashbāh wa-al-naẓā'ir* (Cairo: Maṭba'at 'Īsá al-Bābī al-Ḥalabī).

al-Wansharīsī, al-Mi'yār al-mu'rib (Morocco, 1981).

______, īḍāḥ al-masālik īla Qawā'id al-Imām Mālik, ed. Aḥmad Abū Ṭāhir (Morocco: Ṣundūq Iḥyā' al-Turāth, 1400 AH).

al-Zanjānī, Takhrīj al-furū' 'alá al-uṣūl, ed. Muḥammad Adīb Ṣāliḥ, university of Damascus, 1382 AH.

al-Zarkashī, al-baḥr al-muḥīṭ, edition of Kuwait.

al-Zarkashī, Badr al-Dīn Muḥammad ibn Bahādur ibn *'Abd* Allāh al-Shāfi'ī, al-Manthūr fī al-qawā'id, ed. Taysīr Fā'iq (Mu'assasat al-Khalīj, Kuwaiti Ministry of Endowment, 1402 AH).

al- Zayla'ī Naṣb al-rāyah *fī* takhrīj aḥādīth al-Hidāyah (Beirut: Iḥyā' al-Turāth al-*'Arabī*).

al-Zurqānī, sharḥ al-Zurqānī (UAE: Ministry of Endowment).

Bakr Abū Zayd, al-madkhal almufaṣṣal ilá Madhhab al-Imām Aḥmad (Medina: Dār al-'Āṣimah, 1417 AH).

Fakhr al-Dīn al-Zayla'ī, Tabyīn al-Ḥaqā'iq Sharḥ Kanz ad-Daqā'iq (Egypt: al-Sayyid, 'Umar, 1313 AH).

Fiqh Encyclopedia of Kuwait, (Published by Kuwaiti Ministry of Endowment and Islamic Affairs).

Group of Scholars, al-Fatawā Hindīyah (Beirut: Dār Iḥyā' al-Turāth al-'Arabī).

Ibn 'Abd al-Barr, al-Istidhkār al-jāmi' li-madhāhib fuqahā' al-amṣār wa-'ulamā' al-aqṭār, Mu'assasat al-Risālah.

______, jāmi' bayān al-'ilm wa-faḍlihi, ed. Abū al-Ashbāl Zuhayrī (Dammam: Dār Ibn al-Jawzī, 1414 AH).

Ibn Abī Ḥātim, Kitāb al-jarḥ wa-al-ta'dīl (Cairo: Dā'irat al-Ma'ārif al-'Uthmānīyah, 1952).

Ibn Abī Uṣaybi'a, 'Uyūn al-anbā' fī ṭabaqāt al-aṭibbā' (Beirut: Maktabat al-ḥayāh, 1965).

Ibn 'Ābidīn, Ḥāshiyat ibn 'Ābidīn (Cairo: Maṭba'at 'Īsá al-Bābī al-Ḥalabī).

______, Tanqīḥ al-Fatāwá al-Ḥāmidīyah (Beirut: Dār al-Ma'rifah, n.d.).

______, 'Uqūd rasm al-muftī (Damascus: Dār al-Risālah al-ūlá).

Ibn al-'Arabī, Aḥkām al-Qur'ān, ed. Bajāwī (Cairo: Maṭba'at 'Īsá al-Bābī al-Ḥalabī, 1387).

Ibn al-Najjār, Sharḥ al-Kawkab al-munīr (KSA, Jāmi'at al-Malik 'Abd al-'Azīz).

Ibn al-Qayyim, al-Ṭuruq al-ḥikmīyah fī al-siyāsah al-shar'īyah (Mecca: Dār 'Ālam al-Fawā'id, 1428 AH).

______, *I'lām al-muwaqqi'īn* 'an Rabb al-'Ālamīn, ed. Ṭaha *'Abd* al-Ra'ūf Sa'd (Cairo: Dār al-nahḍah al-jadīdah; Sharikat al-ṭib*ā*'ah al-fannīyah).

______, Sharḥ Sunan Abī Dāwud (Medina: al-Maktabah al-Salafīyah, 1388 AH).

Ibn al-Ṣalāḥ al-Shahrazūrī, *ādāb* al-muftī wa-al-mustaft*ī*, ed. Muwaffaq *'Abd* Allāh (al-Madīnah al-Munawwarah: Maktabat al-*'Ulūm* wa-al-Ḥikam: 1407 AH).

Ibn al-Subk*ī*, *al-Ashbāh wa-al-naẓā'ir* (Beirut: Dār al-Kutub al-'Ilmīyah, 1411 AH).

______, Fatawā Ibn al-Subk*ī* (Beirut: Dār al-Ma'rifah).

______, Jam' al-jawāmi' (Cairo: Dār Iḥyā' al-Kutub al-'Arabīyah).

Ibn Amir al-Ḥājj, al-Taqrīr wa al-Tahbīr (Beirut: Dār al-Kutub al-'Ilmīyah, 1999).

Ibn ʿĀshūr, *Maqāṣid al-sharīʿah al-Islāmīyah*, ed. Muḥammad al-Ḥabīb ibn al-Khūjah, edition of IIFA.

Ibn Ḥajar, Fath al-bārī fī sharḥ ṣaḥīḥ al-Bukhārī (Cairo: al-Maṭba'ah al-Salafīyah, 1380).

______, Talkhīṣ al-ḥabīr fī takhrīj aḥādīth al-Rāfi'ī al-kabīr (Medina: Sharikat al-ṭib*ā*'ah al-fannīyah).

Ibn Ḥazm, al-Muḥalla (Cairo: Maktabat al-Jumhūrīyah al-ʿ*Arabī*ya).

______, Iḥkām *al-Aḥkām fī uṣūl* al-*aḥkām* (Beirut: Dār al-*Āfāq* al-Jadīda, 1983).

Ibn Juzayy, al-Qawānīn al-fiqhīyah (Beirut: Dār al-Kitāb al-*'Arabī*).

Ibn Khaldūn, al-Muqaddimah, Egypt.

Ibn Manẓūr, Lisān al-*'Arab* (Cairo: Dār al-Ma'ārif).

Ibn Nujaym, *al-Ashbāh wa-al-naẓā'ir* (Cairo: Maṭbaʿat 'Īsá al-Bābī al-Ḥalabī).

______, *Al Baḥr al Ra'iq* (Beirut: Dār al-Ma'rifah).

Ibn Qudāmah, al-Kāfī (Beirut: al-Maktab al-Islāmī).

______, al-Mughnī (Maktabat al-Riyāḍ al-Ḥadīthah).

Ibn Rushd, al-Muqaddimāt al-mumahhidāt (Beirut: Dār al-Gharb al-Islāmī).

______, Bidāyat al-mujtahid wa-nihāyat al-muqtaṣid (Cairo: Maṭbaʿat 'Īsá al-Bābī al-Ḥalabī, 1395 AH).

Ibn Taymīyah, majmū' fatāwá Shaykh al-Islām Ibn Taymīyah, compiled by 'Abd al-Raḥmān b. Muḥammad b. Qāsim (KSA, 1398 AH).

Ibrāhīm al-Mālikī, Ṭabṣirat al-al-ḥukkām (Riyadh: 'Ālam al-Kutub, 2003).

'Izz al-Dīn b. 'Abd al-Salām, al-Qawā'id al-kubrá (Qatar: Ministry of Endowments).

______, al-Qawā'id al-kubrá, ed. Ḥammād, Nazīh & 'Uthmān Jum'ah (Damascus: Dār al-Qalam, 1421 AH).

______, Qawā'id al-aḥkām (Beirut: Dār al-Kutub al-'Ilmīyah).

Jalāl al-Dīn Muḥammad ibn Aḥmad Maḥallī, sharḥ al-Waraqāt fī uṣūl al-figh, 1420 AH.

Jamāl al-Dīn 'Aṭīyah, al-tafkīr al-fiqh (Cairo: Maṭbaʿat al-Madīnah).

Kamāl b. al-Humām, Fatḥ al-Qadīr (Cairo: al-Maṭba'ah al-Amīrīyah, 1316 AH).

Khayr al-Dīn al-Ziriklī, al-A'lām, edition of Beirut.

Muḥammad 'Abd Allāh Darāz, *Dustūr al-akhlāq fī al-Qur'ān*, trasn. 'Abd al-Ṣabūr Shāhīn (Beirut: Mu'assasat alrisāla, 1416).

Maḥmūd b. Isma'īl, Qāḍī Simāwnah, jāmi' al-Fuṣūlayn (Būlāq : Maṭba'at Būlāq, 1300 AH).

Mālik, al-Mudawwanah al-kubrá (Cairo: Maṭba'at al-Sa'ādah, 1323 AH).

Muḥammad b. Abī Bakr al-Rāzī, Mukhtār al-Ṣiḥāḥ (Cairo: Dār al-Ma'ārif).

Muḥammad b. Sa'd, al-Ṭabaqāt al-kubrá (Beirut: Dār al-'Ilm).

Muḥammad 'Alī al-Mālikī, Tahdhīb al-furūq wa al-qawā'id al-sunnīya (Beirut: Dār al-Ma'rifah).

Muḥammad al-Kharshī, Sharḥ al-Kharshī (Cairo: al-Maṭba'ah al-Kubrá al-Amīrīyah, 1317).

Muḥammad Amin, Taysīr al-taḥrīr (Cairo: Maṭba'at 'Īsá al-Bābī al-Ḥalabī, n.d.).

Muḥammad b. Aḥmad ibn 'Arafah al-Dusūqī, ḥāshiyat al-Dusūqī (Cairo: al-istiqāmah).

______, al-Sharḥ al-kabīr (Cairo: al-istiqāmah).

Muḥammad b. Maḥmūd al-Bābartī, al-'Ināyah fī sharḥ al-Hidāyah (Beirut: Dār Ṣādir).

Muṣṭafá al- Suyūṭī, maṭālib ulī al-nuhá (Beirut: al-Maktab al-Islāmī, 1961).

______, almadkhal al-Fiqhī al-'Āmm (Damascus: Dār al-Qalam).

______, Sharḥ al-qawā'id al-fiqhīyah (Beirut: Dār al-Gharb al-Islāmī).

Ṣāliḥ al-Azharī, Jawāhir al-iklīl (Kuwait, 1415 AH).

Shams al-Dīn al-Ramlī, Nihāyat al-muḥtāj (Cairo: Maṭba'at 'Īsá al-Bābī al-Ḥalabī, 1386 AH).

Shihāb al-Dīn al-Samarqandī, Tuḥfat al-muḥtāj (Egypt: Dār al-Ḥadīih).

Journals, Encyclopedias & Websites

- Muslim World League -Islamic Fiqh Council Journal.
- OIC-International Islamic Fiqh Academy Journal.
- Islamic Organization for Medical Sciences Publications.
- Papers submitted to the Research Center for Islamic Legislation and Ethics.
- Fiqh Encyclopedia of Kuwait, (Published by Kuwaiti Ministry of Endowment and Islamic Affairs.
- al-Mawsūʻah al-fiqhīya al-ṭibbīya (Encyclopedia of Medical Fiqh)
- Encyclopedia Britannica, 15th ed., 1982
- https://ar.wikipedia.org/wiki
- www.qaradaghi.com